ISRAEL ON HIGH ALERT

RON RHODES

HARVEST HOUSE PUBLISHERS
EUGENE, OREGON

Cover by Bryce Williamson, Eugene, OR

Cover image © RomanSotola, tzahiV / iStock

ISRAEL ON HIGH ALERT

Published by Harvest House Publishers
Eugene, Oregon 97408
www.harvesthousepublishers.com

ISBN 978-0-7369-7122-5 (pbk.)
ISBN 978-0-7369-7123-2 (eBook)

Library of Congress Cataloging-in-Publication Data

Names: Rhodes, Ron, author.
Title: Israel on high alert / Ron Rhodes.
Description: Eugene, Oregon : Harvest House Publishers, [2018] | Includes bibliographical references.
Identifiers: LCCN 2017029360 (print) | LCCN 2017048677 (ebook) | ISBN 9780736971232 (ebook) | ISBN 9780736971225 (pbk.)
Subjects: LCSH: Bible—Prophecies—Israel. | Israel—History—21st century.
Classification: LCC BS649.P3 (ebook) | LCC BS649.P3 R46 2018 (print) | DDC 220.1/5—dc23
LC record available at https://lccn.loc.gov/2017029360

Printed in the United States of America

17 18 19 20 21 22 23 24 25 26 / BP-KBD / 10 9 8 7 6 5 4 3 2 1

To all who yearn for
—and pray for—
the peace of Jerusalem
(Psalm 122:6).

ACKNOWLEDGMENTS

I've always been fascinated by Bible prophecy. After becoming a Christian, I gravitated toward prophecy books written by certain professors at Dallas Theological Seminary—John F. Walvoord, J. Dwight Pentecost, and Charles C. Ryrie. Little did I know then that in the not-too-distant future, I would study under these men at the seminary. I remember those years with great fondness, and I acknowledge my personal indebtedness to these great teachers of the Word.

I certainly remain appreciative of Bob Hawkins and the entire staff at Harvest House Publishers, not only for their commitment to excellence in Christian publishing but also for their unbending commitment to biblical truth. It is a pleasure working with such committed believers.

I also want to offer continued praise to God for the wonderful family He has blessed me with—my wife, Kerri, and my two grown children, David and Kylie. With every year that passes, I grow in appreciation for these three.

Most of all, I express profound thanks and appreciation to our Lord Jesus Christ, who Himself is the heart and center of biblical prophecy. May He be glorified and exalted in this book.

Come soon, Lord!

CONTENTS

INTRODUCTION:

ISRAEL ON HIGH ALERT

Israel is on high alert—more so than ever before. The reasons are not hard to understand:

Israel is surrounded by Muslim nations who passionately seek to bring an utter and complete end to her.

Israel is a mere 8,000 square miles. It is minuscule compared to the 5,000,000 square miles of hostile Arab real estate that surrounds her.

Islamic fundamentalism is a religious philosophy that seeks to establish Islamic dominance in the Middle East and eventually the rest of the world. Israel, a symbol of Jewish power, is viewed as a grievous insult to Allah and cannot be permitted to exist in the Islamic world. Israel must therefore be pushed into the sea.

Hezbollah—literally, the "party of God"—is a Lebanese umbrella organization of radical Islamic Shiites who hate Israel. They advocate the establishment of Shiite Islamic rule in Lebanon and the liberation of all "occupied Arab lands," including Jerusalem. Hezbollah has been relentless in vowing to destroy Israel. Iran has continually backed Hezbollah to the tune of hundreds of millions of dollars.

Hamas—literally, the "Islamic Resistance Movement"—believes that negotiations with the Israelis are a waste of time because the

Arabs and the Israelis cannot coexist. The military wing of the organization has committed countless terrorist attacks and atrocities against Israel, including hundreds of suicide bombings. Hamas has received widespread funding, including from Iran, Saudi Arabia, the Gulf States, the United Arab Emirates, Syria, and Iraq.

Iran's Supreme Leader Ayatollah Khamenei claims that Iran has *the* major role to play in the destruction of Israel, and for that reason must obtain the strongest weapons possible. Khamenei has promised that Israel will not survive the next 25 years. With that threat in mind, it is sobering to realize that Iran is seeking to develop nuclear weapons and obtain missiles capable of delivering nuclear payloads.

Arab nationalism is a movement that seeks to unify Arabs as one people by appealing to a sense of their common history, culture, and language. This movement is secular, and seeks to gain and maintain Arab power in the Arab lands of the Middle East. Arab nationalists seek to end—or at least minimize—direct Western influence (by the United States) in the Arab world. As well, Arab nationalists view Israel as a cancerous tumor that must be excised.

It appears that the stage is now being set for what has been called the Ezekiel invasion (Ezekiel 38–39). Scripture reveals that Russia and a group of Muslim nations—Iran, Sudan, Turkey, Libya, Kazakhstan, Kyrgyzstan, Uzbekistan, Turkmenistan, Tajikistan, Armenia, and possibly northern Afghanistan—will launch a massive invasion into Israel. It is alarming that these very nations have already developed—or are now developing—alliances with each other. They all have a strong motive for seeing Israel obliterated. (More on this later in the book.)

Israel is indeed on high alert!

This seems ironic, for the city name of *Jerusalem*, in Hebrew, literally means "city of peace." Peace has been elusive in Jerusalem in modern times. In fact, peace has been elusive throughout the entire

Middle East. The truth is, the Middle East has been an arena of conflict for the past 70 years. Wars in the region include the War of Independence (which brought Israel's statehood—1947–1948), the Suez War/Sinai Campaign (1956), the Six-Day War (1967), the War of Attrition (1968–1970), the Yom Kippur/October War (1973), the Lebanese Civil War (1975–1990), the Iran-Iraq War (1980–1988), the Lebanon War (1982–1985), the Persian Gulf War (1991), the War with Iraq (1991–2003), and the War on Terror (2001 to present).

Fast-forward to 2017. Hardly a day passes that we do not witness a TV or Internet news report about yet another horrifying act of violence in the Middle East. Atrocities are relentlessly committed by terrorists that are so brutal—*so utterly inhumane and egregious*—that a dark sense of angst has descended upon much of the civilized world. At the epicenter of it all is the tiny nation of Israel.

Of course, this is not a surprise to those familiar with biblical prophecy. Prophetic Scripture tells us that Israel will increasingly be a sore spot in the world in the end times. In Zechariah 12:2 we read, "Behold, I am about to make Jerusalem a cup of staggering to all the surrounding peoples" (ESV). This can also be translated, "I am going to make Jerusalem a cup that sends all the surrounding peoples reeling" (NIV). If there's one thing this verse tells us, it's that even though Israel is small, the end-times turmoil generated by this nation will affect many large nations. The nations that surround Israel are Islamic. They are brutally anti-Semitic. We may expect plenty of "reeling" in the years to come.

In past decades, Israel has enjoyed at least some level of security based on its friendship with the United States. But over the past decade, the United States's commitment to Israel has waned. In late 2016, the United Nations Security Council passed a resolution condemning Israel's settlement construction on territory that the Palestinians have claimed for their future state (as part of the so-called "two-state solution"). Contrary to how past US presidents have stood by Israel in vetoing such resolutions, Barack Obama, in his last month in office, chose not to veto the resolution.

Prime Minister Benjamin Netanyahu of Israel understandably charged, "From the information that we have, we have no doubt that the Obama administration initiated it, stood behind it, coordinated on the wording, and demanded that it be passed."[1] Many saw this as a betrayal of friendship on the part of the United States.

Meanwhile, Obama's action was praised by terrorist organizations: "Palestinian terrorist factions, including the Islamist groups Hamas and Islamic Jihad, welcomed the UN Security Council resolution condemning Israel's settlement policy." Indeed, "the Iran-backed Islamic Jihad announced that the UNSC resolution is 'a clear condemnation of Israel's occupation and aggression, and a victory for the Palestinian people, securing a global consensus in their favor.'"[2]

It concerns me to hear such things. Part of my concern is rooted in the Scripture I just cited, Zechariah 12:2: "Behold, I am about to make Jerusalem a cup of staggering to all the surrounding peoples" (ESV). But more importantly, in verse 3 God unequivocally states: "On that day I will make Jerusalem a heavy stone for all the peoples. *All who lift it will surely hurt themselves*" (emphasis added). This means that in the end times, Jerusalem will be at the center of international controversy. Various nations will become intoxicated with a desire to possess and control Jerusalem. The nations of the world—perhaps the United Nations—will seek to internationalize Jerusalem and control its future. But Zechariah prophetically warns that all who attempt to control Jerusalem for their own purposes will quickly suffer calamity.

This is one reason I fear for the future of the United States. If our country seeks to influence and control Jerusalem—or to internationalize it—we may find ourselves on the receiving end of God's judgment.

I also fear for the future of the United States in light of the Abrahamic covenant, in which God promises in regard to Israel: "I will bless those who bless you and curse those who treat you with contempt" (Genesis 12:3). I have said it many times before: My reading of biblical prophecy leads me to believe that the United States will weaken in the end times. The reasons for this weakening may well include a desertion of Israel, and God's subsequent judgment.

A lack of US support for Israel is especially concerning given that radical Islamists have a vitriolic hatred of Israel. They not only want to annihilate the Jews, but they also want the land of Israel back. As prophecy expert Mark Hitchcock put it, "Israel is the ultimate prize for radical Islam."[3]

A big part of that prize relates specifically to the city of Jerusalem—a city considered holy by both Jews and Muslims. Because of Muslim-Jewish animosity, the tiny city of Jerusalem in the tiny nation of Israel is "ground zero" for a gargantuan end-time conflict.

In this book, I will explore the many components that have led to the current Middle East conflict. This, in turn, will help us to understand why Israel is perpetually on high alert these days. I will address Israel's rebirth as a nation and the conflict this has caused among Muslim nations. I will zero in on Jewish Zionism, Arab nationalism, and radical Islam—including the current activities of ISIS. I will clarify the beliefs of both mainstream Muslims and radical Islamists. I will also touch on the claim that Islam is a religion of peace.

In addition, I'll explore the historic role of the United States as a friend to Israel, and how that friendship has waned to some degree in recent years. I will pay special attention to what prophetic Scripture reveals about how Russia and a group of Muslim nations will one day launch a massive end-times invasion into Israel. I'll also talk about God's destruction of these Islamic invaders, and how this will lead to a shift in the global balance of power in the end times.*

Finally, I will address the trouble Israel will experience during the tribulation period—that future seven-year interval that precedes the second coming of Jesus Christ. I'll talk about the rising persecution of the Jews, both before and during the tribulation period. I'll address the current efforts related to the rebuilding of the Jewish temple, and the role this temple will play during the tribulation period. I'll investigate how the antichrist will initially seem a friend to Israel, but will ultimately double-cross Israel and seek to destroy her. I'll close by explaining how the future Jewish remnant—those who survive through the tribulation period—will be saved by Christ at His second coming, and how God's ancient covenant promises to Israel will finally be fulfilled during Christ's millennial kingdom.

These are exciting days to be alive. We are witnessing the stage being set for the fulfillment of many end-time prophecies related to Israel. That's a major reason I wrote this book.

One thing that will become progressively clear as you read along is that God is in control of human history. God Himself asserts, "Everything I plan will come to pass, for I do whatever I wish" (Isaiah 46:10). God assures us, "It will all happen as I have planned. It will be as I have decided" (14:24). In view of such scriptural facts, theologian Robert Lightner advises us:

> When viewed from the perspective of Scripture, history is more than the recording of the events of the past. Rather, what has happened in the past, what is happening

* At the time of this writing, Donald Trump—in the first month of his presidency—seems more favorable toward Israel. If, however, the United States weakens due to nuclear jihad, an EMP attack, moral implosion, an economic collapse, or even the rapture, the United States will not be in much of a position to render aid to Israel.

> now, and what will happen in the future is all evidence of the unfolding of the purposeful plan devised by the personal God of the Bible. All the circumstances of life—past, present, and future—fit into the sovereign plan like pieces of a puzzle.[4]

In like manner, well-known author C.S. Lewis—once a professor at Oxford University—commented: "History is a story written by the finger of God." His point was that God controls the nations (Job 12:23; Psalm 22:28; Daniel 4:17); He sets up kings and deposes them (Daniel 2:21); and He does all according to His sovereign plan (Acts 4:27-28).

Israel has a special place in God's sovereign plan of the ages. As my friend David Reagan put it:

> The Scriptures reveal the Jews as "the apple of God's eye" (Zechariah 2:8). Their land is described as "holy" (Zechariah 2:12). Their city of Jerusalem is termed the "center of the nations" (Ezekiel 5:5). They are pictured as the wayward wife of God (see Ezekiel 16 and the book of Hosea). And the Bible makes it clear that they will be the object of both God's wrath (Jeremiah 30:7) and His grace (Zechariah 13:1) in the end times.[5]

The way I see it, one of the most magnificent manifestations of God's grace is His *miraculous preservation of Israel for the past 2,700 years*. Just think about it:

- After Jerusalem and the temple were destroyed in AD 70, the Jews were dispersed to more than 130 nations around the world.

- The Jews were mistreated and relentlessly persecuted wherever they went.

- And yet—thousands of years later—their national existence and even their language have been fully restored.

The preservation of the Jews is probably best summed up in Psalm 124, which was originally written in the context of Israel's wilderness wanderings. I think that all who read it will see its modern application:

> What if the LORD had not been on our side? Let all Israel repeat: What if the LORD had not been on our side when people attacked us? They would have swallowed us alive in their burning anger. The waters would have engulfed us; a torrent would have overwhelmed us. Yes, the raging waters of their fury would have overwhelmed our very lives. Praise the LORD, who did not let their teeth tear us apart! We escaped like a bird from a hunter's trap. The trap is broken, and we are free! Our help is from the LORD, who made heaven and earth.

The amazing survival of Israel over thousands of years—against all odds—has led one commentator to speculate:

> If the story of Israel were submitted as a movie script, it would be rejected for being too fantastic to believe. After all, the restoration of sovereignty in our ancestral homeland after 2,000 years, the return of the exiles of our people from across the globe, the defense of Israel against implacable enemies, and the transformation of Israel from a desert backwater to a global technological power, seems to defy both history and logic.[6]

Israel's preservation is an incredible thing to ponder!

1

CORRECTLY INTERPRETING BIBLICAL PROPHECIES ABOUT ISRAEL

Christians love to debate issues related to biblical prophecy. Sometimes the debate relates to when the rapture of the church will occur—before the tribulation period, during it, or after it. Another debate is whether the antichrist will be a Roman Gentile or a Muslim leader. Still another is whether America is mentioned in Bible prophecy. And there is much discussion about whether the mark of the beast will be some kind of tattoo on the skin, or an electronic chip implanted under the skin.

For our purposes, the most important debate relates to the proper method to use in interpreting prophecy—the *literal* method or the *allegorical* method? Obviously, one's decision on this matter will affect one's entire prophetic viewpoint.

For example, one's position on this issue will determine whether the reference to Christ's 1,000-year kingdom in Revelation 20 should be interpreted as a literal kingdom in the future, or Christ's present reign over the church from heaven. It will determine whether the 144,000 Jews—with 12,000 from each tribe—should be interpreted to refer to literal Jews, or is a metaphorical reference to the church. It will determine whether the two prophetic witnesses of Revelation 11 should be viewed as two literal prophets, or they are a figure of speech referring in some way to the church. And it will determine whether the covenant promises made to Israel in Old Testament times (the Abrahamic and Davidic covenants) should be interpreted in reference to Israel, or in reference to the church in some kind of an allegorical way.

What's more, one's position on this debate will determine whether the various judgments referred to in prophetic Scripture—the judgment seat of Christ (Romans 14:10-12), the judgment of the nations (Matthew 25:31-46), the judgment of Israel (Ezekiel 20), and the great white throne judgment (Revelation 20:11-15)—should be seen as separate and distinct judgments (as literalism holds), or as perhaps one general judgment at the end of the age (as allegorism holds). Obviously, one's interpretive approach will lead to very different views on end-time issues, particularly in relation to Israel.

Interpretive Approaches to Understanding Bible Prophecy

A Survey of the Allegorical Approach

Early in church history (by the second century AD), an allegorical school of prophetic interpretation arose in Alexandria, Egypt. This school of thought interpreted Scripture in a nonliteral sense. Hidden, symbolic meanings were sought in biblical texts.

The emergence of this allegorical school of interpretation soon led to the rise of amillennialism in the early church. Amillennialism is the view that the prophecy in Revelation 20 regarding the millennial kingdom should not be interpreted as a literal 1,000-year reign of Christ on earth, but rather must refer to Christ's present spiritual rule over the church from heaven. The terms "a thousand years" and "the thousand years" are allegorically understood to mean a very long time.

The grammatical-historical (literal) approach to Scripture was largely regained by the church fathers by the third century. Nevertheless, premillennialism—based on a literal interpretation of prophecy, which holds to a literal 1,000-year reign of Christ on earth following the second coming—eventually fell by the wayside. The allegorical approach to interpretation gained huge momentum.

History reveals that this early emergence of the allegorical method had enormous influence upon subsequent generations of church history. The well-known theologian Augustine adopted the point of view that Scripture, with the exception of prophecy, should be interpreted naturally and literally. He was inconsistent on how to understand Bible prophecy, however. While he accepted a literal second coming of Christ, as well as a literal heaven and hell, he concluded that prophecies of a future millennial kingdom should not be understood literally. He believed that if these prophecies were taken literally, one would have to conclude that people in the millennial kingdom would regularly engage in excessive feasting, which he viewed as carnal and unworthy of believers. He thus concluded that the church was already living in the millennium, and, as such, is part of the spiritual kingdom of God. Indeed, he believed that Christ is even now reigning through the hearts of Christians.

Augustine's view became the dominant view of the Roman Catholic Church. As well, Reformation luminaries such as Martin Luther and John Calvin adopted his view. Because such well-known theologians in church history adopted the allegorical understanding of the millennial kingdom, many today have adopted the same view. In fact, some today apply the allegorical method not just to the millennium but to other aspects of biblical prophecy as well. For example, many argue that *virtually all* the prophecies related to Israel are somehow fulfilled allegorically in the church. (This is known as *replacement theology*.)

A Survey of the Literal Approach

Based on decades of research, I've concluded that the proper approach to use in interpreting biblical prophecy is the literal approach. The word *literal*, as used in hermeneutics (the science of interpretation), comes from the Latin *sensus literalis*, which refers to seeking a plain, straightforward sense of the text, as opposed to a nonliteral or allegorical sense of it.

Bible expositor J. Dwight Pentecost, one of my former professors at Dallas Theological Seminary, said that "the literal method of interpretation is that method that gives to each word the same exact basic meaning it would have in normal, ordinary, customary usage, whether employed in writing, speaking, or thinking. It is called the grammatical-historical method to emphasize the fact that the meaning is to be determined by both grammatical and historical considerations."[1]

Here are some of the key reasons for adopting a literal interpretation of prophetic Scripture:

1. It is the normal approach in all languages.
2. The greater part of the Bible makes great sense when taken literally.
3. The literal approach allows for a secondary or allegorical meaning when demanded by the context.
4. It is the only sane and safe check on the subjectively prone imagination of human beings.
5. It is the only approach in line with the nature of biblical inspiration—the idea that the words of Scripture are "God-breathed."[2]

Within the biblical text itself, we find multiple confirmations for using the literal method of interpretation. For example, later biblical texts take earlier ones as literal, as when the creation events in Genesis 1–2 are taken literally in later passages (see Exodus 20:10-11). This is likewise the case regarding the creation of Adam and Eve (Matthew 19:6; 1 Timothy 2:13), the fall of Adam and his resulting death (Romans 5:12,14), Noah's flood (Matthew 24:38), and the accounts of Jonah (Matthew 12:40-42), Moses (1 Corinthians 10:2-4,11), and numerous other historical figures.

Further, Old Testament prophecies about the Messiah (Jesus) were fulfilled literally in New Testament times. More specifically, more than 100 predictions about the Messiah were fulfilled literally at Jesus's first coming, including the prophecies that He would be (1) from the seed of a woman (Genesis 3:15); (2) from the line of Seth (Genesis 4:25); (3) a descendant of Shem (Genesis 9:26); (4) the offspring of Abraham (Genesis 12:3); (5) from the tribe of Judah (Genesis 49:10); (6) the son of David (Jeremiah 23:5-6); (7) conceived of a virgin (Isaiah 7:14); (8) born in Bethlehem (Micah 5:2); (9) the heralded Messiah (Isaiah 40:3); (10) the coming King (Zechariah 9:9); (11) the sacrificial offering for our sins (Isaiah 53); (12) the one pierced in His side at the cross (Zechariah 12:10); (13) predicted to be "cut off" or die about AD 33 (Daniel 9:24-26 NASB); and (14) the One who would rise from the dead (Psalm 2; 16).

Moreover, the prophecies about Israel in the Old Testament were fulfilled literally. David Reagan summarizes it this way:

> *Dispersion*—The Jews were warned repeatedly that they would be dispersed worldwide if they were not faithful to their covenant with God. Consider the words of Moses: "The LORD will scatter you among all peoples, from one end of the earth to the other..." (Deuteronomy 28:64; see also Leviticus 26:33).
>
> *Persecution*—The Lord also warned the Jews that they would be persecuted wherever they went. Again, the

> words of Moses are graphic in this regard: "And among those nations you shall find no rest, and there shall be no resting place for the sole of your foot; but there the LORD will give you a trembling heart, failing of eyes, and despair of soul" (Deuteronomy 28:65).
>
> *Desolation*—God promised that after their dispersion, their land would become "desolate" and their cities would become "waste" (Leviticus 26:33). Moses put it more graphically when he said, "The foreigner who comes from a distant land...will say, 'All its land is brimstone and salt, a burning waste, unsown and unproductive, and no grass grows in it'" (Deuteronomy 29:22-23).
>
> *Preservation*—But God in His marvelous grace promised He would preserve the Jews as a separate people during their worldwide wanderings. (See Isaiah 66:22; Jeremiah 30:11; 31:35-37.) Isaiah puts it in a colorful way. He says the Lord could no more forget Israel than a mother could forget her nursing child (Isaiah 49:15). He then adds that God cannot forget Israel because He has them tattooed on the palms of His hands! (Isaiah 49:16).[3]

Now, here is the significant thing: God fulfilled *all* these prophecies literally over the past few thousand years. The Jews, for an extended time, had not been faithful in their covenant relationship with God. In AD 70, Titus and his Roman warriors overran Jerusalem and destroyed its temple, and the Jewish people were scattered across the face of the earth. Wherever the Jews went, they were persecuted, often severely. This culminated in the Nazi Holocaust of World War II. But through it all, God preserved the Jews—both their culture and their ancient language. As Reagan puts it, "the fulfillment of this latter prophecy has been one of the most remarkable miracles of history. No other people have ever been so dispersed and yet been able to retain their identity as a nation."[4]

Because God's past prophecies about Israel were fulfilled literally, we have every reason to believe that His future prophecies about Israel will likewise be fulfilled literally. The precedent for interpreting prophecy literally has therefore been set. As theologian Charles Ryrie put it, "in the interpretation of unfulfilled prophecy, fulfilled prophecy forms the pattern." Indeed, "the logical way to discover how God will fulfill prophecy in the future is to discover how He fulfilled it in the past. If the hundreds of prophecies concerning Christ's first coming were fulfilled literally, how can anyone reject the literal fulfillment of the numerous prophecies concerning His second coming and reign on the earth?"[5]

Prophecy scholar Mark Hitchcock observes,

> The Bible contains about 1000 prophecies, about 500 of which have already been fulfilled down to the minutest detail. With this kind of proven track record—500 prophecies fulfilled with 100 percent accuracy—we can believe with confidence that the remaining 500 yet-to-be-fulfilled prophecies will also come to pass at the appointed time.[6]

We even find examples of Jesus Himself interpreting Old Testament prophecy literally (Luke 4:16-21 is a good example). Jesus thereby indicated His acceptance of the literal method.

Also, by specifically indicating within the text the presence of "parables" (see Matthew 13:3) or an "allegory" (Galatians 4:24), the Bible makes it clear that the ordinary meaning is a literal one. And by providing the interpretation of two of the parables, Jesus revealed that there is a literal meaning behind such parables (Matthew 13:18-23). (More on this shortly.)

There is another observation we can make here. When Jesus rebuked those who did not interpret the resurrection as a literal event, He indicated that the literal interpretation of Old Testament prophetic verses on the resurrection was the correct one (see Matthew 22:29-32; Psalm 2; 16). Jesus's use of Scripture constitutes one of the most convincing evidences that Scripture—including the prophetic portions—ought to be interpreted literally, unless the context indicates otherwise (such as Jesus telling a parable).

The Literal Method and Figures of Speech

The literal method of interpretation does not disregard the fact some passages include figures of speech. For example, when the Bible speaks of the eyes, arms, or wings of God (Psalm 34:15; Isaiah 51:9; Psalm 91:4), these references should not be taken literally. We know that God does not have these physical features because He is said to be pure Spirit (John 4:24). Likewise, He cannot literally be a rock (Psalm 42:9), which is material. But we would not know *what is not literally true* of God unless we first knew *what is literally true*. (You may have to read that sentence a couple times.)

For example, if it were not literally true that God is pure Spirit and infinite, then we would not be able to say that certain things attributed to God elsewhere in the Bible are not literally true. When Jesus said, "I am the true vine" (John 15:1 NIV), the literal method of interpretation does not take this as physically true. Rather, we understand this as a figure of speech that communicates the literal truth that believers derive their spiritual life and sustenance from Christ, our spiritual vine. It is important to understand all this, for prophetic apocalyptic literature—such as the books of Daniel and Revelation, which speak a great deal about Israel—make heavy use of figures of speech.

I grant that sometimes it may be difficult to determine when a passage should not be taken literally. But certain guidelines are helpful in making this determination.

Briefly put, a text should be taken figuratively…

- when the text itself authorizes the figurative sense, as when Paul said he was using an "allegory" (Galatians 4:24), or when Jesus was telling parables (Matthew 13:3);
- when it is *obviously* figurative, as when Jesus said He was a door (John 10:9); and
- when a literal interpretation would contradict other truths inside or outside the Bible, such as when the Bible speaks of the "four corners of the earth" (Revelation 7:1).

In sum, Bible expositor David Cooper suggests that we ought to "take every word at its primary, ordinary, usual, literal meaning, unless the facts of the immediate context, studied in the light of related passages and axiomatic and fundamental truths, indicate clearly otherwise."[7] Likewise, prophecy scholar Arnold Fruchtenbaum suggests that "unless the text indicates clearly that it should be taken symbolically, the passage should be understood literally."[8]

This is in keeping with what we learn from Genesis, the first book in the Bible. When God created Adam and Eve in His own rational image, He gave them the gift of intelligible speech. This enabled them to communicate objectively with the Creator and each other (see Genesis 1:26; 11:1,7). Scripture is clear that God sovereignly chose to use human language as a medium of revelational communication, often through the "Thus says the Lord" pronouncements of the prophets (for example, see Isaiah 7:7; 10:24; 22:15; 28:16; 30:15; 49:22; 51:22; 52:4).

If the primary purpose of God's originating of language was to make it possible for Him to communicate with human beings, as well as to enable humans to communicate with each other, then it must follow that when speaking to people, He would use language in its normal and plain sense. This view of language is a prerequisite to understanding not only God's spoken word but His written word (Scripture) as well. This is why the following dictum is important: *When the plain, literal sense of Scripture makes good sense, seek no other sense.*

Pentecost thus comments:

> Inasmuch as God gave the Word of God as a revelation to men, it would be expected that His revelation would be given in such exact and specific terms that His thoughts would be accurately conveyed and understood when interpreted according to the laws of grammar and speech. Such presumptive evidence favors the literal interpretation, for an allegorical method of interpretation would cloud the meaning of the message delivered by God to men.[9]

A relevant example relates to the specific promises God has made to Israel, including the land promises in the Abrahamic covenant (Genesis 12:1-3; 15:18-21; 17:21; 35:10-12; see also Isaiah 60:18,21; Jeremiah 23:6; 24:5-6; 30:18; 31:31-34; 32:37-40; 33:6-9; Ezekiel 28:25-26; 34:11-12; 36:24-26; 37; 39:28; Hosea 3:4-5; Joel 2:18-29; Micah 2:12; 4:6-7; Amos 9:14-15; Zephaniah 3:19-20; Zechariah 8:7-8; 13:8-9). The plain sense of these verses make perfect sense. There is no good reason to say that such verses will not be fulfilled with Israel, but are rather "spiritually fulfilled" in the modern church—a position held by proponents of replacement theology.

The Literal Method and Symbols

It is likewise critical to understand that the literal method does not disregard Scripture's use of symbols. The Bible includes symbolic language—especially in apocalyptic books like Daniel and Revelation. But each symbol is emblematic of something literal.

For example, there are symbols in the book of Revelation that represent literal things. John said the "seven stars" in Christ's right hand were "the angels [or messengers] of the seven churches" (Revelation 1:20). Likewise, he said "the seven lampstands" were "the seven churches" (1:20), the "gold bowls filled with incense" were "the prayers of God's people" (5:8), and "the waters" represent "masses of people of every nation and language" (17:15). Clearly, then, each symbol represents something literal. There are often textual clues that point us to the literal truth found in a symbol—either in the immediate context, or in the broader context of the whole of Scripture.

The Literal Method and Parables

Finally, as noted earlier, the literal method of interpretation does not disregard the use of parables. Jesus often used parables that are not to be taken literally. Yet each parable has a literal point to convey.

That Jesus wanted His parables to be clear to those who were receptive is evident in the fact that He carefully interpreted two of them for the disciples—the parables of the sower (Matthew 13:3-9) and the tares (13:24-30). He did this not only so there would be no uncertainty as to their correct meaning, but to guide believers as to the proper method to use when interpreting the other parables. The fact that Christ did not interpret His subsequent parables indicates that He fully expected believers to understand the literal truths behind the parables by applying the methodology He illustrated for them.

Israel in Bible Prophecy

In this book, I will explore a variety of prophecies—*all interpreted literally*—that relate directly to Israel and her circumstances in the end times, including…

- Israel's rebirth as a nation;
- the continual flow of Jews back to the holy land from all the countries of the world following Israel's rebirth;
- the increasing persecution of the Jews;
- the nearing Ezekiel invasion against Israel;
- the eventual rebuilding of the Jewish temple;
- Israel during the tribulation period;
- the conversion of the Jewish remnant toward the end of the tribulation period;
- Christ's rescue of the Jewish remnant from the forces of the antichrist at the end of the tribulation period; and
- the fulfillment of the Abrahamic and Davidic covenants in Christ's millennial kingdom.

In the next chapter, we will begin by considering one of the most important of all end-time prophecies—the rebirth of the nation of Israel. This single prophetic event sets the stage for everything that follows.

2

THE AMAZING REBIRTH OF ISRAEL

It is appropriate that, through the ages, the city of Jerusalem has been called the Holy City. The city is famous worldwide for being the scene of Jesus's arrest, trial, crucifixion, and resurrection.

Jerusalem rests in the Judean hills at about 2,640 feet above sea level. During the time of Jesus, the city was probably home to about a quarter of a million people.

In the Jewish thinking of biblical times, no city could possibly compare with Jerusalem. People from neighboring towns and villages would go to Jerusalem for the three major Jewish festivals, as well as to pay the annual temple tax. Jerusalem was the geographical heart of the Jewish religion. Jesus Himself made many visits there (see, for example, Luke 2:22-51; 10:38-42; 13:34).

Historically, King David of Israel captured the city in the tenth century BC. During the reign of his son, Solomon, Jerusalem became the center of Jewish religious life with the magnificent temple that was built there. Tragically, however, Jerusalem was utterly destroyed in AD 70 by Titus and his Roman warriors, as prophesied by Jesus (Matthew 24:2). After Jerusalem was laid in ruins, the Jewish people scattered worldwide.

Israel's Rebirth as a Nation

One of the most significant end-time prophecies in the Bible is that Israel would become a nation again after a long and worldwide dispersion. It seemed like an impossibility, but amazingly, it has happened. In their book *Target Israel*, Tim LaHaye and Ed Hindson wrote, "Never has a nation or a group of people who were expelled from their land returned after nearly 2000 years with their language, their heritage, and their commitments largely intact...The very fact that Israel exists today is evidence of the fact that Bible prophecy is true and can be trusted."[1]

Israel's rebirth as a self-governing nation in 1948 represented the beginnings of an actual fulfillment of specific Bible prophecies about an international regathering of the Jews, even though—as of yet—they've not yet trusted in Jesus the Messiah. This is a regathering *in unbelief*, and it was prophesied to occur before the judgments that will fall upon the world during the future tribulation period.

Some 2,600 years ago, the prophet Ezekiel spoke of God's promise to the Jews: "I will greatly increase the population of Israel, and the ruined cities will be rebuilt and filled with people" (Ezekiel 36:10). God also promised, "I will gather you up from all the nations and bring you home again to your land" (verse 24).

This has never happened before in Israel's past. In Bible times, Israel had been in bondage to single nations. The Babylonian exile is a good example. After 70 hard years of captivity in Babylon, God delivered the Jews and they returned *from that one nation* back to their land. But never in biblical history have the Israelites been delivered from "all the nations." This event did not find fulfillment until 1948 when Israel finally became a national entity again, and Jews have been streaming back to their homeland from various countries around the world ever since.

In 2006, Christian author Joel Rosenberg wrote a book appropriately titled *Epicenter: Why the Current Rumblings in the Middle East Will Change Your Future*. In the book, Rosenberg speaks of the significance of the tremendous number of Jews who are now returning to Israel from around the world, all in fulfillment of biblical prophecy:

> Consider the numbers. When Israel declared her independence on May 14, 1948, the country's population stood at only 806,000. Yet by the end of 2005, nearly 7 million people lived in Israel, 5.6 million of whom were Jewish. Thousands more arrive every year. In 2005 alone, some 19,000 Jews immigrated to Israel. In fact, today more Jews live in the greater Tel Aviv area than in New York City, as many Jews live in Israel as in the United States, and it will not be long before more Jews live in Israel than Jews who do not.[2]

The more I study Israel's recent history, the more it becomes clear that the divine program of restoring Israel had been making steady progress even prior to 1948, thereby setting the stage for the future tribulation period. Consider just a few highlights:

- *1881–1900:* More than 30,000 Jews who had been persecuted in Russia relocated to Palestine.
- *1897:* The goal of reestablishing a home in Palestine for the Jews received great impetus when the First Zionist Congress convened in Basel, Switzerland, and adopted Zionism as a program.*

* Zionism is a form of Jewish nationalism that has the goal of reestablishing the Jewish ancestral homeland. It involves not just the idea that the Jews have returned to the Land, but involves the return of Jewish sovereignty to the ancestral homeland.

- *1904–1914:* Over 32,000 more Jews who had been persecuted in Russia relocated to Palestine.
- *1924–1932:* About 78,000 Polish Jews relocated to Palestine.
- *1933–1939:* Some 230,000 Jews who had been persecuted in Germany and central Europe relocated to Palestine.
- *1940–1948:* About 95,000 Jews who had been persecuted in central Europe relocated to Palestine.
- *1948:* Against all odds, the new state of Israel was born.
- *1967:* Israel captured Jerusalem and the West Bank during the Six-Day War, which was precipitated by an Arab invasion.
- *1968 to the present:* Jews have continued to stream back to the Holy Land from various countries around the world.

All of this was foreseen by the prophet Ezekiel. In fact, in Ezekiel's vision of the dry bones recorded in Ezekiel 37, the Lord is miraculously portrayed as bringing scattered bones back together into a skeleton, and the skeleton becomes wrapped in muscles and tendons and flesh. God then breathes life into the body. There can be no doubt that this chapter is speaking about Israel, for we read that "these bones represent the people of Israel" (verse 11). Hence, this chapter portrays Israel as becoming a living, breathing nation, brought back from the dead, as it were.

And notice that it's portrayed as a process: dispersed bones forming into a skeleton, then becoming wrapped in muscle, and then receiving a breath of life. The process began prior to 1948 as Jews from various parts of the world began relocating to Palestine. It greatly escalated when Israel became a nation again in 1948. And the process has continued ever since, with Jews streaming back to the Holy Land from around the world. Ezekiel's prophecy is being fulfilled before our very eyes.

This, in turn, is setting the stage for other key biblical prophecies relating to the tribulation period to be fulfilled. For example, the return of the Jews to the Holy Land prior to the tribulation period is clearly implied in the peace covenant that will one day be signed between the antichrist and the leaders of Israel (Daniel 9:27). When this pact is signed, it will signal the actual beginning of the tribulation. Of course, such a treaty would make absolutely no sense if the Jews had not previously returned to their land, with Israel having become a viable political entity. Israel's rebirth as a nation is a *precondition* to the signing of this covenant.

We can make the same point in relation to the prophesized "Ezekiel invasion," in which Russia and a group of Muslim nations—Iran, Sudan, Turkey, Libya, Kazakhstan, Kyrgyzstan, Uzbekistan, Turkmenistan, Tajikistan, Armenia, and possibly northern Afghanistan—will launch a massive attack against Israel in the end times (see Ezekiel 38–39). Obviously, Israel's rebirth as a nation is a *precondition* to this invasion. Israel cannot be invaded unless Israel first exists as a nation.

The same is true regarding the rebuilding of the Jewish temple that is prophesied to exist during the tribulation period (see Matthew 24:15-16; 2 Thessalonians 2:4). Israel's rebirth as a nation is a *precondition* to this rebuilding.

The point also holds true regarding Jesus's instructions to the Jews to get out of Jerusalem quickly at the midpoint of the tribulation, when the antichrist sets up his headquarters there. Israel's rebirth as a nation is a *precondition* to the escape of the Jews out of Jerusalem.

All of this means that 1948 is a year to remember!

Now, while the current regathering of the Jews to the Holy Land is what we might call a *gathering in unbelief*, there is a day in the future, according to Joel 2:28-29, during which there will be a spiritual awakening in Israel. Armageddon—the campaign of battles that erupts at the end of the tribulation period—will apparently be the historical context in which the people of Israel will finally become converted to Christ (Zechariah 12:2–13:1). At the end of the tribulation, the forces of the antichrist will decisively move against the Jewish remnant to annihilate them, and it is at this time that the Jewish remnant will finally recognize that Jesus is the Messiah and place their belief in Him. Israel's rebirth will include the confession of Israel's national sin (Leviticus 26:40-42; Jeremiah 3:11-18; Hosea 5:15), after which time Israel will be saved, thereby fulfilling the apostle Paul's prophecy in Romans 11:25-27. In dire threat at Armageddon, Israel will plead for their newly found Messiah to return and deliver them (they will "mourn for him as for an only son"—Zechariah 12:10; see also Matthew 23:37-39, as well as Isaiah 53:1-9), at which point their deliverance will surely come (see Romans 10:13-14).

Israel's leaders will have finally realized the reason the tribulation has fallen upon them. This realization will likely be due to the Holy Spirit's enlightenment of their understanding of Scripture, or the testimony of the 144,000 Jewish evangelists (Revelation 7; 14), or perhaps the testimony of the two prophetic witnesses (Revelation 11).

Later, in the millennial kingdom, which follows the second coming of Christ, Israel will experience a full possession of the Promised Land and the reestablishment of the Davidic throne. This will be in fulfillment of the ancient unconditional covenants God made long ago with Abraham and David. It will be a time of physical and spiritual blessing, the basis of which is the new covenant (Jeremiah 31:31-34). *It will be a glorious time.*

Meanwhile, the Middle East Conflict Continues to Escalate

How ironic that *Jerusalem* literally means "city of peace." There is anything but peace in Jerusalem nowadays. In fact, due to external threats, there is little peace in all of Israel. The Muslim nations that surround the Jewish nation are strongly motivated to annihilate her.

A large part of today's Middle East conflict centers on the dispute over who the Holy Land really belongs to. Israel claims that the God of the Bible promised the Holy Land to the Jews. Muslims retort that Allah promised the land to the Arabs and Muslims. Let's take a brief look at the details.

God's Promises to the Jewish Patriarchs

The name *Abraham* means "father of a multitude." Abraham lived around 2000 BC, originating from the city of Ur, in Mesopotamia, on the River Euphrates. He was apparently a wealthy and powerful man.

Genesis 11 reveals that God called Abraham to leave Ur and go to a new land—the land of Canaan, which God was giving to Abraham and his descendants. Abraham promptly left with his wife, Sarah, and his nephew, Lot. Upon arriving in Canaan, his first act was to construct an altar and worship God. This was typical of Abraham; *God is of first importance.*

God made a pivotal covenant with Abraham around 2100 BC. In this covenant, God promised Abraham a son, and said that his descendants would be as numerous as the stars in the sky (Genesis 12:1-3; 13:14-17; 22:17). The promise may have seemed unbelievable to Abraham because his wife had been childless (11:30). Yet Abraham did not doubt God; he knew the Lord would faithfully give what He had promised.

God reaffirmed the covenant in Genesis 15, perhaps to emphasize to Abraham that even in his advanced age, the promise would come to pass. Abraham was also told that he would be personally blessed, that his name would become great, that those who bless him would be blessed and those who curse him would be cursed, and that all the families of the earth would be blessed through his posterity.

As time went by and Abraham and Sarah still remained childless, Sarah impatiently suggested that their heir might be procured through their Egyptian handmaiden, Hagar. Ishmael was thus born to Abraham, through Hagar, when Abraham was 86 years old. But Ishmael was not the child of promise. In God's perfect timing, His promise of a son was fulfilled when Abraham was 100, and Sarah was 90—far beyond normal childbearing age (Genesis 17:17; 21:5). Their son was named Isaac. As promised, the entire Jewish nation eventually developed from his line. *Isaac* means "laughter," a meaning that is fitting because it points to the joy derived from this child of promise. Recall that when Abraham and Sarah heard they would have a son in their old age, they laughed (see Genesis 17:17-19; 18:9-15).

Isaac's significance is found in the fact that he would carry on the covenant first given to his father Abraham. The New Testament calls him a child of promise (Galatians 4:22-23), and he was a man of good character.

In a famous episode in the Bible, Abraham's faith was stretched when he was commanded by God to sacrifice his beloved son of promise, Isaac—a command he obeyed without hesitation. In his heart, Abraham believed God would provide a substitute lamb for the burnt offering (Genesis 22:8). God, of course, intervened before

Isaac was sacrificed, and the episode serves to demonstrate the tremendous faith Abraham had in God. In God's providence, Isaac indeed was the son of promise.

Of critical importance in all this is the fact that God made specific land promises to Abraham. We read in Genesis 15:18-21: "The LORD made a covenant with Abram that day and said, 'I have given this land to your descendants, all the way from the border of Egypt to the great Euphrates River—the land now occupied by the Kenites, Kenizzites, Kadmonites, Hittites, Perizzites, Rephaites, Amorites, Canaanites, Girgashites, and Jebusites.'"

The land promises made to Abraham were then passed down through Isaac's line. Indeed, in Genesis 26:3-4 we read the Lord's very words to Isaac:

> Live here as a foreigner in this land, and I will be with you and bless you. I hereby confirm that I will give all these lands to you and your descendants, just as I solemnly promised Abraham, your father. I will cause your descendants to become as numerous as the stars of the sky, and I will give them all these lands. And through your descendants all the nations of the earth will be blessed.

The land promises then passed from Isaac to Jacob (not to Esau). The Lord said to Jacob,

> I am the LORD, the God of your grandfather Abraham, and the God of your father, Isaac. The ground you are lying on belongs to you. I am giving it to you and your descendants. Your descendants will be as numerous as the dust of the earth! They will spread out in all directions—to the west and the east, to the north and the south. And all the families of the earth will be

> blessed through you and your descendants (Genesis 28:13-14).

Prophecy scholar Randall Price has written a concise, helpful book entitled *Fast Facts on the Middle East Conflict.* In it he summarizes the significance of these land promises to the Jewish patriarchs:

> The Bible states that the covenant was re-established not with Ishmael, but only with Isaac and his descendants (see Genesis 17:18-21). This means that the Abrahamic Covenant and the land promise contained within it (Genesis 15:18-21) is exclusive to the Jewish people as the sole descendants of Isaac. This promise, in turn, was selectively passed on to Isaac's son Jacob (who was renamed "Israel") rather than his son Esau (Genesis 28:13-15; 35:12).[3]

This distinct family line through which God's covenant promises were to be fulfilled is affirmed later in the Bible. For example, in Psalm 105:8-11 we read, "He always stands by his covenant—the commitment he made to a thousand generations. This is the covenant he made with Abraham and the oath he swore to Isaac. He confirmed it to Jacob as a decree, and to the people of Israel as a never-ending covenant: 'I will give you the land of Canaan as your special possession.'"

Many additional prophecies after this continue to speak of Israel possessing the land in the future (see Isaiah 60:18,21; Jeremiah 23:6; 24:5-6; 30:18; 31:31-34; 32:37-40; 33:6-9; Ezekiel 28:25-26; 34:11-12; 36:24-26; 37; 39:28; Hosea 3:4-5; Joel 2:18-29; Micah 2:12; 4:6-7; Amos 9:14-15; Zephaniah 3:19-20; Zechariah 8:7-8; 13:8-9). In fact, every Old Testament prophet except Jonah spoke of a permanent return to the land of Israel by the Jews.

Clearly, then, the land promises made by God and recorded in the Bible are for the descendants of Abraham, Isaac, and Jacob—*the Jewish people*. From a biblical perspective, there is virtually no question about God's intended recipients of the land.

The Muslim Response

Muslims explain all of this away. It is typically claimed that while the original Bible was the Word of God—apparently still in good shape during the time of Muhammad in the seventh century[4]—it quickly thereafter became corrupted by devious Jews and Christians. We are told that the Bible of today has been mingled with many "untruths." These untruths relate particularly to areas where the Bible disagrees with the Quran. World religion scholar Stephen Neill observes that "it is well known that at many points the Quran does not agree with the Jewish and Christian Scriptures. Therefore, from the Muslim point of view, it follows of necessity that the Scriptures must have been corrupted."[5]

Muslim apologist Alhaj Ajijola puts it this way:

> The first five books of the Old Testament do not constitute the original Torah, but parts of the Torah have been mingled up with other narratives written by human beings and the original guidance of the Lord is lost in that quagmire. Similarly, the four Gospels of Christ are not the original Gospels as they came from the prophet Jesus...The original and the fictitious, the divine and human are so intermingled that the grain cannot be separated from the chaff. The fact is that the original Word of God is preserved neither with the Jews nor with the Christians.[6]

Muslims therefore hold that what used to be the Word of God

in the Bible has been so adulterated by human hands that it is now hardly distinguishable from the word of man. In some verses, there may be a remaining glimmer of the truth, but these are few and far between in "the jungles of interpolations and contradictions with which the Bible is dense."[7]

Muslims typically claim that sometime after the life of Muhammad, the Jews inserted many statements into the Old Testament that served to personally benefit them. Muslim apologist Maurice Bucaille, for example, claims that "a revelation is mingled in all these writings, but all we possess today is what men have seen fit to leave us. These men manipulated the texts to please themselves, according to the circumstances they were in and the necessities they had to meet."[8]

Muslims say that through Ishmael, who gave rise to the Arab nations, they are the rightful heirs to the promises made to Abraham. They allege that the Jews, for personal gain, concocted a story—and inserted it into the manuscript copies of the Old Testament—to the effect that Isaac became Abraham's heir of the Palestinian land promises. In this Jewish version, Ishmael and his descendants became outcasts and thus have no right to the land.[9] The original Old Testament, we are told, did not say this. Palestine, by divine right, thus belongs to the Muslims and not to the Jews.

As for the New Testament, Muslims claim that Christians altered it by inserting statements about Jesus being the Son of God, and by teaching the doctrine of the Trinity. The original New Testament did not contain such ideas, we are told. The original Jesus presented Himself as a mere prophet of Allah. Christians then took it upon themselves to deify this prophet. Today's New Testament, then, is not viewed as containing the actual words of Jesus, but rather words that were "put into His mouth" by Christians. The New Testament—like the Old Testament—is said to be corrupted.

The Folly of Muslim Reasoning

Muslims have literally rewritten history to suit their own theological and political agenda. But their explanation is impossible to fathom. After all, by Muhammad's time, there were countless thousands of copies of biblical manuscripts dispersed over a large part of the world. For Christians to have successfully corrupted these biblical manuscripts would have required that they all be meticulously gathered—assuming people everywhere would have been willing to surrender them, an impossible-to-believe scenario—so that the changes be made to all of them.

Another scenario is that countless thousands of people from around the world who were in possession of biblical manuscripts met together and colluded to make the changes. But if most of these people were believers, how likely is it that they would tamper with the Scriptures upon which they were basing their eternal salvation? What's more, would collusion on such a massive scale even be physically possible?

It's important to keep in mind that hundreds of years before Muhammad was even born, biblical manuscripts had already been translated into a number of different languages. The Syriac, Coptic, Old Nubian, Ethiopic, and Georgian translations were available before Muhammad arrived on the scene. Would Muslims have us believe that these and other translations were somehow identically altered all over the world so they would contain a uniformly corrupt message? Such would have been impossible.

Moreover, if the Jews had gone through the trouble of corrupting their Scriptures, wouldn't they have at least changed all the horrible things we read about them in the Torah? For example, why leave in the description of their total unfaithfulness to God during the wilderness sojourn and their participation in rampant idolatry?

Likewise, if Christians had changed the New Testament, why

didn't they remove the unflattering portions? Why not hide the facts that Peter denied Christ three times and the disciples scattered like a bunch of faithless cowards when Christ was arrested? It doesn't make sense.

Christians have hard evidence to support their claim that the Bible is reliable. For example, the Bible's accuracy and trustworthiness have been confirmed over and over again by archeological finds produced by both Christian and non-Christian scholars and scientists. This includes verification for numerous customs, places, names, and events mentioned in the Bible.

To date, more than 25,000 sites in Bible lands have been discovered. These have established the accuracy of the accounts given in the Bible. Nelson Glueck, a specialist in ancient literature, did an exhaustive study and concluded, "It can be stated categorically that no archaeological discovery has ever controverted a biblical reference."[10] Well-known scholar William F. Albright, following a comprehensive study, wrote, "Discovery after discovery has established the accuracy of innumerable details, and has brought increased recognition of the value of the Bible as a source of history."[11]

The Dead Sea Scrolls provide even further hard evidence of the reliability of Bible manuscripts. In these scrolls discovered at Qumran in 1947, we have Old Testament manuscripts that date about 1,000 years earlier (150 BC) than any of the Old Testament manuscripts previously in our possession (which date to AD 980). It is noteworthy that when the two sets of manuscripts are compared, they are essentially the same, with very few changes. The fact that manuscripts separated by 1,000 years are virtually the same indicates that the original message of the Old Testament has been well preserved in the course of repeated transmission.

The copy of the book of Isaiah discovered at Qumran illustrates this accuracy. Dr. Gleason Archer, who personally examined both the AD 980 and 150 BC copies of Isaiah, made this comment:

> Even though the two copies of Isaiah discovered in Qumran Cave 1 near the Dead Sea in 1947 were a thousand years earlier than the oldest dated manuscript previously known (A.D. 980), they proved to be word for word identical with our standard Hebrew Bible in more than 95 percent of the text. The 5 percent of variation consisted chiefly of obvious slips of the pen and variations in spelling.[12]

Similarly, Christian apologist Paul Little comments,

> In comparing the Qumran manuscript of Isaiah 38–66 with the one we had, scholars found that the text is extremely close to our Massoretic text. A comparison of Isaiah 53 shows that only 17 letters differ from the Massoretic text. Ten of these are mere differences in spelling, like our "honor" or "honour," and produce no change in the meaning at all. Four more are very minor differences, such as the presence of the conjunction, which is often a matter of style. The other three letters are the Hebrew word for "light" which is added after "they shall see" in verse 11. Out of 166 words in this chapter, only this one word is really in question, and it does not at all change the sense of the passage. This is typical of the whole manuscript.[13]

The Dead Sea Scrolls prove that the copyists who worked on the biblical manuscripts took great care in going about their work. These copyists knew they were duplicating God's Word. Hence, they went to incredible lengths to ensure that no errors crept into the copies they were producing. The scribes carefully counted every line, word, syllable, and letter to guarantee accuracy.[14]

So that you do not miss the significance of all this, the early manuscripts of Isaiah date to 150 BC. This is more than 700 years *before* Muhammad was born. The manuscripts dated at AD 980 are centuries *after* Muhammad's time. When one compares the two sets of manuscripts, *there are hardly any differences.* This fact alone annihilates the Muslim claim that the Old Testament manuscripts were corrupted on a massive scale. And one of the truths found in the book of Isaiah is that the Jews "will possess their land forever" (Isaiah 60:21).

When all the facts are considered, it becomes obvious to the unbiased observer that not only are the Old and New Testament manuscripts reliable, but God also promised the land to the Jewish people.

An Important Distinction

I don't want to sound like a broken record, but it is important—indeed, *critically important*—for us to keep in mind the distinction between Bible verses which speak of Israel's gathering to the land *before* the tribulation period, and verses that speak of Israel's full possession of the land *after* the tribulation, following the Jewish people's conversion to the Lord. Unless this distinction is recognized and maintained, the prophecy student will end up confused. Prophecy scholar Thomas Ice advises,

> To properly understand the end-time homecoming or regathering of the Jews to their promised land, we need to keep in mind that the Bible predicts that Israel will experience two worldwide, end-time regatherings to the Promised Land. The first regathering will be partial, gradual, and in unbelief, while the second regathering will be full, instantaneous, and will occur when Israel enters into belief in Jesus as their personal and national Messiah.

> Dozens of biblical passages predict this global event. It is a common mistake, however, to lump all of these passages into one fulfillment time frame, especially in relation to the current state of Israel. Modern Israel is prophetically significant and is fulfilling Bible prophecy. But when we read God's Word, we need to be careful to distinguish which verses are being fulfilled in our day and which await future fulfillment.
>
> In short, there will be two end-time regatherings: one before the tribulation and one after the tribulation. The first worldwide regathering will be a return in unbelief, in preparation for the judgment of the tribulation. The second worldwide regathering will be a return in faith at the end of the tribulation, in preparation for the blessing of the millennium, or thousand-year reign of Christ.[15]

Tim LaHaye also speaks of this:

> We may expect two regatherings. The one we are seeing in our day under the direction of world Zionism—this occurs in unbelief. It is a partial regathering which will, as we shall see, give Jews opportunity to rebuild their temple. But it will not be a permanent regathering, for the coming world dictator [the antichrist] will desecrate their temple and drive them out of the Holy Land. The second and final regathering, accomplished by Christ Himself, will be universal in that all believing Israelites will be included. And they will never again leave the Land of Promise (Ezekiel 36:24-38; 11:17-20).[16]

At the end of the tribulation period, when Israel finally recognizes Jesus as her divine Messiah, the covenant stipulations regarding full possession of the Promised Land will finally have been met. And the Jews will take complete possession of the land during Christ's millennial kingdom. Prophecy scholar Randall Price explains it this way:

> Israel will fulfill the conditional terms of the covenant because in the Last Days, every Israelite will know the Lord (Jeremiah 31:34), for God will have given them a new heart and a new spirit and put His Spirit within them and caused them to walk in His ways (see Ezekiel 36:25-28). According to the prophets, it will be at this time...that the territorial aspects of the Abrahamic Covenant (such as possession of the full extent of the promised boundaries and the universal blessing of all mankind) will find fulfillment (Isaiah 2:2-4; Hosea 3:4-5; cf. Ezekiel 37:24-28; Zechariah 8:7-8,11-13).[17]

Meanwhile, Muslims Want the Land Back

It is wonderful to contemplate what lies ahead for the Jewish people in the millennial kingdom. But current world circumstances call us back to the present. Walid Phares, author of *Future Jihad*, is correct in his assessment that "as the Jewish state became a reality [in 1948] and prospered, Islamists viewed the entire existence of Israel as an aggression. The initial settlement was illegitimate to start with; Jews had no right to 'return' or come back to an Islamic land." Muslim resentment toward the Jews is based on a longstanding Islamic policy: "Following the logic of the Fatah and of jihad, any territory that was at some time 'opened' by a legitimate Islamic authority cannot revert to a non-Islamic authority."[18] In other words, once a land is under Muslim control, it cannot be allowed to pass out of Muslim control.

While Muslims want the land back, Israel has been welcoming

Jewish immigrants and offering repatriation to all Jews who return. This is based on an important piece of legislation adopted by the new state of Israel called the "Law of Return"—a law that provides all Jews the legal right to immigrate to Israel and immediately become citizens if they so choose. The Arabs, by contrast, say Jewish immigration to Palestine must stop.

As a result of the ongoing conflict between the Israelis and Arabs, many Palestinians have been displaced and have taken up residence in refugee camps in Jordan, the West Bank, and Gaza. Today, there are millions of Palestinian refugees. While Jews from anywhere in the world are welcomed as Israeli citizens in Israel, Palestinian refugees are prevented from becoming citizens in neighboring Arab countries—except in Jordan.

While all the Arab nations except Jordan have refused to help solve the refugee problem, Israel has been willing to offer some limited assistance. The challenge for Israel is the danger of allowing large numbers of unhappy Palestinians into the Jewish state who could later become allies with Arab nations seeking to attack Israel. That's the reason Israel has allowed only a limited number of Palestinians to live outside of Israel proper, and has segregated the Jews and Palestinians via a perimeter wall and demilitarized the Palestinian area.

Palestinians, by contrast, want permission to return to their former homes or be given compensation for choosing not to return. They claim Israel is not honoring the UN Security Council's Resolutions 194 and 242, which grant repatriation and war reparations to the ousted Palestinians.

Resentment among Arabs and Muslims is thus at an all-time high today. The extremist Muslims want to "wipe Israel off the map." They want to destroy this "lesser Satan," along with the "greater

Satan" that supports Israel—that is, the United States. The Middle East conflict is escalating by the day, with no peaceful resolution in sight.

I will continue to address Muslim hostilities toward the Jewish people in the next chapter and those that follow.

3

MUSLIM HOSTILITIES AGAINST JEWS: THE CURRENT MIDDLE EAST CONFLICT

Since the terrorist attacks that took place on September 11, 2001, 35 percent of Americans say they are now paying closer attention to the news, and how specific news events might relate to the coming of the end of the world. One poll reveals that 42 percent of Americans say they agree that Israel's rebirth as a nation, the instability of the Middle East, and other such events are indications that we are living in what the Bible calls the last days. Some 52 percent of Americans say they agree that the rebirth of Israel as a nation in 1948 and the return of millions of Jews to the Holy Land is a direct fulfillment of biblical prophecies.

In the previous chapter, I noted that Muslims view the mere existence of Israel as an aggression. They say the initial settlement of Jews in the land was illegitimate, and that the Jews had no right to "return" or "come back" to a land that was now under Islamic authority. The Jews have therefore committed a grievous offense against Allah, and Muslims want the land back.

When Israel became a nation again in 1948 after a long and worldwide dispersion, the rest of the Middle East was utterly enraged. Aaron Klein, in his book *The Late Great State of Israel*, says that "the declaration of the state of Israel set off the chain of events that has led to the modern terrorism we see today."[1] Moreover,

> the Islamic/Arabic world erupted like a volcano. The call of jihad was pronounced throughout the Islamic-Arab world. The first call to jihad came from the founder of the Muslim Brotherhood in Egypt (the forerunner of today's terrorist organizations). Al-Azhar also openly condemned Israel. All the people in the Arab countries were pushing their governments to send their militaries to fight Israel.[2]

After all, when the Jewish people declared the birth of the nation of Israel, it was considered an affront to every Islamic country because it was viewed as taking the land away from Islam.[3] That's when the call to jihad came.

Jihad comes from the Arabic word *jahada*, which principally means "to struggle" or "to strive in the path of Allah." Muslims today often use the term in reference to armed fighting and warfare in defending Islam and standing against evil. For most Muslims today, any war that is viewed as a defense of one's own country, home, or community is called a jihad.

Radical Islamic fundamentalists are well known for their use of arms and explosives—as well as knives used in beheading—to defend their version of Islam. Jihad, in their thinking, has the goal of terrorizing perceived enemies of Islam into submission and retreat. Many Muslims believe Muhammad's mission was to conquer the world for Allah. The goal of jihad, for them, is to establish Islamic authority over the whole world. In their view, Islam teaches that Allah is the only authority, and all political systems must be based on Allah's teaching.

The religious motivation for participating in jihad is that any Muslim who loses his or her life in service to Allah is guaranteed entrance into Paradise (Hadith 9:459). According to Muslim tradition, Muhammad said, "The person who participates in (holy battles) in Allah's cause and nothing compels him to do so except belief in Allah and His Apostles, will be recompensed by Allah either with a reward, or booty (if he survives) or will be admitted to Paradise (if he is killed in the battle as a martyr)" (Hadith 1:35).

Despite the Muslim threat, the Jews in Israel are not about to budge. They believe the land is *their* land. It is *their* possession, *their* inheritance from God. It is not hard to see why the tension between Jews and Muslims has never been greater.

Conflicting Ideologies

Three significant ideologies have emerged in the Middle East that directly relate to the current conflict over the land: Zionism, Arab nationalism, and Islamic fundamentalism. Let's take a brief look at these.

Zionism. Zionism gets its name from Mount Zion, the hill in ancient Jerusalem where King David's palace once stood. Zion became a symbol for Jerusalem during David's reign (2 Samuel 5:7). Zionism is another name for a type of Jewish nationalism that has the goal of reestablishing the Jewish ancestral homeland. It involves not just the idea that the Jews have returned to the Holy Land, but also the return of Jewish sovereignty to the ancestral homeland. Zionism, then, is essentially a national liberation movement of the Jewish people. Christians who uphold the right of the Jewish people to return to the Land and establish an independent state are often referred to as Christian Zionists.

Arab nationalism. Arab nationalism is a movement that seeks to unify Arabs as one people by appealing to a sense of their common history, culture, and language. It is a secular movement that seeks to gain and maintain Arab power in the Arab lands of the Middle East. In more recent decades, Arab nationalists have sought to end—or at least minimize—direct Western influence in the Arab world.

As well, Israel is viewed as a cancerous tumor that must be removed. Arab nationalists heavily permeate the entire Middle East.

Islamic fundamentalism. Islamic fundamentalism is a religious philosophy that seeks to establish Islamic dominance in the Middle East and eventually the rest of the world—including the United States. Israel, a symbol of Jewish power, is viewed as a grievous insult to Allah and cannot be allowed to continue to exist, and must therefore be "pushed into the sea."

Here is the point I am building up to: The coexistence of Jewish Zionism, Arab nationalism, and Islamic fundamentalism might be likened to a powder keg with a lit fuse. It's a recipe for disaster. *It's an explosion just waiting to happen.* And the explosive nature of this conflict shows no signs of decompressing.

The Multifaceted Nature of the Middle East Conflict

The Middle East conflict is truly multifaceted. There are so many different Arab and Muslim groups that have emerged amid the strife that it's hard to keep up with them all. Following is a brief primer that provides a handle on the most important of these groups. I believe this overview will help reveal just how intensely Arabs and Muslims feel about Israel, as well as Israel's longtime ally, the United States.

The Palestinian Liberation Organization. The Palestinian Liberation Organization (PLO) was created by the Arab League in 1963.* It was originally intended to be the primary Arabian vehicle for the utter annihilation of Israel. It utilized terrorist tactics to attain this goal. The PLO undertook militant activities against both the Israeli civilian population and military targets. Hijackings, kidnappings,

* The term *Palestinian* has not always referred to the Arab population west of the Jordan River. Prior to 1948, when Israel was reborn as a state, both Arabs and Jews were recognized as Palestinian. There were Palestinian Jews and Palestinian Arabs. Once Israel was reborn as a state in 1948, the Jews were identified as Israelis while non-Israeli Arabs were increasingly identified as Palestinians. By the time the Palestinian Liberation Organization was formed in 1963, the term *Palestinian* was being used in reference to Arab nationalists, who wanted the land back from the Israelis.

and assassinations were commonplace. All the while, the PLO was busy promoting a one-state doctrine: Arab Palestine. The PLO sought to drive the Israelis into the sea. By the 1980s, the PLO shifted its strategy to gain more global political influence. The new goals were to (1) proclaim an independent Palestinian state, (2) renounce terrorism, and (3) recognize Israel's right to exist. This shift marked the beginning of a two-state doctrine: Palestine and Israel. Over the years that followed, talks between Israel and the PLO took place, but they broke down and the conflict continued.

Al-Qaeda. This term literally means "the base" (or military base) in Arabic. Al-Qaeda has sought to diminish American influence in the Middle East, particularly in Israel and Iraq, and has sought to oust American troops from Saudi Arabian soil. The al-Qaeda network seeks to fund, recruit, train, and coordinate Islamic militants and extremist organizations across the globe. Many members of al-Qaeda envision the establishment of a caliphate—a single Islamic state ruled by a caliph, a successor of Muhammad—across all Muslim lands. While al-Qaeda has been on the run from the US military in recent times, it is still alive and well.

Al-Qaeda was first established in Afghanistan in 1982 by Palestinian sheikh Abdallah Yussuf Azzam and Osama bin Laden, the seventeenth of 52 children of a wealthy Saudi construction magnate. The bin Laden family wealth is calculated to hover around $5 billion. Osama's cut was around $300 million.

To date, al-Qaeda terrorist cells have penetrated 94 countries around the world, and they are growing. Al-Qaeda training camps in Afghanistan and Pakistan have equipped around 70,000 Islamic fighters from some 55 countries. They spread like a hidden virus, forging alliances with both Muslim and non-Muslim terrorists, as well as with organized crime. One US defense official testified before the Senate that "al Qaeda is not a snake that can be killed by lopping off its head…it is more analogous to a disease that has infected many parts of a healthy body."[4]

As for the funding of al-Qaeda, the smoking gun clearly points to the Saudis. Rachel Ehrenfeld, author of a groundbreaking book entitled *Funding Evil: How Terrorism Is Financed—and How to Stop It*, says al-Qaeda receives funds from the oil-rich Saudi royal family, Saudi charitable organizations, Saudi banks and financial networks, Saudi businesses (including real estate, publishing, software, and construction companies), and Saudi criminal activities (for example, related to credit card fraud, the pirating of compact discs, prostitution rings, and the sale of illegal drugs). While there are multiple sources of funding, the lion's share of the money comes from Saudi oil wealth.[5]

One might be surprised that Saudi charitable organizations are helping to fund al-Qaeda. The truth is, these charities do not operate the way you might think. The backdrop is that Muslims are expected to give alms (*zakat*) to the Muslim community that amount to one-fortieth (or 2 1/2 percent) of one's income. *Zakat* is a word that means "to be pure" and signifies the purifying of one's soul.[6] The offering is supposed to benefit widows, orphans, and the sick, or it can be used toward furthering Islam (for example, building mosques and religious schools). Giving to charity is considered an extremely meritorious act in Islam (see Suras 24:56; 57:18). The gift is to be given with the conscious awareness that all things ultimately belong to Allah, and that each person is a mere trustee for a limited time on earth.[7]

Muslim tradition affirms that Allah withholds his blessing from those who withhold alms (Hadith 2:515). Tradition also indicates that one can nullify salvation by withholding charity (Hadith 2:486). "Save yourself from Hell-fire even by giving half a date-fruit in charity" (Hadith 2:498). Muhammad said almsgiving was important because society is like a body with many parts. If one part of society suffers, all of society suffers, and hence the other "body parts" of society should rally in response.[8]

Different Muslim communities handle charity in different ways. In some communities, it is up to the individual Muslim to make a charitable contribution to the Islamic cause of his choice—generally a local charity. Some Muslims give the money to their local mosque, or to a respected Islamic leader, who then decides how to apply the funds. In other Muslim communities there is a *zakat* tax collected by the government. The income derived from this tax is then used either for social benefit (building schools, for example) or for religious purposes.

The key point in all this is that in Saudi Arabia, Kuwait, the United Arab Emirates, and other oil-rich Islamic countries, the governments control the charities as well as make substantial contributions to them. We are talking major bucks here, for these charities collectively have a treasury chest worth more than $4 billion. Although much of the money has gone to support humanitarian tasks in Islamic territories, it is also true that a significant amount of money has been diverted, directly or indirectly, to fund terrorism.[9] More to the point, Saudi charities have helped to fund al-Qaeda and jihad. Al-Qaeda thus remains alive and well because the finances are there to fuel it.

Hezbollah. Hezbollah, or the "party of God," is a Lebanese umbrella organization of radical Islamic Shiites who hate Israel and oppose the West. Founded in 1982, they are deeply entrenched in terrorism. They believe Israel occupies land that belongs only to the Muslims, and they will resort to any level of violence and terror to rectify the situation. They advocate the establishment of Shiite Islamic rule in Lebanon and the liberation of all "occupied Arab lands," including Jerusalem. Hezbollah has thus continually vowed to destroy Israel and establish an Islamic state in Lebanon. They also seek to eliminate Jews worldwide.

From the inception of the organization, Hezbollah has had deep ties to both Iran and Syria. This is highly significant, for Yossef Bodansky—former director of the Congressional Task Force on Terrorism and Unconventional Warfare—affirmed that "ultimately the key to effective terrorism in and out of the Arab world is firmly in the hands of the two main sponsoring states—Iran and Syria."[10] These two states have consistently provided large infusions of cash to Hezbollah.

In fact, the late Hassan Nasrallah—formerly Hezbollah's secretary general—was very open about how Hezbollah received funding from oil-rich Tehran to support its terrorist activities against Israel. In earlier years, Iran provided some $60 to $100 million annually to Hezbollah, and then increased the amount to $10 million per month. This money has been provided by Iran specifically to enable terrorist activities against Israel. Iran also assists in providing weaponry, explosives, organizational aid, instructors, and political support.[11]

Multiple news reports have indicated that, in years past, Syria has provided not only shelter and financing to Hezbollah, but also weaponry from its own stockpiles, as well as thousands of long-range rockets. Training facilities have also been provided, along with logistical and technological support for attacks against Israel.

Hamas. Hamas is an Arabic term that means "Islamic Resistance Movement." This fundamentalist organization was founded by Sheikh Ahmed Yassin in 1987 to wage jihad to liberate Palestine and to establish an Islamic Palestinian state. Hamas has a 36-article covenant that outlines its current position toward Israel. In it we read this: "The land of Palestine is an Islamic Waqf [Holy Possession] consecrated for future Moslem generations until Judgment Day" (Article 11). "Palestine is an Islamic land...Since this is the case, the liberation of Palestine is an individual duty for every Moslem wherever he may be" (Article 13).[12]

Members of Hamas believe that negotiations with the Israelis are a waste of time because the Arabs and the Israelis cannot coexist. The military wing has committed countless terrorist attacks against Israel, including hundreds of suicide bombings. Yassin once called on Iraqis to "become human bombs, using belts and suitcases aimed at killing every enemy that walks on the earth and pollutes it."[13] Former President George W. Bush categorized Hamas as one of the deadliest terrorist organizations in the world. Even today, one often finds Hamas supporters carrying signs saying, "Death to USA."

There is no question that Hamas has received widespread funding, including from Iran, Saudi Arabia, the Gulf States, the United Arab Emirates, Syria, and Iraq, among other sources. Untold millions of oil dollars are sent to Hamas by these nations in order to continue Hamas's jihad. This is clearly oil-sponsored terrorism.

Palestinian Islamic Jihad. The Palestinian Islamic Jihad is a militant Islamic group that has long been based in Damascus, Syria. It is dedicated to the destruction of Israel and the establishment of an Islamic state in Palestine. It emerged in the 1970s, and has engaged in large-scale suicide bombing attacks against Israeli civilians as well as military targets. Not surprisingly, Iran's oil money helps to underwrite this organization. As well (again, not surprisingly), Syria has provided safe haven, finances, arms, and training for the group. According to Palestinian intelligence documents discovered by the Israelis in 2002, money transferred from Iran and Syria to Palestinian terrorist groups is used for preparing terrorist attacks against Israel, supporting families of dead and detained terrorists, procuring arms, and purchasing physical equipment for terrorist attacks.[14]

ISIS. ISIS is an acronym for the Islamic State in Iraq and Syria. It started as an al-Qaeda splinter group. It has now become the most powerful terrorist group in history, as well as the richest terrorist group in the world, bringing in one to two million dollars per day.

They have more than enough money to effectively finance global terror operations.

ISIS aims to create an Islamic caliphate across Iraq, Syria, and beyond. Everywhere that the group is in control, it seeks to implement Sharia law, which is rooted in eighth-century Islam. ISIS fighters have executed countless people—typically using barbarous and cruel means—in enforcing its view of Sharia law. ISIS is so brutal that even al-Qaeda activists have urged ISIS terrorists to tone down their actions.

ISIS is well known for using social media to promote its radical politics and religious fundamentalism. The group has successfully recruited young people around the world through the use of the Internet.

The group has also enslaved many of the peoples it has conquered—including women and girls who are sexually abused. Most recently (as of early 2017), ISIS members have remained undeterred in killing the perceived enemies ("infidels") of their version of Islam. Their various attacks seem engineered to demonstrate that their reach is far and wide—with atrocities in Belgium, Turkey, Bangladesh, Baghdad, and more.

Of great concern to many is that ISIS members have apparently secured radioactive uranium in Iraq. This could easily be used to construct a "dirty bomb" that could potentially spread lethal radiation into the atmosphere. There is no doubt that ISIS would love to get its hands on nuclear weaponry.

ISIS leaders have put the Jews in Israel on notice that their days are numbered. Head leader Abu Bakr al-Baghdadi said to the Jewish people: "You will never find comfort in Palestine, Jews. Palestine will not be your land or your home, but it will be a graveyard for you. Allah assembled you in Palestine so that the Muslims kill you."[15]

There is so much more information we could learn about the

various terrorist groups in the Middle East. The main point I wish to emphasize is that these organizations—and others—want to bring down the lesser Satan (Israel) as well as the greater Satan (the United States). And all of them seek the absolute dominance of Islam.

Failed Peace Efforts

Temporary peace has, on occasion, been achieved in the Middle East, such as that which resulted from the Oslo Accords in 1993. However, unresolved issues—invariably related to the city of Jerusalem—have always led to the reemergence of conflict.

A substantial peace came with the Camp David Accords, signed in 1978, in which Jimmy Carter brought Anwar Sadat and Menachem Begin together at Camp David. This meeting led to an Israeli agreement to withdraw from the Sinai in exchange for Egypt normalizing relations between the countries. The Camp David Accords changed the political landscape, but problems remained. More specifically, while the Accords led to a peace treaty between Egypt and Israel, they did not result in peace between Israel and other Arab states. The two sides have been unable to make substantial progress on a broader Arab-Israeli peace.

American presidents since Carter have consistently sought to initiate peace, but no lasting progress has resulted. To make matters worse, the vacuum created by the recent withdrawal of US troops from the Middle East arguably led to the emergence of ISIS, a supremely radical group that has escalated the conflict to ever-new heights.

The Present and the Near-Term Future

My personal assessment is that the situation in the Middle East will continue to escalate from bad to worse. Prophetic Scripture assures us that Israel will increasingly be a sore spot in the world in the end times. In Zechariah 12:2 we read, "Behold, I am about to make Jerusalem a cup of staggering to all the surrounding peoples" (ESV). The "surrounding peoples" of Israel are Islamic, and they are strongly motivated to see Israel destroyed.

No one can deny that Israel is in trouble today. Klein, in his book *The Late Great State of Israel*, tells us that Israel is "under relentless pressure from an international community that favors terrorist gangs over a forward-looking Westernized democracy; that balks at any assertion of Israeli self-defense; that pressures the tiny Jewish country to evacuate vital territory; that perpetuates the Israeli-Palestinian conflict by artificially maintaining a festering 'refugee' crisis; and that provides legitimacy, and at times money, weapons, and advanced training, to Israel's terrorist foes."[16]

In the introduction of this book I noted that the United States is presently calling (as of early 2017) for immediate action to salvage a two-state solution to the Israeli-Palestinian conflict. US representatives say that Israel's continued building of Jewish outposts on Palestinian land is corrosive to the cause of peace. Arab governments are obviously seeking to put a halt to these Israeli settlements. Israel is meanwhile unbending in its possession and occupation of the land. And they are continuing to build housing on Palestinian land. *No solution is in sight.*

Meanwhile, Syria has become a massive thorn in the flesh in the Middle East. In the Syrian civil war, the Russians have sided with Syrian leader Assad against Syrian rebels. Many are concerned that this civil war may lead to a wider regional war. Russia and the United States are presently at bitter odds with each other over the conflict. Some are fearful that America and Russia may come to a point of war over this. Tensions are at a fever pitch.*

* At the time of this writing, it remains to be seen what impact President Donald Trump will have in this regard. At the G20 Summit held in Hamburg, Germany, on July 7-8, 2017, the US and Russia agreed on a ceasefire in southwestern Syria. Israeli prime minister Benjamin Netanyahu opposed the ceasefire agreement. Some political analysts suggest the agreement could ultimately be abused by Russia to help the Assad regime consolidate power in the region. Time will tell.

Meanwhile, Turkey has been cooling in its relationship with NATO while buddying up with Russia—a turn of events that the US government is obviously not happy with. Russia is now friendly with Iran, Turkey, and Syria. It is clear that Russia wants to become the major influence in the region—a reality that bears directly on the eventual "Ezekiel invasion" into Israel (which I'll address later in the book).

There is also the continuing problem of ISIS. The problem Western leaders are facing is that ISIS is like a recurring cancer. To use an analogy, you can cut the vast majority of cancerous tissue out of a human body, but if you don't get 100 percent of it, it can regrow and become just as big as it was before (and bigger). Even though the US and its regional allies have attacked and overcome many ISIS strongholds, the concern is that the group will continue to regroup and spread. Moreover, many wonder whether lone-ranger ISIS sympathizers will continue to emerge and engage in terrorist attacks around the world. Even though they are not formally connected to ISIS, they can contribute toward furthering ISIS's goals. Also of concern is whether ISIS members posing as "immigrants" in Europe and the United States will go on to victimize innocent people.

One thing is certain: The multiple variables of the Middle East conflict seem at present to be cascading out of control. Taken in conjunction with the other signs of the times addressed in this book, can there be any doubt that we are living in the end times?

Biblical prophecy is clear that there will not be lasting peace for Israel or the Middle East (or for the world, for that matter) until the Lord Jesus returns at the second coming. The current president of the US, for example, may seek to bring about a lasting peace in the Middle East, but like all others, he will fail at this task. Only the Lord Jesus will succeed.

Please do not get me wrong. We should still seek to do all we can to bring peace to the region and stop the bloodshed. Peace is always God's ideal (Isaiah 19:23-25), and the apostle Paul called God "the God of peace" (Romans 15:33 ESV). Jesus is the "Prince of Peace" (Isaiah 9:6), and He affirmed, "Blessed are the peacemakers" (Matthew 5:9 NIV).

A realistic assessment of Middle East affairs, however, lends credence to the biblical prophecies which reveal that such peace will ultimately be found only at the return of Jesus Christ. Certainly we can look forward to the day prophesied in Scripture when we will experience universal peace (Isaiah 2:4; see also Isaiah 11:1-9; Hosea 2:18; Zechariah 9:9-10). Meanwhile, the apostle Paul encouraged Christians to pray "for kings and all those in authority so that we can live peaceful and quiet lives marked by godliness and dignity" (1 Timothy 2:2). We should pray specifically that God give our leaders supernatural wisdom that will enable them to make the correct decisions with regard to foreign policy.

Many people are crying out today for a leader who can take control of world crises and solve the Middle East problem. This yearning for a solution to the Middle East problem is setting the stage for what is to come. For Scripture prophesies that the antichrist—the leader of a revived Roman Empire, a "United States of Europe"—will one day sign a covenant with Israel (Daniel 9:27) and impose peace on the Middle East. To the amazement of everyone, he will—from a position of great power—*force* peace upon the Middle East (it will be a "*strong* covenant" ESV, emphasis added). The signing of this covenant will constitute the beginning of the tribulation period. More on all this later.

4
UNDERSTANDING ISLAMIC BELIEFS, PART 1

In this chapter and the next, my goal will be to help us see the Islamic worldview from a Muslim's perspective. The better we understand the Islamic worldview, the better we will understand the current Middle East conflict. Indeed, this will help us to realize all the more why Israel today is constantly on high alert.

First we will explore the five primary doctrines of traditional Islam as well as the five religious duties of Muslims. We will see that certain of these doctrines and duties are interpreted by Islamic extremists in a way that supports their radical propensities. Then in the next chapter, we will narrow our attention to specific beliefs of Islamic fundamentalists.

The Five Primary Doctrines of Traditional Islam

There are five essential doctrines Muslims subscribe to: God, angels, holy books, prophets, and a future judgment. Let's consider what mainstream Muslims believe about these issues.

1. God. There is only one true God, whose name is Allah. The term *Allah* is probably derived from *al illah*, which means "the god." Allah is said to have seven primary characteristics: He is

(1) an absolute unity, (2) all-seeing, (3) all-hearing, (4) all-speaking, (5) all-knowing, (6) all-willing, and (7) all-powerful.

Muslims often insert Allah's name in their conversations. If a Muslim sneezes, he might be heard saying, "Praise Allah!" If he witnesses a beautiful sight, he might say, "Glory to Allah!" No matter what he might encounter in day-to-day life, he is likely to say, "Thanks be to Allah!" Allah is absolutely central to every facet of Muslim life.

Muslims stress that Allah is absolutely one. Because he is one, he has no partners or associates. The emphasis on the absolute oneness of Allah is the primary reason Muslims reject the Christian doctrines of the Trinity and Jesus being "the Son of God." They take this latter phrase quite literally, and believe it implies that Allah had a sexual partner in order to beget Christ. It is for this reason that Muslims also reject the idea that Allah is a "Father." In the Muslim mindset, the term *father* cannot be divorced from the physical realm. Hence, to call Allah "Father" or "heavenly Father" is viewed as blasphemous because it amounts to saying Allah had sexual relations to produce a "Son" (see Suras 6:101; 19:35).

Allah is said to be entirely separate from all of creation, and is not manifested in any way. While Allah's *will* is manifested (in the pages of the Quran), Allah himself is not. He is utterly transcendent. He is so separate and divorced from the creation and so unified to himself that he cannot be associated with creation. Any talk of him revealing himself would compromise his transcendence.

One of the more controversial aspects of the Muslim view of Allah relates to his absolute sovereignty. The Quran tells us, "God hath power over all things" (Sura 3:165). According to Muslims, God brings about both good and evil (Suras 32:13; 113:1-2). He can guide men in righteousness, or he can lead them to evil. In some 20 passages of the Quran, Allah is said to lead men astray. Everything that happens in the universe, whether good or bad, is said to be foreordained by the unchangeable decrees of Allah. Muslims believe all our thoughts, words, and deeds (good or evil) were foreseen, foreordained, predetermined, and decreed from all eternity. Everything is irrevocably and fatefully written (Hadith 8:611). One Muslim theologian, Risaleh-i-Barkhawi, goes so far as to say,

> Not only can he (God) do anything, he actually is the only one who does anything. When a man writes, it is Allah who has created in his mind the will to write. Allah at the same time gives power to write, then brings about the motion of the hand and the pen and the appearance upon paper. All other things are passive, Allah alone is active.[1]

There is thus a very strong strain of fatalism in Islam. This strain can lead to a diminished sense of moral responsibility among Muslims. A frequent statement one hears among devout Muslims is *Enshallah*—"If Allah wills." If something good happens, it is assumed to be Allah's will. If something bad happens (like a child falling over a balcony), it is assumed to be Allah's will. Nothing takes place apart from Allah's will.

In view of the Quranic teaching that Allah engages in both good and evil, it is not surprising to learn that there is no suggestion in the Quran that Allah is holy. The Quran seems to emphasize Allah's power rather than his purity, his omnipotence rather than his holiness.

2. Angels. There is believed to be a hierarchy of angels between Allah and humankind, the chief of whom is Gabriel—an archangel who allegedly gave Quranic revelations to Muhammad (Sura 2:97). Angels are viewed as spirits who have "subtle bodies."

Each human being is said to have two angels who keep a record of all of his or her deeds, good or bad (Sura 50:17). These deeds will then be recalled at the coming judgment.

Angels also play a role when a person dies. We read, "Every soul shall have a taste of death" (Sura 3:185). Indeed, at death "the angels stretch forth their hands, [saying], 'Yield up your souls'" (Sura 6:93). Following this, the Muslim faces a future day of resurrection and judgment, and because there is no assurance of salvation among Muslims, this can be a frightening prospect. The death of unbelievers is especially frightful, for the angels "smite their faces and their backs, [saying]: 'Taste the penalty of the blazing Fire'" (Sura 8:50).

3. Holy Books. Muslims believe there are four inspired books: the Torah of Moses, the Psalms of David, the Gospel of Jesus Christ, and the Quran (which contains the teachings of Muhammad). Muslims believe Allah's revelation is eternal, and hence the substance of all the holy books that derive from him are the same. Why, then, are there differences between, for example, the Quran and the Christian Bible? The answer most often given is that the Bible was tampered with by Jews and Christians so that what passes as the Bible today is not the same as what was originally given to man. Other Muslims point out that there is a progressive nature to Allah's revelation to humankind, for man was not always ready for the fullness of his message. Hence, man was only given as much as he could digest at a given time. These progressively more comprehensive revelations from Allah culminated in the Quran, which is Allah's final and complete revelation.

The Quran is composed of 114 Suras (chapters) arranged in order according to length, with the longer chapters first and the shorter ones last. Because the material is arranged in order from longest to shortest Suras, non-Muslim readers are often confused because they are more used to books having a topical or chronological arrangement. The Quran contains a total of 6,247 verses, and is about four-fifths the length of the New Testament.

Muslims believe the Quran is an exact and faithful reproduction of the original in heaven—an engraved tablet that has existed for all eternity in the presence of Allah. The angel Gabriel took more than 20 years to bring the revelations of the Quran to Muhammad, communicating only isolated sections at any single time, portion by portion, while Muhammad was in a prophetic trance. The Quran is thus viewed not as the words of Muhammad but as the very words of Allah.

Because the Quran was brought from heaven to earth via Gabriel in its original Arabic form, the Arabic language is considered an essential component of the Quran. Many Muslims believe the Quran cannot be divorced from the Arabic language in which it was communicated. Unlike Christians, who have long sought to translate the Bible into as many languages as possible, Muslims have always been reluctant to publish the Quran in other languages for non-Arabic readers.

Muslims say that a prerogative of the Quran is *abrogation*, which involves the annulling of a former law by a new law (Sura 16:101). What this means is that Allah is not bound to his revelations. If he wants, he is free to bring forth new revelations that completely contradict former revelations. If circumstances call for it, Allah is free to rescind earlier revelations and bring about entirely new and different ones.

For example, Muhammad originally ordered his followers to pray toward Jerusalem (Suras 2:150; 2:142). However, when the Jews rejected Muhammad and called him an imposter, he received new revelation to the effect that the correct direction of prayer should be Mecca (Sura 2:125). This change is in keeping with what we read in Sura 2:106: "If we abrogate a verse or consign it to oblivion, we offer something better than it or something of equal value."

The respect the Quran receives in Islamic lands cannot be

overstated. The Quran is the most revered book in any Muslim home. It is called "the mother of books." Verses from the Quran are often inscribed on the walls of Muslim homes. The Quran is also a textbook on Islam for Muslim children.

4. Prophets. The Quran says Allah has sent a prophet to every nation to let people know there is only one true God. Among these "prophets" mentioned in the Quran are Adam, Saleh, Lut (Lot), Hud, Yüacub (Jacob), Ibrahim (Abraham), Yunus (Jonah), Musa (Moses), Daud (David), Al-Yaüsa (Elisha), Zakara (Zachariah), Dhul-Kifl (Ezekiel), Isa (Jesus), Nuhu (Noah), Shuüaib, Ismaiüil (Ishmael), Yusuf (Joseph), Ishaq (Isaac), Harun (Aaron), Sulaiman (Solomon), Yahya (John the Baptist), Ayyub (Job), Ilyas (Elijah), Idrees, and Muhammad. Islamic tradition claims 124,000 prophets have been sent to humankind, but the actual number of books given to the prophets is said to be just 104. Even prophets like Adam, Noah, and Abraham wrote prophetic books, but those books are said to no longer exist.

Each prophet's revelation is stated to have been appropriate only for the age in which he lived. When God gives a new book to one of the prophets, he thereby abrogates the previous books. This means the revelation that came through Muhammad abrogated all previous revelations, including that of the Bible. Each of the great prophets allegedly foretold the coming of the prophet who would succeed him. The last and greatest of the prophets, Muhammad, is called "the Seal of the Prophets" (Sura 33:40). Whereas the previous prophets presented revelation only for their age, Muhammad's revelation is said to be for *all time*. He is said to be a greater prophet than Jesus.

Muslims believe all the prophets raised up by Allah taught the same basic message—that there is only one true God, that people must submit to his laws, and that they must do good works in view of the coming day of judgment. Different prophets may appear to have delivered different messages, but that is due to people's distortions of the prophets' fundamentally identical teachings. The Jews are said to have distorted Old Testament Scripture, and Christians supposedly have distorted the New Testament. Jesus's *original* teachings are said to have been in full agreement with those of Muhammad.

5. A Future Judgment. Muslims believe Allah will one day resurrect all who have died. The day and the hour are not known to mortals. At the last day, Allah will sound a trumpet, the earth will be split, and the bodies of human beings will rejoin their souls. Allah will recreate each individual's body and rejoin his or her soul to it (Sura 46:33). While many Muslims believe this to be a physical resurrection, others believe it is a spiritual one.

Following the resurrection, all humans will be judged. They will be face to face with Allah and will have to give an account for all their actions. The Quran teaches that "only on the day of judgment shall you be paid your full recompense" (Sura 3:185).

Allah will judge people based on the scale of absolute justice. This scale is used to balance one's good deeds against one's bad deeds. The good deeds will be placed in one pan of the balance, and the evil deeds in the other. If the good deeds are heavier, the person will go to Paradise. If, however, one's evil deeds are heavier, he will be cast into the fires of hell. The Quran affirms, "Then those whose balance (of good deeds) is heavy, they will attain salvation: But those whose balance is light, will be those who have lost their souls, in Hell will they abide" (Sura 23:102-103). This essentially means that one must be at least 51 percent good to get into Paradise. This judgment will be based on the records of the two angels who kept track of a person's good and bad deeds throughout life.

Now, for the purposes of this book, three of the aforementioned beliefs are important to remember:

1. Allah is the only true God.
2. Muhammad is the greatest of all prophets.
3. The Quran is the final and definitive Scripture from Allah.

In the next chapter, we will see that Islamic extremists approach these doctrines in such a way as to lend support to their terrorist activities. Here's a brief summary:

- ***Allah:*** Islamic fundamentalists believe Allah is the only true God and say he is on their side in the goal of achieving Islamic dominion over the entire world via a global caliphate. He is on their side in the goal of enforcing Sharia law on a global scale. When the fundamentalists engage in terrorist acts against non-Muslims, they do so in the name of Allah.
- ***Muhammad:*** Islamic fundamentalists believe they are following on the path of Muhammad, for he was *the prophet of the sword.* It is noteworthy that it was only after Muhammad sanctioned use of the sword among his followers that Islam began to grow rapidly. Muhammad's movement eventually took on the character of religious militarism. He transformed his followers into fanatical fighters by teaching them that if they died while fighting Allah's cause, they would be instantly admitted to Paradise. Another motivation for fighting was that the spoils of all their caravan raids in those early days were divided among Muhammad's men, with Muhammad keeping one-fifth of everything.

- ***Quran:*** Islamic fundamentalists believe that the smiting off of the heads of infidels is an act sanctioned in the pages of the Quran. They often cite verses said to support their view that arms are permissible and even compulsory in the defense of Islam. We read, "Fighting is prescribed for you, and ye dislike it. But it is possible that ye dislike a thing which is good for you" (Sura 2:216). Sura 47:4 says, "Therefore, when ye meet the unbelievers (in fight), smite at their necks; at length, when ye have thoroughly subdued them, bind a bond firmly (on them)." Sura 9:5 says, "When the forbidden months are past, then fight and slay the pagans wherever ye find them, and seize them, beleaguer them, and lie in wait for them in every stratagem (of war)."

Chrislam's Distortion of Islam and Christianity

There are many today who subscribe to what is known as Chrislam. It is a view that advocates that Christianity and Islam are compatible with each other—claiming (among other things) that the Bible and the Quran are in agreement, and that Christians and Muslims worship the same God. It is thus reasoned that Christians and Muslims should seek unity with each other. The truth is, however, that Chrislam is based upon false premises.

The Bible and the Quran are Not Compatible

This is easily illustrated by the fact that there are numerous contradictions between the Quran and the Bible—such that if one of them came from God, there is no way the other could have come from Him as well.

Following are some of the notable contradictions between the Quran and the Bible:

- Genesis 8:4 says Noah's ark rested on the mountains of Ararat, while the Quran says Noah's ark rested on Mount Judi (Sura 11:44).
- Genesis 11:27 says Terah was Abraham's father, whereas the Quran says Azar was his father (Sura 6:74).
- Exodus 2:5 says the daughter of Pharaoh found the baby Moses in a basket and adopted him as her son, while the Quran says Pharaoh's wife adopted Moses (Sura 28:8-9).
- Matthew 27:35 says Jesus was crucified, while the Quran says He was not crucified nor even killed (Sura 4:157).
- Luke 1:20 indicates Zechariah's punishment for doubt was that he would not be able to speak until his son was born, while the Quran says he would not be able to speak for three nights (Sura 3:41).
- Luke 2:6-7 says Mary gave birth to Jesus in a stable, whereas the Quran says she gave birth under a palm tree (Sura 19:23).
- Hebrews 1:1-3 indicates Jesus is the brightness of God's glory and the express image of His person, while the Quran says Jesus was no more than a messenger (Sura 5:75).
- John 3:16 says God loves all people, while the Quran says Allah loves only those who follow him (Sura 3:32,57).
- Romans 5:8 indicates that God loves even sinners, while

the Quran indicates that Allah does not love transgressors (Sura 2:190).

- Ephesians 5:25-28 says husbands are to love their wives as Christ loved the church, whereas the Quran says husbands can beat their wives if there is reason for it (Sura 4:34).

That's just a sampling. There are many more points at which the Bible and the Quran are in stark disagreement.

The God of Christianity Is Not the God of Islam

Though those who adhere to Chrislam argue that the Allah of Islam and the God of the Bible are one and the same, the differences between the two are so substantive as to make such a suggestion impossible:

- Whereas the God of the Quran is a radical unity, the God of the Bible is a Trinity—one God eternally manifest in three persons (Matthew 28:19).
- Whereas the God of the Quran cannot have a son, the God of the Bible has an eternal Son named Jesus Christ, the second person of the Trinity (John 3:16).
- Whereas the God of the Quran is not spirit, the God of the Bible is spirit (John 4:24).
- Whereas the God of the Quran is wholly transcendent, the God of the Bible is both transcendent and immanent—both high above us and also near us (Deuteronomy 4:39; Isaiah 57:15; Jeremiah 23:23-24).
- Whereas the God of the Quran brings about both good and evil, the God of the Bible never engages in evil (1 John 1:5).

- Whereas the God of the Quran is not a "Father" (Sura 19:88-92; 112:3), the God of the Bible is addressed as Father (Matthew 6:9).
- Whereas the God of the Quran loves only those who love and obey him, the God of the Bible loves all people, including sinners (Luke 15:11-24).
- Whereas the God of the Quran reveals only his laws and not himself, the God of the Bible has revealed Himself from the beginning.
- Whereas the God of the Quran has no objective basis for forgiving people, the God of the Bible does have an objective basis—the death of Jesus Christ on the cross (Romans 5:8; 1 Corinthians 15:3; 1 Peter 3:18).

There are many other differences between the God of Islam and the God of the Bible. We are left to conclude, then, that Chrislam is misguided.

The Five Pillars of the Faith

Muslims not only believe in five primary doctrines; they also believe every Muslim is obligated to follow five religious duties:

1. Recite the Creed

Every Muslim is obligated to publicly recite the *Shahadah* (literally, "to bear witness"). The creed reads, "There is no god but Allah and Muhammad is the Prophet of Allah." The reciting of this creed is said to make one a Muslim. Of course, a mere mechanical reciting of the words is insufficient. There are six conditions that must be met for the creed to render one a Muslim: (1) The creed must be repeated aloud; (2) it must be perfectly understood; (3) it must be believed in the heart; (4) it must be professed until one dies; (5) it must be recited correctly; and (6) it must be professed and declared without hesitation.[2]

Of course, when a radical Muslim affirms, "There is no god but Allah," his mindset is that Allah is on his side in the goal of establishing a global caliphate and enforcing Sharia law. When he affirms that "Muhammad is the Prophet of Allah," he is keeping in mind that Muhammad is the prophet of the sword. This is the way radical Muslims "read" the creed.

2. Pray Five Times Daily

Every Muslim is expected to perform *salat*, or offer prayers, five times a day: dawn, noon, afternoon, evening, and night. Prayer is compulsory for everyone over the age of ten. The prayers involve specific words and a series of postures—standing, kneeling, hands and face on the ground, and so forth—while facing Mecca, the holy city for Muslims.[3] It is permissible to pray at home, at work, or even outdoors, so long as the place of prayer is free from distractions and is clean. Radical Muslims no doubt pray to Allah for victory in the goal of establishing Islamic dominion over the entire world.

3. Be Charitable

Every Muslim is expected to give alms (*zakat*) to the Muslim community that amount to one-fortieth (or 2 1/2 percent) of one's income. Giving to charity is considered an extremely meritorious act in Islam (see Suras 24:56; 57:18). This donation is intended to benefit widows, orphans, and the sick, or it can be used toward furthering Islam (for example, building mosques and religious schools). There is hard evidence that some of the funds given to Muslim charities are channeled toward supporting Islamic terrorist groups.

4. Fast During the Month of Ramadan

Every Muslim is expected to fast during the month of Ramadan, the ninth month of the Muslim lunar year. During this month Muslims are called to abstain from food, drink, smoking, and sexual relations during the daylight hours. Muslims say that as soon as there is enough light to distinguish a white thread from a black thread each morning, the fast is to begin. At sundown—when there is not enough light to distinguish the threads—Muslims are allowed to partake of these things again until sunrise the next morning. The fast is intended to be a time of purifying both body and soul, as well as increasing one's self-awareness.[4] Terrorist groups such as ISIS encourage Islamic sympathizers around the world to increase their acts of violence during the month of Ramadan.

5. Engage in a Pilgrimage to Mecca

Every Muslim is expected to make an official pilgrimage to Mecca (Hajj) at least once in his or her life. It is believed that going on this journey is meritorious and greatly enhances one's chances for salvation. A highlight of the pilgrimage is running around the Ka'ba (religious shrine) seven times. It is believed that Abraham, Ishmael, and Muhammad did this.

There is a sixth "unofficial" religious duty: engage in violent jihad in the cause of Muhammad and Allah. We will see this illustrated in the next chapter as I focus our attention on the primary beliefs of radical Islamists. These radicals take quite literally Allah's instruction in the Quran to "do battle for the cause of Allah" and fight "against the friends of Satan" (Sura 4:76).

5

UNDERSTANDING ISLAMIC BELIEFS, PART 2

There has been a lot of discussion over the past decade about whether Islam is a religion of peace. I certainly know Muslims who are peaceful, and who have never given any indication of interest in violence against others. I have encountered Muslims who have been nothing but kind to me. And for that I am thankful.

That said, one must also acknowledge the historical reality that Muhammad was quite appropriately known as "the prophet of the sword." Abd El Schafi comments:

> Muhammad and his successors initiated offensive wars against peaceful countries in order to impose Islam by force as well as to seize the abundance of these lands. Their objective was to capture women and children and to put an end to the poverty and hunger from which Arab Muslims suffered. So, Islam was imposed upon Syria, Jordan, Palestine (Jerusalem), Egypt, Libya, Iraq, Iran, all of North Africa, some parts of India and China, and later Spain...Undoubtedly, the concept of an offensive war to spread the faith is a genuine Islamic concept; it is known as a Holy War for the sake of God...If sufficient military power is available to Islamic countries, they

ought to attack all other countries in order to force them to embrace Islam.[1]

There are a number of verses in the Quran that seem to support fighting and slaying and doing battle in the name of Allah (emphasis is added in the following quotations):

- When the forbidden months are past, then *fight and slay the Pagans wherever ye find them. And seize them, beleaguer them. Lie in wait for them* in every stratagem of war; but if they repent, and establish regular prayers and practice regular charity, then open the way for them: For Allah is Oft-Forgiving, Most Merciful (Surah 9:5).
- *Fight those who believe not in Allah* nor the Last Day, nor hold that forbidden which hath been forbidden by Allah and His Apostle, nor acknowledge the Religion of Truth, even if they are of the people of the Book, until they pay the Jizya with willing submission, and feel themselves subdued (Surah 9:29).
- *Go forth, light-armed and heavy-armed*, and strive and struggle with your goods and your persons, *in the Cause of Allah* (Surah 9:41).
- The only reward of those who make war upon Allah and His messenger and strive after corruption in the land will be that *they will be killed or crucified, or have their hands and feet on alternate sides cut off*...Such will be their degradation in the world, and in the Hereafter theirs will be an awful doom (Surah 5:33).
- *Fight in the way of Allah* against those who fight against you...*Slay them wherever you find them*, and drive them

out of the places whence they drove you out... (Surah 2:190-192).

- *Fight against such of those who have been given the Scripture as believe not in Allah* nor the Last Day... *Go forth, light-armed and heavy-armed*, and strive with your wealth and your lives in the way of Allah! (Surah 2:29,41).
- *Those who believe do battle for the cause of Allah*; and those who reject the faith do battle for the cause of evil. So *fight ye against the friends of Satan* (Surah 4:76).

In view of Islam's history—in conjunction with these verses in the Quran—I find myself resonating with Thomas Ice's assessment:

> Muhammad founded Islam with the sword. His followers maintained Islamic rule with the sword. Subsequent generations have always spread Islam's oppressive rule beyond the Arabian Peninsula with the sword. One cannot be a true follower of Islam without holding to the tenets of the Koran, which also advocates forced submission to its rule. How can anyone who knows much about Islam deny this?[2]

The Apocalyptic Beliefs of Islamic Fundamentalism

Today there is an apocalyptic fervor in how radical Muslims view Israel. These radicals go far beyond what traditional Muslims believe (that is, the five Islamic doctrines summarized in the previous chapter). Author Joel Rosenberg had the opportunity to interview Benjamin Netanyahu, the prime minister of Israel. Rosenberg found that Netanyahu is fully aware of this apocalyptic element in the worldview of Islamic radicals:

> I think the West misunderstood, and still misunderstands, the threat of radical Islam…It is a fanatic, messianic ideology that seeks to have an apocalyptic battle for world supremacy with the West. It seeks to correct what it sees—and its disciples see—as an accident of history, where the West has risen and Islam has declined. The correction is supposed to be done by the resurrection of an Islamic empire and the acquisition of nuclear weapons and the use of nuclear weapons, if necessary, to obliterate Islam's enemies, and to subjugate the rest. This is a pathological ideology, much like Nazism was. And it poses a threat, in my judgment, in many ways bigger than Nazism because Hitler embarked on a world conflict and then sought to achieve nuclear weapons, whereas the leading radical Islamic regime, Iran, is seeking to first acquire nuclear weapons and then embark on a world conflict. That is what is not yet understood in the West—and certainly, if it is understood, it is not acted upon.[3]

Dore Gold served as Israel's ambassador to the United Nations from 1997 to 1999 and was a foreign policy advisor to Netanyahu. He also served as a diplomatic envoy to the political leaders of Egypt, Jordan, the Persian Gulf states, and the Palestinian Authority. In his book *The Fight for Jerusalem: Radical Islam, the West, and the Future of the Holy City*, Gold speaks about this apocalyptic aspect of Islam:

> According to Islamic doctrine of recent centuries, the concept of jihad has evolved into an eschatological [end times] concept reserved for the future. Accordingly, pious Muslims are expected to proselytize their religion and gain converts worldwide, an activity known as *da`wa*. Then, at the apocalyptic end of days, mainstream Muslims envision that a great, armed jihad will result in

> the subjugation of the entire world to Islam. Militant Wahhabism, however, reverses the order of *da`wa* and jihad, advancing jihad to the present day as a precursor for spreading Islam.
>
> Hence, almost by definition, militant Islam is an apocalyptic movement preparing in the present for a final confrontation with the West and with others opposed to its agenda. It brings scenarios from the end of days to the here and now. It is therefore not surprising to find apocalyptic references in the speeches of jihadist leaders like Abu Musab al-Zarqawi, the former head of al-Qaeda in Iraq.[4]

Because radical Muslims believe Allah is on their side, they are convinced there is no way they can lose. It is just a matter of time before the entire world becomes subjugated to Islam and Sharia law. This explains why radical Muslims are not afraid of Israel or the United States. In fact, they are emboldened to act as never before. They believe that by their violent acts they are actually preparing the way for the coming "Promised One"—the Muslim Mahdi who will soon publicly emerge and build his global caliphate.[5]

Today there are two Islamic nation-states who hold to this apocalyptic kind of theology—Iran and ISIS. Let's examine both of them here.

Islamic Fundamentalism in Iran

Mainstream Shiites have long believed in the eventual return of the Twelfth Imam, believed to be a direct (bloodline) descendant of Muhammad's son-in-law, Ali (whose family, it is believed, constitutes the only legitimate successors to Muhammad). The Twelfth Imam—who allegedly disappeared as a child in AD 941—will return in the future as the Mahdi ("the rightly guided One"), who will bring about a messianic-like era of global order and justice for Shiites in which Islam will be victorious.

Significantly, it is believed that the time of the appearance of the Twelfth Imam can be hastened through apocalyptic chaos and violence—by unleashing a holy war against Christians and Jews. It is thus within the power of Muslims to influence the divine timetable and bring about the end of days.[6] Interestingly, a number of Shiite leaders in Iran have gone on record as saying they have witnessed physical sightings of the Twelfth Imam, and claim that he will reveal himself to the world soon, presumably following a time of chaos and violence against Christians and Jews.

Ali Ansari, who holds a doctorate from the School of Oriental and African Studies at the University of London, has written numerous books on the history and politics of Iran and the Middle East. In his book *Confronting Iran: The Failure of American Foreign Policy and the Next Great Conflict in the Middle East*, Ansari forcefully suggests that "Iran is not simply *a* problem, it's *the* problem. It's not just a member of the Axis of Evil, but the founding member, the chief sponsor of state terrorism, or to use a more recent characterization, the central banker for terrorism."[7]

This is consistent with the findings of a sobering report published in *U.S. News & World Report*, which tells us that "Iran today is the mother of Islamic terrorism. Tehran openly provides funding, training, and weapons to the world's worst terrorists, including Hezbollah, Hamas, the Palestinian Islamic Jihad, and the Popular Front for the Liberation of Palestine, and it has a cozy relationship with al Qaeda."[8]

Mahmoud Ahmadinejad, the president of Iran from 2005 to 2013, said, "Our revolution's main mission is to pave the way for the reappearance of the Twelfth Imam, the Mahdi."[9] Ahmadinejad believed the appearance of the Twelfth Imam was imminent in view of the coming Muslim annihilation of the Jews in Israel. "For Ahmadinejad, the destruction of Israel is one of the key global developments that will trigger the appearance of the Mahdi."[10] His goal has always been to "wipe Israel off the map"—a phrase he borrowed from the deceased mullah Ayatollah Khamenei.[11]

On one occasion when Ahmadinejad spoke at the United Nations, he concluded his speech by invoking the soon arrival of the Islamic Messiah, the Hidden Imam, the Twelfth Imam, or the Mahdi. He prayed, "O mighty Lord, I pray to you to hasten the emergence of your last repository, the Promised One, that perfect and pure human being, the One that will fill this world with justice and peace."[12]

Once back in Iran, in a videotaped meeting with a prominent ayatollah in Tehran, Ahmadinejad made the claim that during his speech he was surrounded by a light, and that this caused the atmosphere to change: "For 27 or 28 minutes all the leaders did not blink; it's not an exaggeration, because I was looking. They were astonished, as if a hand held them there and made them sit. It had opened their eyes and ears for the message of the Islamic Republic."[13] Ahmadinejad clearly believes Islamic fundamentalists are destined to bring about the end times—the end of the world—by paving the way for the return of the Shia Muslim messiah.

Islamic fundamentalists are convinced that "a world without America and Zionism" is "attainable," and once attained, the Twelfth Imam can be expected to return. They believe humanity will soon know what it is like to live in a Jew-free and USA-free world: "The United States and the Zionist regime of Israel will soon come to the end of their lives," according to the Islamic Republic of Iran Broadcasting's website.[14] The world will soon be without the Great Satan (the USA) and the Little Satan (Israel), and this will bring about the emergence of the Twelfth Imam.

Today's Islamic fundamentalists in Iran believe the apocalypse will occur during their lifetime. They believe they were chosen by Allah himself to play a role in ushering in the end of days. This view is rooted in the apocalyptic theology of the messianic Hojjatieh Society, which is led by Ayatollah Mesbah Yazdi. Interestingly, Iran's state-run television network has aired programs in recent years which delineate the signs of the end of the world. These programs are designed to prepare Iran for the arrival of the Twelfth Imam.[15]

Now, just ponder for a moment what might happen if Iran finally develops a nuclear weapon. The threat against Israel would be beyond grave. After decades of vowing to destroy the Jewish state, Iran's leaders—such as current president Hassan Rouhani, who answers to the Supreme Leader of Iran, Sayyed Ali Hosseini Khamenei—could gain the means to create a new Holocaust simply by pressing a few buttons—buttons that launch nuclear missiles! Israel, about the size of New Jersey, would likely not survive a first nuclear strike by Iran or any other rogue nation.

Iran has long been on track to develop nuclear weapons. To thwart this possibility, the United States signed a nuclear deal with Iran in July 2015, called the Joint Comprehensive Plan of Action. The agreement was engineered to prevent Iran from producing a bomb over the 15-year term of the agreement—and the agreement stipulated that Iran was to permit international inspection of their nuclear facilities beyond that.[16]

The problem is, the deal does not truly eliminate Iran's nuclear program. Specific details of the agreement publicly surfaced about a year after it was signed. We now know that after the first ten years of the agreement's implementation, Iran will be permitted to begin replacing its mainstay centrifuges with more advanced equipment. Iran will end up with fewer centrifuges with which to enrich uranium, but the new machines will be more efficient, capable of enriching uranium at more than twice the former rate.[17]

It is my firm conviction that the Iranians are continuing to move forward on developing nuclear weapons, and that they are not being forthright with their true intentions. A senior Israeli security official was cited in *The Jerusalem Post* as saying, "History has shown that rogue nations tend to use diplomacy as a cover while they complete their work."[18] One political commentator warns, "Iran will stay on track to develop nuclear weapons as fast as possible. Until then, sign any agreement, say anything, cheat—do whatever is necessary to throw the world off track."[19] The entire mentality of the mullahs must be seen as cheating on the agreement: "While buying time, the mullahs are willing to make whatever concessions they have to make, but they are resolved to never lose sight of their ultimate purposes—to get nuclear weapons, to defeat the United States and to wipe Israel from the face of the earth."[20] As noted earlier, Iran's supreme leader Ayatollah Khamenei has promised that Israel will not survive the next 25 years. It would thus seem that any effects of the US agreement with Iran will be short-lived at best.

One analysis I read suggested that we must continue to "be prepared to confront an Iranian regime just as hostile to the West as past ones…There are also real risks that a much bigger and broader war is brewing in the region."[21] I agree with this assessment. In fact, I believe that the "bigger and broader war" that is "brewing in the region" is none other than the prophesied Ezekiel invasion described in Ezekiel 38–39, which I will address later in this book. In that chapter I will demonstrate that one day in the not-too-distant future, there will be a massive invasion into Israel involving not just Iran, but also Russia, Sudan, Turkey, Libya, Kazakhstan, Kyrgyzstan, Uzbekistan, Turkmenistan, Tajikistan, Armenia, and possibly northern Afghanistan.

Islamic Fundamentalism in ISIS

ISIS started as an al-Qaeda splinter group, and its current aim is to create an Islamic caliphate across Iraq, Syria, and beyond. The establishment of this caliphate is central to the end-of-days worldview of ISIS. Mark Hitchcock says,

> For them, the end of days is at hand, and the caliphate is a precursor to the advent of their messiah. The appeal of ISIS and the caliphate is so magnetic and irresistible to young Muslims that by the end of May 2015, nearly 30,000 Muslims from 115 nations had joined ISIS in Iraq and Syria, with an additional 5,000 joining the wing of ISIS in Libya...The Islamic State is positioning itself as the harbinger of the end times—of the final and decisive battle between the Muslims and the enemies of Allah, from which the Muslims will emerge victorious, after which peace—the peace of total Sharia adherence—will prevail over all the earth.[22]

Meanwhile, ISIS has executed countless people as it enforces its commitment to Sharia law. Jews and Christians are among those mercilessly executed, often in barbarous ways, including the slitting of throats, beheading, or even crucifixion, in open mockery of the Christ of Christianity. Former US Secretary of State John Kerry widely publicized how ISIS, over years past, has committed mass genocide against large numbers of Middle Eastern Christians.[23]

Christian churches in the Middle East are also targets of persecution. In areas of Syria and Iraq that are under the control of ISIS, churches have been seized, crucifixes destroyed, and paintings depicting scenes from the Bible are obliterated—they are considered "idolatrous" by ISIS members.[24]

A key target for ISIS, of course, is Israel. ISIS leaders say that the Jewish nation will soon be a thing of the past. with the land becoming a mass graveyard for executed Jews. ISIS members believe they are acting under the direct lead of Allah with their moves against Israel.[25]

And ISIS is not the only extremist Islamic group targeting Israel. Whether we are talking about ISIS or organizations such as al-Qaeda, Hezbollah, Hamas, or the Palestinian Islamic Jihad, they all have the common goal of annihilating Israel. Pastor Robert Jeffress, in his book *Countdown to the Apocalypse*, commented that "in the end all the Islamic terror groups are essentially the same because they are all anti-Israel, anti-West, and all of them pursue their goals using the most violent means possible."[26]

This is why Israel is constantly on high alert. Israel's leaders recognize that their country is the target of many such groups. On September 29, 2014, Benjamin Netanyahu spoke at the United Nations and said,

> Ladies and gentlemen, militant Islam's ambition to dominate the world seems mad. But so too did the global ambitions of another fanatic ideology that swept to power eight decades ago...The Nazis believed in a master race. The militant Islamists believe in a master faith. They just disagree about who among them will be the master of the master faith. That's what they truly disagree about. Therefore, the question before us is whether militant Islam will have the power to realize its unbridled ambitions.[27]

ISIS, of course, does not limit its terrorist activities to the Middle East. Authorities in both Europe and the United States are currently watchful for ISIS attacks on their own soil. ISIS is like an octopus with long tentacles that reach around the world. Intelligence and law enforcement agencies are understandably on constant alert for the next attack. ISIS certainly has the money to finance global terrorism; they are the richest jihad terror group in the world.

Where did ISIS get all its money? They have multiple streams of income. Islamic nations have donated incredibly large sums of money to their cause. ISIS extremists often kidnap people and hold them until a large ransom is paid. ISIS had a massive cash infusion of around $500 million when they invaded Mosul and looted its banks. They made an equal amount by selling black market oil. They also steal and sell precious artifacts.[28] All things considered, they've got more than enough money to inflict an apocalyptic bloodbath upon Israel, the United States, and other countries.

God Is Still in Control

As we study the activities and goals of extremist Muslims, it might seem easy to forget that God is in sovereign control of the universe. There's a lot of negativity documented in this chapter. That's why I feel it necessary, as I close, to point to the Bible's reminders that God reigns! Psalm 66:7 affirms that "by his great power he rules forever." We are assured in Psalm 93:1 that "the Lord is king" and that He is "armed with strength." God asserts, "Everything I plan will come to pass, for I do whatever I wish" (Isaiah 46:10). He assures us, "It will all happen as I have planned. It will be as I have decided" (Isaiah 14:24). Proverbs 16:9 tells us, "We can make our plans, but the Lord determines our steps." Proverbs 19:21 says, "You can make many plans, but the Lord's purpose will prevail." Yes, God is sovereign—over all the nations of the earth (Ezekiel 38:4,8,16; Daniel 2:21; 4:17).

That being so, we must assume that God is now allowing ISIS and other such organizations to influence and even reshape the

Middle East in preparation for the end-time events prophesied in the Bible—including the imminent Ezekiel invasion into Israel:

> ISIS has served as a potent catalyst to bring Russia into Syria—right on the northern border of Israel. Russian tanks, troops, and jet fighters are streaming into Syria under the guise of fighting ISIS. Russia is part of the Gog colossus that will invade Israel in the last days, according to Ezekiel 38. The presence of Russia on Israel's northern border is unprecedented and could be a run-up to the fulfillment of Ezekiel's ancient prophecy.[29]

Don't for a minute think this invading force prophesied by Ezekiel will succeed. Later in this book, I'll share about how God Himself will annihilate these invaders.

I close with a final observation: It is possible that the unrest caused today in the Middle East by ISIS and other terrorist organizations is setting the stage for the forced peace that the antichrist will bring about when he signs a covenant with Israel (Daniel 9:27). The signing of this covenant will mark the beginning of the tribulation period. I say "forced peace" because the covenant is said to be a "*strong* covenant" (Daniel 9:27 ESV, emphasis added)—apparently meaning a covenant enforced from a position of great strength, such as that possessed by the antichrist as the head of a revived Roman Empire. This scenario seems increasingly likely in the day in which we live.

6

THE DIMINISHING SUPPORT FOR ISRAEL

Scripture reveals that as we continue to move into the end times, Israel will increasingly be a "lone ranger" state. The Jewish nation will have very few (if any) true friends in the world.

Historically, the United States has been a solid ally to Israel. During the 1967 Six-Day War, for example, the Russians were poised to attack Israel and had been preparing to do so for a substantial time. Soviet warships, submarines, bombers, and fighter jets were mobilized and ready for action. However, President Johnson—aware of Russia's intentions—ordered the US 6th Fleet to steam toward Israel as a show of solidarity with the country. This served to stare down the mighty Russian bear.

In 1973, the Russians showed renewed military aggression toward Israel. Though it was Egypt, Syria, and some other Arab/Islamic countries that launched the actual attack against Israel, Russia provided the military muscle behind the attack—including weaponry, ammunition, intelligence, and military training to assist this Arabic coalition in their goal of destroying Israel.

While Russia backed the Arabs, the United States provided help to Israel. Things began to heat up between the Russians and the United States. Russian general secretary Leonid Brezhnev fired off a threatening communiqué, couched in diplomatic language, to US President Richard Nixon. Both Soviet and US forces were put on high alert. Nixon promptly returned the favor and fired off a response to Brezhnev, warning him that his actions could lead to "incalculable consequences." This strongly worded communiqué, combined with the presence of US military forces in the region, served to once again stare down the Russian bear.

American presidents since then have consistently sought to initiate peace in the Middle East, but no lasting progress has resulted. To make matters worse, the vacuum created by the withdrawal of US troops from the Middle East—beginning in 2007 and completed by 2011—arguably led to the emergence of ISIS, which has contributed to escalating the conflict.

In recent years, the United States' friendship with Israel has been cooling. In late 2016, the US—at the very end of President Barack Obama's term—called for immediate action to salvage a two-state solution to the Israeli-Palestinian conflict. Obama himself abstained on a UN Security Council vote that condemned Israel—something no other US president has ever done. US representatives, speaking for Obama, later said that Israel's continued building of Jewish outposts on Palestinian land was corrosive to the cause of peace.

Prophecy author Joel Rosenberg commissioned McLaughlin & Associates to do a poll to measure the American response to Barack Obama's abstaining on the UN Security Council vote just before Donald Trump took office. Following are some highlights of the results of the poll:

- 29.4% overall said Obama was right to abstain on the UN vote.
- 37.2% overall said Obama was wrong to betray Israel.
- 50.3% of Democrats said Obama was right to abstain on the UN vote.

- 12.7% of Republicans said Obama was right to abstain on the UN vote.
- 52.9% of political liberals said Obama was right to abstain on the UN vote.
- 12.2% of political conservatives said Obama was right to abstain on the UN vote.[1]

Meanwhile, a poll conducted by the Pew Research Center regarding Israel and the Middle East conflict had similar findings:

- 74% of Republicans say they sympathize more with Israel than the Palestinians.
- 33% of Democrats sympathize with Israel.

This means there is a 41-point gap between Republicans and Democrats on this issue. Which is why Israeli prime minister Benjamin Netanyahu continues to be popular with Republicans and unpopular with Democrats.[2]

I think everyone will agree that one's political viewpoint has a lot to do with one's outlook on Israel. Rosenberg's assessment of US-Israel relations resonates with many Christians today: "It is painful to watch personal tensions growing between the White House and the State Department and the Netanyahu government at a moment when Iran's nuclear threat requires unity between two long-standing allies. Why do we see such intense emotion from the Obama team about Netanyahu, a faithful ally of the US, but never against Khamenei?"[3]

After Barack Obama abstained from the vote, US Senators Marco Rubio and Ben Cardin introduced a Senate resolution that read in part:

> "Efforts to delegitimize Israel have been underway a long

> time at the United Nations and have now sadly been aided by the outgoing administration, but the time has come to turn back the tide and renew America's commitment to the Jewish state," said Rubio. "When it comes to the U.S.-Israel alliance, we believe that senators of both parties must stand firmly with Israel and condemn efforts to undermine Israel's legitimacy. This resolution expresses the Senate's rejection of continued anti-Israel efforts at the United Nations, reiterates our commitment to Israel, and urges the incoming administration [of Donald Trump] to work with Congress on this issue."[4]

At present, it appears that the Trump administration will have a much more favorable relationship with Israel. Time will tell.

Nations Ganging Up on Israel

The UN, as previously noted, is obviously uninterested in fair treatment toward Israel. The condemnations have been piling up on Israel for quite some time. As David Reagan put it:

> Just consider a partial listing of condemnations issued by the United Nations Human Rights Council since it was established in 2006. Israel has been condemned 62 times, Syria 17 times, North Korea 8 times, and Iran 5 times.
>
> Of the 193 members of the United Nations, only 11 nations have been condemned, representing six percent. Of the 116 resolutions of condemnation, 53 percent have been aimed at Israel!
>
> Not a one of the following states have received a single condemnation despite the fact that all of them have horrible records of human rights violations—Cuba, China,

> Pakistan, Russia, Saudi Arabia, Egypt, Somalia, Nicaragua, and Venezuela.
>
> *Yet Israel has been condemned 62 times.*
>
> Or consider this list of terrorist organizations—ISIS, al Qaeda, Boko Haram, Fatah, Hamas, Hezbollah and Islamic Jihad. The only one that has been condemned by the UN Human Rights Council is ISIS, with one condemnation!
>
> *Yet Israel has been targeted 62 times.*[5]

Complaints about the United Nations' anti-Israel bias seem justified. Jay Sekulow, in his book *The Rise of ISIS*, notes that "the UN has made its anti-Israel sentiments known in a number of ways. For example, during the 2014 conflict between Hamas and Israel, the UN refused to denounce Hamas's practice of using human shields in danger zones and blamed Israel when Palestinian civilians died." Moreover, "when UN officials discovered Hamas rockets hidden in UN facilities such as schools, the rockets were handed back to Hamas rather than confiscated."[6] Joel Richardson understandably laments that "the United Nations has morphed into an Israel-hating monstrosity."[7]

Even apart from the UN, nations around the world are ganging up on Israel. A few weeks after Obama's call for immediate action to salvage a two-state solution to the Israeli-Palestinian conflict, there was a meeting of 70 nations in Paris to discuss how to solve the Middle East conflict. Two days before the meeting, *Yahoo News* reported:

> About 70 countries and international organizations will make a new push for a two-state solution in the Middle East at a conference...just days before Donald Trump takes office vowing unstinting support for

> Israel. The Paris meeting aims to revive the moribund Israeli-Palestinian peace process, amid fears of fresh violence if Trump implements a pledge to recognize the contested city of Jerusalem as Israel's capital. But neither Israel nor the Palestinians will be represented in Paris, and Israeli Prime Minister Benjamin Netanyahu has dismissed it as a "rigged" conference.[8]

A day *after* the meeting, it was reported,

> Foreign ministers and other diplomats from some 70 different countries descended on Paris on Sunday, with the intent to renew peace talks between Israel and the Palestinians…"We are here to reiterate strongly that the two-state solution is the only one possible," said French Foreign Minister Jean-Marc Ayrault, in his opening remarks to top envoys at the conference… Israeli Prime Minister Benjamin Netanyahu refused to attend, decrying the conference as biased against Israel from the outset. "It's a rigged conference, rigged by the Palestinians with French auspices to adopt additional anti-Israel stances," he said…U.S. Secretary of State John Kerry participated in Sunday's talks in order to "try to ensure America's continued interest in a two-state solution is preserved."…Trump's incoming administration is expected to adopt a decidedly different tack.[9]

All of this has obvious significance in terms of biblical prophecy. Joseph Farah commented: "I can say with confidence and disappointment as a former Middle East correspondent and prophecy watcher of 40 years that nothing good will come out of this gathering."[10] My friend Jan Markell understandably warned,

> Israel is concerned that round two of an international attack is in the works. This time a two-state solution could be forced on them. Joel 3:2 tells us that in the last days the nation of Israel will have her land "divided." Joel 3 also suggests that the nations that enter into the division of God's land will face judgment. Israel is the only location that God calls "His land." He is jealous for it. He does not want it divided.[11]

In Joel 3:2, God says, "I will gather the armies of the world into the valley of Jehoshaphat. There I will judge them for harming my people, my special possession, for scattering my people among the nations, and for dividing up my land." Markell observes, "The Palestinians don't want a two-state solution. They want the eradication of Israel as we know it and a one-state solution—Palestine."[12]

Meanwhile, anti-Semitism is escalating everywhere. Tim LaHaye and Ed Hindson cite a European study that surveyed 6,000 self-identified Jews. The findings affirm that things are getting worse:

- Two-thirds of respondents said that anti-Semitism was a serious problem in their country; three out of four felt it had worsened in the past five years.
- Close to a quarter said they sometimes refrained from visiting Jewish events or sites out of safety concerns. Nearly two out of five usually avoided public displays of Jewish identity such as wearing a Star of David.
- Almost one in three had considered emigrating because they did not feel safe as Jews.[13]

The April 2015 issue of *U.S. News & World Report* tells us, "Seventy years after the Holocaust, anti-Semitism is again growing more virulent in Europe. From Toulouse to Paris, London to Berlin,

Brussels to Copenhagen, Jews are being harassed, assaulted, and even killed."[14]

Newsweek published an article titled, "Exodus: Why Europe's Jews Are Fleeing Once Again." In the article we read of some recent events:

> France has suffered the worst violence, but anti-Semitism is spiking across Europe...In Britain there were around 100 anti-Semitic incidents...In Berlin a crowd of anti-Israel protesters had to be prevented from attacking a synagogue. In Liege, Belgium, a café owner put up a sign saying dogs were welcome, but Jews were not allowed...Yet for many French and European Jews, the violence comes as no surprise. Seventy years after the Holocaust, from Amiens to Athens, the world's oldest hatred flourishes anew.[15]

A recent report issued by the Pew Research Center indicates that Jews are being persecuted in 34 out of 45 European countries, and anti-Semitic harassment worldwide has reached a seven-year high. A Lamb and Lion Ministries report tells us,

> All over Europe, and particularly in Greece, France, and Belgium, Jews are seeing their religious freedoms violated, their cemeteries vandalized, and their synagogues desecrated. They are also experiencing increasing personal attacks that often result in death. In France, the annual number of anti-Semitic incidents is currently seven times as high as in the 1990s. In 2014, they doubled.[16]

No US Assistance to Israel in the Coming Ezekiel Invasion

It seems from current rhetoric that president Donald Trump intends to restore strong relations with Israel. Despite that, however, we can say rather definitively that *no* nation—*not even the United States*—will stand with Israel when a massive northern military coalition invades Israel. This coalition will involve Russia and a group of Muslim nations—including Iran, Sudan, Turkey, Libya, Kazakhstan, Kyrgyzstan, Uzbekistan, Turkmenistan, Tajikistan, Armenia, and possibly northern Afghanistan—invading Israel in the end times (Ezekiel 38:1-6). (I'll address this invasion in detail in the next chapter.)

Scripture affirms that Israel will stand alone when this attack takes place. Granted, there will be a few nations that voice a lame protest against the invasion. Ezekiel 38:13 tells us, "Sheba and Dedan and the merchants of Tarshish will ask [the invading force], 'Do you really think the armies you have gathered can rob them [that is, the Jews in Israel] of silver and gold? Do you think you can drive away their livestock and seize their goods and carry off plunder?'"

Sheba and Dedan apparently refer to the geographical territory that today is Saudi Arabia. Arnold Fruchtenbaum writes: "Sheba and Dedan are countries in northern Arabia, which shows that at least some of the Arab states will not favor the Russian presence in the Middle East."[17]

Tarshish, however, is much harder to locate. Some Bible expositors believe ancient Tarshish may refer to modern-day Spain. Others say it may be Great Britain. Others say it may refer to the colonies of Western Europe and the nations that have subsequently arisen from them—including the United States. Still others say Tarshish might represent virtually all the Western nations of the end times, which would include the United States.

That being so, some suggest—based on Ezekiel 38:13—that the United States might be among the nations that lodge a protest against the massive Ezekiel invasion. But the protest is a feeble one, with no military action to back the words. My personal assessment is that there is no definitive understanding of what geographical region is meant by Tarshish. But there is no uncertainty on the fact that Israel will stand alone when the Ezekiel invasion takes place.

A Weakening of the United States

According to prophetic scriptures, the United States will not only fail to come to Israel's rescue during the invasion, but apparently is not even mentioned in Bible prophecy, except for general references to "the nations" (for example, Haggai 2:6-7 and Isaiah 66:18-20). This causes one to wonder: *Why not?*

In other books I've written on Bible prophecy, I've held to the position that in the end times the United States will likely weaken in power while the revived Roman Empire—a United States of Europe—will become the superpower of the day. A weakening of the United States would explain (1) why it does not come to Israel's aid during the Ezekiel invasion, and (2) why it is apparently not even mentioned in Bible prophecy.

There are a number of factors that might explain the end-times weakening of the United States. One is that it could be on the receiving end of a nuclear detonation. If even a single major city—such as New York City, or Los Angeles, or Chicago, or Dallas—were destroyed, this would have an absolutely devastating effect on the already-fragile, debt-ridden US economy. And with so many easy entrances across both the northern and southern borders of the country, it would not be difficult for a terrorist to smuggle in a nuclear bomb. As of now, countries that have threatened a nuclear strike against the United States include Iran and North Korea, and Russia could carry out a strike as well.

If such a nuclear detonation were to occur, it could be an expression of Islamic jihad. Radical Islamic fundamentalists are well known for their use of arms and explosives in defending their version of Islam, and if they had the opportunity to get their hands on a nuclear weapon that could be used against the United States, they would surely do so.

It is also possible that the United States could be weakened due to an electromagnetic pulse (EMP) attack. A single nuclear weapon, delivered by a missile to an altitude of a few hundred miles over US air space, would yield catastrophic damage. Such a missile could easily be launched from a freighter off the coast. The electromagnetic pulse produced by such a weapon would have a high likelihood of severely damaging electrical power and information systems that Americans are heavily dependent upon. At high risk would be the infrastructures for handling electric power, sensors and protective systems of all kinds, computers, cell phones and other telecommunications devices, cars, boats, airplanes, trains, and other means of transportation, fuel and energy resources, banking and finance transactions, emergency services, and even food and water. Anything electrical in nature is at risk. Of great concern to US intelligence officials is the fact that Iran has been observed practicing launching missiles a few hundred miles into the atmosphere from a freighter boat.

It is also possible that the United States could weaken due to a moral implosion. There are many statistics that show moral and spiritual decline are widespread. As the downward spiral continues to worsen, it could very well be that God decides to bring judgment upon the nation (see Job 12:23; Daniel 2:20-21; Romans 1:18-28).

Yet another reason the United States may weaken is that the nation might turn its back on Israel in the end times. As we learned earlier, in Genesis 12:3 God promised Abraham and his descendants: "I will bless those who bless you and *curse those who treat you with contempt*" (emphasis added). This ancient promise from God has never been revoked. Should the day ever come when the United States turns against Israel, woe unto this country! It is good for us to remember that God is a promise keeper, and He will bless those who bless Israel, and stand against those who stand against Israel.

Tim LaHaye and Ed Hindson comment,

> Given God's promise to Israel in Genesis 12:3, we can conclude that America's future is closely connected to the kind of relation it has with Israel. Over the decades that America has stood as Israel's ally, the nation has been blessed. Yet we also have to acknowledge that when the US fails to show support for Israel, then God's blessings will be removed. Not only does Israel need America, but America also needs Israel.[18]

I've also long believed that the rapture of the church could cause the United States to weaken. It seems fair to say that this country will be negatively affected by the rapture more so than most other nations. That is because there is such a high concentration of Christians here. Following the moment of the rapture, many workers of all kinds will no longer show up at their workplace. Many bills and mortgages will go unpaid, including college tuition bills and loans. Many business leaders will no longer show up to help run their companies. Many law enforcement personnel will no longer be here to keep the peace, and crime will worsen. The stock market will crash like never before because of the horrific panic over millions of people suddenly vanishing. You can imagine how devastating these developments will be on the United States.

There is another factor to consider here in relation to the rapture: once it occurs, *all Israel-supporting Christians will no longer be on planet Earth*. This will no doubt contribute to the increased anti-Semitism expected to occur during the tribulation period.

Will the United States Ultimately Side with the Antichrist?

It is entirely possible that following the rapture of the church, the United States may end up in some kind of subservient role with the revived Roman Empire, which will be headed by the antichrist. Because many US citizens are from Europe, it would be natural for the US to become an ally of this revived Roman power in the end times. Should this occur, the United States will be subsumed into the globalism that will emerge and prevail during the tribulation.

I hate to say it, but it seems clear that when Armageddon breaks out at the end of the tribulation period, troops from the United States may apparently be there, standing against Israel, and ultimately standing against the Lord at the second coming. Zechariah 12:3 informs us, "On that day I will make Jerusalem an immovable rock. *All the nations* will gather against it to try to move it, but they will only hurt themselves" (emphasis added). The phrase, "all the nations" would certainly seem to include the United States.

Likewise, in Zechariah 14:2 we read, "I will gather *all the nations* to fight against Jerusalem" (emphasis added). Again, "all the nations" would appear to include the United States.

Then, in Revelation 16:14, we are told that "the rulers of the world" will be gathered together "for battle against the Lord on that great judgment day of God the Almighty." The "rulers of the world" would also include the president of the United States.

The rapture may indirectly lead to all of this and more. It is easy to see how a *Christian-less* United States could ally with the revived Roman Empire and then find itself in league with the antichrist against Israel. That is a sobering possibility to ponder.

These are days for discernment!

7

NORTHERN STORM RISING: THE NEARING "EZEKIEL INVASION"

The book of Ezekiel was written by the prophet Ezekiel, the son of Buzi, between 593 and 570 BC. God had called him into service as a prophet when he was about 30 years of age. At the time, he was training to be a priest. Like all the other Jews of his day, however, he soon found himself living in exile in Babylon, and this captivity would last 70 years. Ezekiel's messages, then, were for his fellow Jews in exile.

Ezekiel's name literally means "God is strong" or "strengthened by God." To carry on his work of confronting the people regarding their sins, and bringing comfort to them while in exile, Ezekiel would surely have needed God's strength.

One of the most important end-time prophecies in the Bible is found in Ezekiel 38–39. In this passage the prophet—some 2,600 years ago—stated that some time after Israel becomes a nation again (Ezekiel 37), there would be an all-out invasion against it by a massive northern assault force. The goal of this force will be to utterly obliterate the Jewish people. Mark Hitchcock tells us that the ultimate threat for Israel, according to Scripture, "is not ISIS, but rather, a Russian-Islamic alliance that will involve Iran as a key player. This threat will completely eclipse ISIS and play a key role in God's end-time drama."[1]

What nations make up this assault force? Ezekiel 38:1-6 specifies Rosh, Magog, Meshach and Tubal, Persia, Ethiopia, Put, Gomer, and Beth-togarmah. A comparison of Ezekiel's prophecy with ancient historical records, archeological discoveries, and current linguistic studies reveals the identity of these various nations:

Rosh apparently refers to modern-day Russia. There is considerable historical evidence that a place known as Rosh—sometimes using alternate spellings such as Rus, Ros, and Rox—was very familiar to the ancient world and was located in the territory now occupied by Russia. Rosh also appears as a place name in Egyptian inscriptions as Rash, dating as early as 2600 BC. One inscription that dates to 1500 BC refers to a land called Reshu that was located to the north of Egypt (as is the case with modern Russia).

Rosh (or its equivalent) is found in a variety of other ancient documents as well. Placing Rosh in the area today known as Russia has long been a tradition in the Christian church, going back to as early as AD 438. In Ezekiel 39:2, Rosh is said to be "from the uttermost parts of the north" (ESV). The term "north" is to be understood in relation to Israel. If you were to take a map and draw a line from Israel and go straight north, you would end up in Russia.

Magog refers to the geographical area in the southern portion of the former Soviet Union—probably including the former southern Soviet republics of Kazakhstan, Kyrgyzstan, Uzbekistan, Turkmenistan, Tajikistan, and possibly even northern parts of Afghanistan. Significantly, this entire area is Muslim-dominated, with more than enough religious motivation to move against Israel.

Meshech and Tubal refers to the geographical territory to the south of the Black and Caspian Seas of Ezekiel's day—what is now Turkey. Meshech and Tubal are apparently the same as the Mushki and Tabal of the Assyrians, and the Moschi and Tibareni of the Greeks, and they inhabited the territory that constitutes modern Turkey. This is confirmed by the ancient historian Herodotus.

Persia is modern Iran. Persia became Iran in 1935, and the Islamic Republic of Iran in 1979. The borders on the east and west sides of ancient Persia were wider than the modern borders of Iran, so Persia could actually refer to Iran plus territories extending to the east and the west, all of which are Islamic. Iran hates Israel and seeks to wipe it out.

Ethiopia refers to the geographical territory to the south of Egypt on the Nile River—what is today known as Sudan. Sudan is a hardline Islamic nation that is a kindred spirit with Iran in its venomous hatred of Israel. These nations are already such close allies that a mutual stand against Israel would not in the least be unexpected. Sudan is infamous for its ties to terrorism and its harboring of the late Osama bin Laden from 1991 to 1996.

Put, a land to the west of Egypt, is modern-day Libya. However, ancient Put was larger than the Libya that exists today, and hence the boundaries of Put, as referenced in Ezekiel 38–39, may extend beyond those of Libya, perhaps including portions of Algeria and Tunisia.

Gomer apparently refers to part of the geographical territory in modern Turkey. The ancient historian Josephus said Gomer founded those whom the Greeks called the Galatians. The Galatians of New Testament times lived in central Turkey. Hence, there is a direct connection of ancient Gomer to modern Turkey. Moreover, many claim Gomer may be a reference to the ancient Cimmerians or Kimmerioi. History reveals that from around 700 BC on, the Cimmerians occupied the geographical territory that is modern Turkey.

Beth-togarmah also apparently refers to modern-day Turkey. In Hebrew, "Beth" means "house." "Beth-togarmah" is a Hebrew term that means "the House of Togarmah." Ezekiel 38:6 makes reference to Beth-togarmah as being from the remote parts of the north.

Hence, Beth-togarmah must be located to the north of Israel, which is true of present-day Turkey.

There are several intriguing things about the prophecy of these attacking nations that immediately grab my attention. First, this specific alignment of nations described by Ezekiel has never occurred in history. It is, however, occurring in the present day. All these nations are now aligning together. This lends credence to the idea that we are living in the end times, and that the stage is presently being set for this Ezekiel invasion.

Second, an alliance between these nations likely did not make good sense back in Ezekiel's day. After all, they were not even located near each other. A person living back then might have wondered, "Why would these geographically separated nations want to invade Israel?"

Today, however, an alliance between these nations makes great sense, for they are almost all Islamic, except for Russia. Of course, Islam did not even exist back in Ezekiel's day. So there is no way people living back then would have seen this connecting point. But now the connection is obvious. These nations are predominantly Islamic, and their hatred of Israel is what will motivate the invasion.

What About Iraq?

We know from Ezekiel 38:1-6 that the northern coalition of nations will include Russia, Iran, Sudan, Turkey, Libya, Kazakhstan, Kyrgyzstan, Uzbekistan, Turkmenistan, Tajikistan, Armenia, and possibly northern Afghanistan. *But what about Iraq?*

It's not beyond the realm of possibility that Iraq will indeed be a part of this invading coalition. I say this because in addition to the nations mentioned in Ezekiel 38:1-6, we find that the invading force will include "many peoples with you" (verse 15 ESV). It may be that Iraq is among these "many peoples."

The Ezekiel Invasion—an End-Times Prophecy

How do we know Ezekiel 38–39 is an end-times prophecy? First and foremost, Ezekiel was clear that the things of which he spoke would be fulfilled "in the latter years" (Ezekiel 38:8 ESV) and "in the latter days" (verse 16 ESV) from the standpoint of his day. The Old Testament use of the term "latter days" (and similar terms) refers to the time leading up to the coming of the Messiah to set up His millennial kingdom on earth. More specifically, such terms are generally used to speak of Israel during her future time of tribulation.

Second, there has never been an invasion of Israel on the scale of what is described in Ezekiel 38–39. Nor has there ever been an invasion that includes the specific nations mentioned in the passage. Because the prophecy has not been fulfilled yet, its fulfillment must yet be future.

Moreover, Ezekiel affirmed that the invasion would occur *after* Israel has been regathered from all around the earth—"from exile in many nations" (Ezekiel 38:12)—to a land that had been a wasteland. The only regathering of Jews "from exile in many nations" is that which is occurring in modern days—especially since 1948, when Israel achieved statehood.

Now, because chapters 36–37 are being literally fulfilled (that is, because Jews are presently returning to Israel from out of many nations), it is reasonable and consistent to assume that chapters 38–39 will also be literally fulfilled. This is in keeping with the well-established precedent of biblical prophecies throughout the Old Testament being literally fulfilled.

Gog—the Commander of the Northern Military Coalition

In Ezekiel 38, "Gog" is a reference to the powerful leader of the end-times northern military coalition that will launch an invasion against Israel. Gog is referred to as the "prince of Rosh, Meshech and

Tubal" (verse 2 NASB). This term appears 11 times in Ezekiel 38–39, thereby indicating that he plays a significant role in this end-times invasion.

"Gog" may or may not be a proper name. There is reference to an altogether different Gog in 1 Chronicles 5:4, where we read that among the sons of Joel were "Shemaiah his son, Gog his son, Shimei his son" and others (NASB). This verse at least indicates that the term can be used as a proper name. It would seem, however, that the term is not intended as a proper name in the context of Ezekiel 38–39.

Rather, the term may refer to a king-like role—such as Pharaoh, Caesar, czar, or president. The term means "high," "supreme," "a height," or "a high mountain." Apparently, then, this leader—this czar-like military leader—will be a man of great stature who commands tremendous respect.

We must be clear that Gog is not just another name for the antichrist. You will end up in prophetic chaos if you try to make this identification. The antichrist heads up a revived Roman Empire (Daniel 2, 7), while Gog heads up an invasion force made up of Russia and a number of Muslim nations (Ezekiel 38:1-6). Further, Gog's moment in the limelight is short-lived (it's all over when God destroys the invading force—Ezekiel 39). The antichrist, by contrast, is in power over the span of a significant part of the tribulation period.

Some have wondered whether Russia's president, Vladimir Putin, may be Gog. Interestingly, though Joel Rosenberg—author of the book *Epicenter: Why Current Rumblings in the Middle East Will Change Your Future*—does not believe one can definitively say that Putin is Gog, he doesn't rule out the possibility either:

> Am I saying that Putin is Gog, the Russian dictator described by the Hebrew prophet Ezekiel who will form an alliance with Iran and other Middle Eastern countries and attack Israel in "the last days"? I am not. As of this

edition of *Epicenter*, it remains too early to draw such a firm conclusion. But I maintain that such a possibility cannot be ruled out. For though it is not yet clear that Putin is Gog, he most certainly is Gog-esque.[2]

The Motivation for the Invasion

Not only do Muslims hate the Jews because they believe the land of Israel belongs to them by divine right (Allah allegedly gave it to them), they also want Israel's wealth (see Ezekiel 38:11-12). Ezekiel states that the invaders—both Russians and Muslims—want Israel's "silver and gold" and "livestock" and "goods" (38:13).

It is noteworthy that there are quite a number of wealthy people who live in Israel—more than 6,600 millionaires with total assets exceeding $24 billion. Moreover, the mineral resources of the Dead Sea—including 45 billion tons of sodium, chlorine, sulfur, potassium, calcium, magnesium, and bromide—are worth virtually trillions of dollars. There have also been recent discoveries of gas and oil reserves in Israel. The three to five trillion cubic feet of proven gas reserves beneath Israel's soil could be worth up to $6 billion. All in all, whoever controls the land of Israel can look forward to an incalculably large economic boost. Russia may also view the land of Israel as being a strategic location from a military perspective.

Precondition—Israel Must Be at Peace in the Land

A precondition for this end-times invasion is that Israel must be living in security and at rest. Ezekiel makes this quite clear in his prophecy addressed to the invading nations: "A long time from now you will be called into action. In the distant future you will swoop down on the land of Israel, *which will be enjoying peace*" (Ezekiel 38:8, emphasis added). We are told that when this invasion force moves against Israel, it will be "an unprotected land filled with unwalled villages" (verse 11). The people will be "living in peace in their land" (verse 14).

From a timing standpoint, then, this invasion by the northern military coalition cannot take place until this state of security and rest exists for Israel. And what will bring this about? There are at least two possible interpretive scenarios.

Scenario #1: A Present Reality. One possibility is that Israel *as she is today* is already in a relative state of security. Israel's present level of security may be based on a number of relevant factors, including...

- Israel's well-equipped army
- Israel's first-rate air force
- Israel's effective missile-defense system
- Israel's strong economy
- and Israel's historically strong relationship with the United States (even though this friendship may currently be weakening)

As one prophecy expert said,

> The Hebrew prophet does not go so far as to say there will be a comprehensive peace treaty between Israel and all of her neighbors, or that all or even most hostilities in the Middle East will have ceased. But he does make it clear that in "the last days" (Ezekiel 38:16 NASB) before the Russian-Iranian attack, the Jewish people are "living securely" in "the land that is restored from the sword" (Ezekiel 38:8 NASB).[3]

With Israel's present military capabilities, and her historically strong relationship with the United States, Israel may be considered to be "living securely" in the land. One of the more well-known proponents of this view is Arnold Fruchtenbaum, who writes,

> This is not a security due to a state of peace, but a security due to confidence in their own strength. This...is a good description of Israel today. The Israeli army has fought four major wars since its founding and won them swiftly each time. Today Israel is secure, confident that her army can repel any invasion from the Arab states. Hence, Israel is dwelling securely.[4]

Scenario #2: A Future Reality. Another view held by many Christians is that Israel's state of peace is something that is yet future. Proponents of this view suggest that since Israel became a nation in 1948, she has been on high alert because of the danger she is in from all her Arab and Muslim neighbors. There has never been a time when Israel has been able to let her guard down. It is because of the constant conflict and tension in the Middle East that one Western leader after another has tried to broker a peace deal for the region. After all, stability in the Middle East and the Persian Gulf is a high priority for the entire world, especially with regard to ensuring the uninterrupted flow of oil to world markets.

In view of this, some believe that true security will be experienced by Israel only when the leader of a revived Roman Empire—a European superstate—signs a peace pact or covenant with Israel, an event that will officially begin the tribulation period (Daniel 9:27). This leader—the antichrist—will seemingly accomplish the impossible, solving the Middle East peace puzzle. It is thus suggested that from the moment of the signing of this covenant, Israel will enjoy a heightened sense of security, and this security will be backed by the military might of the most powerful political leader in the world.

Notice that in Daniel 9:27 this peace pact is called a "strong covenant" (ESV). The Holman Christian Standard Bible (HCSB) translates this as "firm covenant." The Amplified Bible translates it as "binding and irrevocable covenant." Such terminology has led some to conclude that the peace that comes upon Israel and the Middle East will be an *imposed* peace—that is, imposed by the antichrist. It will be a *forced* peace backed up by military might.

My Assessment. Though both views have merit, I believe Israel is already in a state of relative security. I think it makes best sense to conclude that the invasion will take place sometime after the rapture but *before* the beginning of the tribulation period. Prophecy scholar Thomas Ice agrees, and suggests that the invasion "will be during the interval of days, weeks, months, or years between the rapture and the start of the seven-year tribulation."[5] There are a number of arguments that support this view:

1. The world will likely be in a state of chaos following the rapture. Because the United States has such a large population of Christians, the rapture will have a devastating effect on the country. This being the case, Russia and her Muslim allies may well "seize the moment," considering this the ideal time to launch a massive attack against Israel, which, up until this time, had been protected by the United States.
2. Once God destroys Russia and the Muslim invaders prior to the tribulation period, this may open the door for the rapid rise of the antichrist as the leader of the revived Roman Empire—a European superstate. Thomas Ice observes, "I have always thought that one of the strengths of this view is the way in which it could set the stage for the biblical scenario of the tribulation. If the tribulation is closely preceded by a failed regional invasion of Israel (by Russia and her Muslim allies), then this would remove much of the Russian and Muslim

influence currently in the world today and allow a Euro-centric orientation to arise."[6]

3. With the Muslim invaders having already been destroyed prior to the beginning of the tribulation, this might make it easier for the antichrist to sign a peace pact with Israel (Daniel 9:27)—a pact that guarantees Israel will be protected. This makes sense, for Israel will be easier to protect if the Muslim forces have been taken out of the picture.
4. This scenario may account for Israel's ability to construct the Jewish temple on the Temple Mount in Jerusalem. With Muslim forces decimated, Muslim resistance will be greatly minimized.
5. If the invasion takes place after the rapture, and the rapture takes place at least three-and-a-half years prior to the beginning of the tribulation, then this scenario would allow for the weapons used in the invasion to be burned for seven years (Ezekiel 39:9-10) by the midpoint of the tribulation, at which time the people of Israel will flee from Jerusalem due to the antichrist's persecution (Matthew 24:15-21). It may well be, then, that there is a significant lapse of time between the rapture and the beginning of the tribulation.

These things being so, here is something to think about: If we are presently seeing the stage being set for the Ezekiel invasion, then the rapture must be all the nearer.

Today's Russia-Muslim Alliances

We already know the Muslim nations are strongly motivated to attack Israel. But some might be surprised at the idea of the Russians partnering with the Muslims against Israel. From a historical perspective, however, the precedent for such a partnership has already been set. As noted in the previous chapter, when Egypt, Syria, and some other Arab/Islamic countries attacked Israel in 1973, Russia provided the weaponry, ammunition, intelligence, and military training for the Muslim troops. Likewise, during the 1967 Six-Day War, when Egypt, Jordan, and Syria were doing battle with Israel, the Russians were poised to attack as well, but backed down due to US intervention.

Later, in 1982, then-Israeli prime minister Menachem Begin revealed that a secret but massive cache of Russian weaponry had been discovered in deep underground cellars in Lebanon, apparently prepositioned for later use in a future ground invasion of Russia into Israel. Discovered were large quantities of ammunition, armored vehicles, tanks, small arms, heavy weapons, communications devices, and other paraphernalia useful to military forces. Much of what was found was highly sophisticated—equipment that crack military units would use. So much was uncovered that hundreds of trucks were required to remove it all. Israel's leaders admitted they had no idea that such extensive plans had been made for a future ground assault into their country.

It seems clear that the Russians are seeking to build political, military, and economic alliances with the Arab and Islamic world. Russia seeks to be *the* major player in the Middle East.

Russia and Iran

An illustration of Russia's strong ties with Muslim nations is the current Russia-Iran partnership. Over the past decade, the two nations have developed strong ties, largely military in nature. This is extremely relevant, for no such alliance has ever existed previously in the history of these nations. Formerly, the relationship between Russia and Iran was characterized by sheer hatred. But circumstances changed. Following the Iran-Iraq war (1980–1988), Iran needed to rebuild its military. Russia needed money from weapons sales. The rest is history.

Iran is today spending about a half a billion dollars annually purchasing military equipment from Russia. Ilan Berman, in his book *Tehran Rising*, informs us, "In late 2000, buoyed by its expanding ties with the Kremlin, the Iranian government announced plans for a massive, twenty-five-year national military modernization program—one entailing upgrades to its air defense, naval warfare, land combat capabilities and built almost entirely around Russian technology and weaponry."[7] The modernization program includes the purchase of fighter aircraft for use by the Iranian air force, assistance in constructing military submarines, anti-aircraft missile systems, surface-to-air missile systems, radar stations, infantry fighting vehicles, naval landing craft, and patrol equipment.[8] Russia has also assisted Iran in the past with its nuclear program.

More recently, a 2016 report affirms a new military agreement between Russia and Iran that allows Russian jets to use the Nojeh Airbase in western Iran for attacks against Syrian rebels. This is the first time that the Islamic regime in Iran has allowed a foreign power—in this case, Russia—to use Iranian territory as a base of operations for military offensives against another country in the region.[9]

It is also highly significant that Iran's anti-Semitism has reached unprecedented levels. As of late 2016, Iranian leaders are declaring that Iran now possesses the capability to destroy Israel. The deputy commander of Iran's Revolutionary Guard Corps boasts that they have "more than 100,000 missiles" ready to strike at the heart of the Jewish nation.[10] Indeed, he says, "Today, the grounds for the annihilation and collapse of the Zionist regime are present more than ever."[11] A senior adviser to the Iranian Revolutionary Guards' elite unit Quds Force, Ahmad Karimpour, likewise affirmed that "Iran could destroy Israel in eight minutes if the Supreme Leader, Ayatollah Ali Khamenei, gave the order."[12]

We are assured that "tens of thousands of other high-precision, long-range missiles, with the necessary destructive capabilities, have been placed in various places throughout the Islamic world. They are just waiting for the command, so that when the trigger is pulled, the accursed black dot will be wiped off the geopolitical map of the world, once and for all."[13]

Why do the Iranians so hate Israel? The Iranian head of the Strategic Research Center at the Expediency Council, Ali Akbar Velayati, says that Iran will not recognize Israel because "it is a usurper entity." Indeed, "Iran believes Israel has stolen the Palestinians' land."[14] They want the land back. It belongs to Allah.

Russia and Turkey

Russia has also been building a relationship with Turkey in recent days. This is a bit of a surprise, given the fact that Turkey has long been committed to NATO.

In July 2016 there was an attempted coup in Turkey that made headlines around the globe. As it happened, Turkey's president Tayyip Erdogan was unaware of this imminent threat. Vladimir Putin, the president of Russia, warned him about the impending coup about an hour before it happened. Erdogan promptly made haste to escape danger.

Following the attempted coup, Erdogan felt that NATO showed less-than-satisfactory support. Then-US Secretary of State John Kerry explained that it would be unwise for US forces to stand against Turkey's military personnel, for "the actions could have consequences for the NATO alliance."[15]

To make things worse, the US declined to cooperate with Turkey in bringing immediate justice to the mastermind of the attempted coup. The coup was directed by former Turkish imam Fethullah Gülen, founder of the Gülen movement. At the time of this writing, Gülen resides in Saylorsburg, Pennsylvania. Erdogan understandably wants him extradited to Turkey, but US officials have said Turkey must go through the US legal process.

It wasn't long before Erdogan called Vladimir Putin "my dear friend" during a subsequent news conference. Erdogan pledged close relations for the future—including a military alliance.

This represents a weakening of NATO ties, something of great concern to the White House. One Middle East analyst suggests that "Erdogan's recent cozying up to Putin sends the message to the United States and its allies that Turkey can make new friends in the region. It certainly appears that the Russian leader took advantage of cracks in the NATO alliance."[16]

Things are shifting these days in the Middle East. As one Middle East analyst put it:

> It is a very dynamic situation. I think Turkish President Erdogan basically has given up on NATO and even on the EU [European Union]—He is pivoting more towards the East at this point. For Turkey and Russia now to begin to talk as they are—particularly in terms of military alliances—this offers a whole new opportunity for not only bilateral cooperation [between the two], but also regional cooperation in a very intriguing sense.[17]

Indeed:

> Turkey and Iran are simultaneously moving toward Russia, while Russia is expanding its global military and strategic reach, all to the detriment of the United States and our allies. This will have a major impact across the

> region, potentially leaving U.S. ally Israel isolated to face a massive hostile alliance armed with nuclear weapons... Believers in Bible prophecy see this new alignment as a step closer to the alliance mentioned in Ezekiel 37–38.[18]

More recently, on July 27, 2017, Joel Rosenberg reported in his blog that "this once-loyal and trustworthy NATO ally is now planning to buy an advanced, state-of-the-art military system from Czar Putin amidst the growing political, economic, and military ties between Russia and Turkey."[19] This military system includes S-400 missiles that are capable of destroying ground and air targets, including ballistic and cruise missiles.

Russia and Muslim Nations

It seems obvious from Russia's recent actions that it has and *will continue* to seek political, military, and economic alliances with Muslim nations beyond just Iran and Turkey. It is not without significance that about 20 million people in Russia's population are Muslims. There are also more than 7,000 Muslim mosques on Russian soil.

What all this means is that ultimately, the northern military coalition prophesied by Ezekiel is slowly but surely coming together in our day—with alliances or strategic agreements forming between Russia, Iran, Turkey, Libya, various former Soviet republics, and others. It appears as if the day is drawing near.

As massive and powerful as this military coalition will be, however, God will completely annihilate it. More on this in the next chapter.

8

GOD'S DEFEAT OF THE NORTHERN COALITION

A look at a map reveals how tiny a piece of real estate Israel is when compared to the immense tracts of Islamic land that surrounds her. Israel, on her own, will stand virtually no chance of survival against the massive northern military coalition. And yet, against all odds, Israel will not be harmed. How can this be so? Scripture reveals that God Himself will be Israel's protector.

This should surprise no one, for God has long watched over Israel. God once promised His people, "No weapon turned against you will succeed" (Isaiah 54:17). In fulfillment of this promise, we often witness God in the Old Testament playing the definitive role in battling against Israel's enemies (see, for example, Exodus 15:3 and Psalm 24:8). God is even sometimes described in military terms—"the LORD of Hosts" (2 Samuel 6:2,18 ESV), also translated "the LORD of Heaven's Armies" (NLT).

God will be angered when this overwhelming Islamic force moves against His people Israel. He affirms, "My fury will boil over" (Ezekiel 38:18). This can also be translated, "My wrath will flare up" (HCSB), or "My rage will mount up in my anger" (NET), or "My wrath shall come up into My nostrils" (AMP). God understandably promises, "In my jealousy and blazing anger, I promise a mighty shaking in the land of Israel on that day" (verse 19). Such words express the unrestrained intensity of God's display of vengeance against those who attack His covenant people. Despite the size of the invading force, it will be no match for Israel's supreme Protector.

Scripture often speaks of God as all-powerful (Jeremiah 32:17). He has the power to do all that He desires and wills. Some 56 times, Scripture declares that God is almighty (for example, Revelation 19:6). God is said to be abundant in strength (Psalm 147:5) and has incomparably great power (2 Chronicles 20:6; Ephesians 1:19-21). No one can hold back His hand (Daniel 4:35). No one can reverse Him (Isaiah 43:13) and no one can thwart Him (14:27). Nothing is impossible with Him (Matthew 19:26), and nothing is too difficult for Him (Genesis 18:14; Jeremiah 32:17,27). Scripture reveals that this all-powerful God will utterly thwart the northern military coalition's invasion.

The Bible also reveals that God is always watchful—"He who watches over Israel never slumbers or sleeps" (Psalm 121:4). The invaders may think their success is all but guaranteed. But God sees all. He's always watchful on behalf of His people. Israel's attackers stand no chance of success.

These attackers will learn the hard truth that Israel's God is *a God of judgment*. J.I. Packer forcefully reminds us of this in his classic book *Knowing God*:

> The reality of divine judgment, as a fact, is set forth on page after page of Bible history. God judged Adam and Eve, expelling them from the Garden and pronouncing curses on their future earthly life (Gen. 3). God judged the corrupt world of Noah's day, sending a flood to destroy mankind (Gen. 6–8). God judged Sodom and Gomorrah, engulfing them in a volcanic catastrophe (Gen. 18–19). God judged Israel's Egyptian

> taskmasters, just as He foretold He would (see Gen. 15:14), unleashing against them the terrors of the ten plagues (Ex. 7–12). God judged those who worshipped the golden calf, using the Levites as His executioners (Ex. 32:26-35). God judged Nadab and Abihu for offering Him strange fire (Lev. 10:1ff.), as later He judged Korah, Dathan, and Abiram, who were swallowed up in an earth tremor. God judged Achan for sacrilegious thieving; he and his family were wiped out (Josh. 7). God judged Israel for unfaithfulness to Him after their entry into Canaan, causing them to fall under the dominion of other nations (Judg. 2:11ff., 3:5ff., 4:1ff.).[1]

It is *this* God—all-powerful and always watchful—who will sovereignly exercise judgment against the northern military coalition when it invades Israel. The judgment will be thorough, effective, and comprehensively lethal. The Islamic invading force will be annihilated.

God's Fourfold Defeat of the Invading Armies

The invading force—made up of Russia, Iran, Sudan, Turkey, Libya, Kazakhstan, Kyrgyzstan, Uzbekistan, Turkmenistan, Tajikistan, Armenia, and possibly northern Afghanistan—will seem unstoppable. Israel will seem doomed. Humanly speaking, there's no way tiny Israel could repel this tsunami.

But then God will act! And He will do so through a fourfold judgment:

1. A Massive Earthquake (Ezekiel 38:19-20). Ezekiel describes a God-inflicted earthquake of gargantuan proportions: "Mountains will be thrown down; cliffs will crumble; walls will fall to the earth" (Ezekiel 38:20). Countless enemy troops will die. As well, transportation will be disrupted, and the armies of the multinational forces will be thrown into utter chaos. God says people "will quake in terror at my presence" (verse 20).

2. Infighting Among the Invading Troops (Ezekiel 38:21). Suddenly the invading forces will turn and start firing on and killing each other. It is possible that this may be at least partially due to the confusion and chaos that results following the massive earthquake. My former mentor John F. Walvoord, now with the Lord, suggested that "in the pandemonium, communication between the invading armies will break down and they will begin attacking each other. Every man's sword will be against his brother (Ezek. 38:21). Fear and panic will sweep through the forces so each army will shoot indiscriminately at the others."[2]

The confusion will be exacerbated by the fact that the armies of the various nations speak different languages—including Russian, Farsi, Arabic, and Turkic. Communication will be difficult at best. Perhaps the Russians and Muslim nations turn on each other. Or, in the midst of the chaos, they will mutually suspect that the other has double-crossed them, and they respond by opening fire on each other. There will be countless casualties.

3. The Outbreak of Disease (Ezekiel 38:22a). As a result of the catastrophic earthquake and the infighting of the invading troops, there will be many dead bodies lying around everywhere. Transportation will be disrupted so it will be difficult, if not impossible, to transfer the wounded or bring in supplies such as food and medicine. Meanwhile, a myriad of birds and other predatory animals will have a feast on this unburied flesh. All this is a recipe for the outbreak of pandemic disease—disease which, according to Ezekiel, will take many more lives.

Of course, these days there is always the possibility that biological warfare—also known as germ warfare—may be utilized. This type of warfare involves unleashing on one's enemy lethal biological infectious agents such as bacteria, viruses, and fungi with a view to killing or incapacitating them. The invading forces may have with them a supply of such biological agents with the intention of using them against Israel, but instead they may end up using them on each other following the great earthquake. Whether or not biological weapons will be used, many of the invaders will die due to the outbreak of disease.

4. Torrential Rain, Hailstones, Fire, and Burning Sulfur (Ezekiel 38:22b). God will also pour torrential rain (with heavy flooding), hailstones, fire, and burning sulfur upon the invading troops. Some Bible expositors suggest that the powerful earthquake may set off volcanic eruptions in the region, thrusting molten rock and burning sulfur (volcanic ash) into the atmosphere, which would then fall upon the enemy troops, thereby destroying them.

The irony of all this is hard to miss. The northern military coalition will seek to kill all the Jews in Israel, but instead they themselves will be killed. They will seek to overwhelm Israel, but instead will be overwhelmed by the greater power of God. They will seek to possess a new land (Israel), but instead will end up getting buried in the land.

Even after all that, God will not have been finished yet. He says, "I will rain down fire on Magog and on all your allies who live safely on the coasts" (Ezekiel 39:6). The term "Magog" apparently refers to the geographical area in the southern part of the former Soviet Union—perhaps including the former southern Soviet republics of Kazakhstan, Kyrgyzstan, Uzbekistan, Turkmenistan, Tajikistan, and possibly even northern parts of modern Afghanistan. We are told in this prophetic passage that God will rain fire down upon this area of the world, as well as upon Magog's allies, "who live safely on the coasts." That could include Russia and other targets that were once a part of the Soviet Union.

This "fire" judgment will be catastrophic. Joel Rosenberg comments:

> This suggests that targets throughout Russia and the former Soviet Union, as well as Russia's allies, will be supernaturally struck on this day of judgment and partially or completely consumed. These could be limited to nuclear missile silos, military bases, radar installations, defense ministries, intelligence headquarters, and other government buildings of various kinds. But such targets could very well also include religious centers, such as mosques, madrassas, Islamic schools and universities, and other facilities that preach hatred against Jews and Christians and call for the destruction of Israel. Either way, we will have to expect extensive collateral damage, and many civilians will be at severe risk.[3]

Tim LaHaye and Ed Hindson, in their book *Target Israel*, suggest that those on the coastlands will be destroyed because they may be among the ones either planning or secretly taking part in the attack against Israel: "God will defeat even the secret terrorists who come against Israel. He will protect Israel from even clandestine efforts against it. God's intervention will save Israel and rescue it from every possible attempt made against it."[4]

This judgment will nullify any possible reprisal or future attempts at invasion. No further attack against Israel by Russia and these Islamic nations will be possible! God's judgment will be complete. He will have fulfilled His promise to Israel: "No weapon turned against you will succeed" (Isaiah 54:17).

We cannot help but notice that God's deliverance of Israel may also be rooted in the ancient covenant He made with His friend, Abraham. In Genesis 12:3, God promised Abraham: "I will bless those who bless you and *curse those who treat you with contempt*" (emphasis added). The Russians and Muslims, by attempting this invasion, will have demonstrated the utmost contempt for Israel. God will therefore curse the invading forces by destroying them.

God's Exaltation

The Muslim forces in this invasion will attempt to attack Israel with fervor in honor to their god Allah. One can easily envision these Muslims shouting "Allahu akbar" (meaning "Allah is the greatest") as they attack. The true God, by His destruction of these Muslim invaders, will demonstrate that He alone is God. He will give a mighty testimony of Himself before a watching world, proving that He—and not Allah—is the one true God:

- God affirms, "I will show my greatness and holiness, and I will make myself known to all the nations of the world. Then they will know that I am the LORD" (Ezekiel 38:23).
- Of the invaders God says, "They will know that I am the LORD" (Ezekiel 39:6).
- God then affirms, "The nations...will know that I am the LORD, the Holy One of Israel" (Ezekiel 39:7).
- Of the Israelites God says, "My people will know that I am the LORD their God" (Ezekiel 39:28).

In short, the destruction of the northern military coalition will be a powerful testimony to God's power, glory, and majesty. It will be a testament to the one true God, as opposed to the false god of Islam. Following Yahweh's mighty judgment against the invaders, no one will be found on the battlefield shouting, "Allahu akbar."

All of this is quite similar to how God gave a testimony of Himself when He delivered the Jews from Egyptian bondage—from Egyptians who also believed in false gods:

- To His people God said: "You will know that I am the LORD your God who has freed you from your oppression in Egypt" (Exodus 6:7).
- To the pharaoh He said: "I will show you that I am the LORD" (7:17); "You will know that I am the LORD and that I am present even in the heart of your land" (8:22); "You will know that the earth belongs to the LORD" (9:29).
- Of the Egyptians God said: "The Egyptians will know that I am the LORD!...All Egypt will see my glory and know that I am the LORD!" (14:4,18).

The invading Muslims will receive the same kind of rude awakening suffered by the Egyptians of old.

Burial of Enemy Invaders

When soldiers are slain on the battlefield, they are normally gathered and buried by their own respective countries. Such will be impossible in the aftermath of the Ezekiel invasion, for all the invading forces will be dead. Hence, in this case, the dead invaders will be buried by the Jews of Israel.

Burial efforts will begin immediately after God destroys the northern military alliance. The number of slain invaders will be staggering. The casualties will be so vast—so innumerable—that nothing but a deep valley will suffice for their corpses (Ezekiel 39:11). It will take a full seven months to accomplish the gruesome task of burial.

Following the seven months, another Jewish crew will traverse the land as they engage in what might be called a final "mopping up" operation. They will search with precision for any bones that might have been missed by the initial burial crews. This will be necessary in order to cleanse the land perfectly from all the uncleanness arising from the bones of the dead (see Numbers 19:11-22; Deuteronomy 21:1-9). Markers will be placed wherever bones are found, and grave diggers will follow up by taking the bones to the burial site—the Valley of Hamon-gog (Ezekiel 39:11).

Burning of Enemy Weapons

Another task the Israelis will engage in following God's destruction of the invading forces is that enemy weapons will be gathered and burned for seven years. If it will take that long to burn the weapons, this can only mean that a formidable arsenal will be collected from among the dead soldiers.

This brings up an interesting point. If the seven years of burning weapons is parallel to the seven-year tribulation period, how can this be reconciled with Israel taking flight from Jerusalem at the middle of the tribulation? Jesus warned that when the antichrist sets up his headquarters in Jerusalem at the midpoint of the tribulation, the Jews will need to exit Jerusalem immediately:

> Those in Judea must flee to the hills. A person out on the deck of a roof must not go down into the house to pack. A person out in the field must not return even to get a coat. How terrible it will be for pregnant women and for nursing mothers in those days. And pray that your flight will not be in winter or on the Sabbath (Matthew 24:16-20).

In view of this exodus from Jerusalem, here is the problem: How will the Jews be able to continue the task of burning weapons—for a total of seven years—if they have to near-instantly take flight from Jerusalem at the midpoint of the tribulation?

One possible solution is that the Jews will simply grab the

weapons as they escape from the city. Their motivation for doing this might be rooted in the fact that there will be a shortage of combustible materials in those days. Revelation 8:7 tells us what will have happened in that time: "One-third of the earth was set on fire, one-third of the trees were burned, and all the green grass was burned." So, combustible materials will be of high value in that day.

Another possible solution is to place the Ezekiel invasion at least three-and-a-half years prior to the beginning of the tribulation. In that case, the burning of the weapons will have been completed by the midpoint of the tribulation.

Keep in mind that the tribulation does not begin immediately after the rapture. There is nothing in Scripture that would negate the possibility of a number of years passing between the rapture and the beginning of the tribulation. The signal for the beginning of the tribulation is the antichrist's signing of a covenant with Israel (Daniel 9:26-27). So it is feasible that after the rapture, some three-and-a-half years before the tribulation begins, the Ezekiel invasion will take place.

A Shift in the Balance of Power

Following God's destruction of the massive northern military coalition, there will be a shift in the world's balance of power—both politically and religiously. This shift will make things much easier for the antichrist.

More specifically, the destruction of the northern invaders will make it easier for the antichrist to quickly rise into power. With both Russia and many of the Muslim nations out of the way, there will be far fewer nations with political clout to challenge the antichrist's authority when he comes into power early in the tribulation period. As prophecy scholar Arnold Fruchtenbaum puts it, "the eastern balance of power will collapse with the fall of Russian forces and her Muslim allies in Israel and the destruction of Russia itself. With the eastern power destroyed, this will open the way for a one-world government."[5]

John Walvoord likewise suggests:

> With Russia out of the way, the head of the revived Roman Empire, in control of the Mediterranean area at that time, will be able to proclaim himself as dictator of the whole world. There will be, accordingly, a fulfillment of the Scriptures which prophesy that the Roman government of that time will not only rule over all the territory of the ancient Roman Empire, but will extend its suzerainty to every people, land, kindred, and tongue (cf. Rev. 13:4-8). Chapters 38 and 39 of Ezekiel may well fit into the prophetic picture, and the defeat of Russia and its military force may be the occasion of the establishment of the world government by the world rulers pictured in Scripture.[6]

It will also be easier for the antichrist to sign a peace pact with Israel (Daniel 9:27), and guarantee that Israel will be protected. After all, Muslim forces will no longer be a threat.

This, in turn, likely explains why Israel will finally be able to rebuild its temple on the Temple Mount early in the tribulation period. If Muslims were still in power at the time, it would be very difficult for Israel to build anything on the Temple Mount. But if the Muslim armies are decimated by God prior to the beginning of the tribulation, then this major obstacle to Israel's rebuilding of the temple will have been removed. There will be much less Muslim resistance.

Today's Islamic Threat Against Israel

At the time of this writing, Islamic leaders continue to make vitriolic threats to the effect that Israel will soon be a thing of the past. They are claiming that the world will soon know what it is like to live in an Israel-free and United States-free world. They are promising that Israel will soon be annihilated. We are told that it is imminent that Israel will become a mass graveyard for Jewish people. Such ominous threats are eye-opening when one considers that thousands of years ago, the prophet Ezekiel gave us "history in advance" by revealing that the future invaders will be "covering their land like a cloud" (Ezekiel 38:16).

When it comes to end-time events, we should not engage in date-setting (see Acts 1:7). Nor should we participate in sensationalism (see Mark 13:32-37). But we *are* called upon by Jesus to be accurate observers of the times (see Matthew 16:1-3; Luke 21:29-33). A studied consideration of the world scene today seems to indicate that things are shaping up for the military invasion envisioned by Ezekiel so long ago. One day, it will surely come to pass. God Himself assures everyone: "Behold, it is coming and it will be brought about...That is the day of which I have spoken" (Ezekiel 39:8 ESV).

Consider how the stage is now being set:

- Multiple Islamic nations are now positioned to attack Israel.
- The motive for Islamic nations to attack Israel is sheer hatred of the Jews. They want the Holy Land back—land they believe was promised to them by Allah.
- Russian alliances with these Muslim nations—including with Iran and Turkey—continue to grow and solidify.
- The precedent has already been set for the Russians to partner with Muslim nations against Israel.

Understandably, *Israel presently remains on high alert.*

9

THE 70 WEEKS OF DANIEL: THE COMING TRIBULATION PERIOD

The ancient prophet Daniel revealed a great deal about Israel's future—including Israel's future suffering. In that regard he was much like one of his contemporaries, Ezekiel.

Daniel was uncompromising in his faithfulness to God, and those who knew him acknowledged both his righteousness and his wisdom (see Ezekiel 14:14,20; 28:3). He was taken captive as a youth to Babylon by King Nebuchadnezzar in 605 BC. He was likely 15 or 16 years old when this happened. Though he didn't know it at the time, he would spend the rest of his life there—perhaps 85 years or more. He became a governmental official in charge of assisting with the imported Jews.

This was an important job because there were three separate deportations involved in Babylon's victory over Judah. The first took place in 605 BC and included Daniel and his friends. The second took place in 597 BC and included Daniel's contemporary, Ezekiel. The third took place in 586, when the Babylonians destroyed both Jerusalem and its temple.

Daniel authored the biblical book that bears his name (see Daniel 8:15,27; 9:2; 10:7; 12:4-5). His book was titled "Daniel" not only because he was one of the chief characters in the book, but also because it was customary in Bible times to affix the author's name to the book he wrote. Part of the book deals with Daniel's experiences and the kings who ruled Babylon, and part of it deals with Israel's future.

The book of Daniel is categorized as apocalyptic literature. This type of literature is a special kind of writing that arose among the Jews and Christians to reveal certain mysteries about heaven and earth, especially regarding the world to come. It is often characterized by visions—and there are plenty of them in the book of Daniel.

Certain themes are common to apocalyptic literature. These include: (1) A growing sense of hopelessness as wicked powers grow in strength; (2) the promise that God, who is sovereign, will intervene; (3) heavenly visions which provide readers with a heavenly perspective that helps them endure their present suffering; (4) the intervention of God in overcoming and destroying evil; (5) the call to believers to live righteously; (6) the call to persevere under trial; and (7) God's final deliverance and restoration, with the promise that He will dwell with His people. We see all of these themes in the book of Daniel, and we also see them in the book of Revelation.

Daniel Prophesies about the Seventy Weeks

In Daniel 9:20-27 we read the following account:

> I went on praying and confessing my sin and the sin of my people, pleading with the LORD my God for Jerusalem, his holy mountain. As I was praying, Gabriel...came swiftly to me at the time of the evening sacrifice. He explained to me, "Daniel, I have come here to give you insight and understanding. The moment you began praying, a command was given. And now I am here to tell you what it was, for you are very precious to God.

> Listen carefully so that you can understand the meaning of your vision.
>
> "A period of seventy sets of seven has been decreed for your people and your holy city to finish their rebellion, to put an end to their sin, to atone for their guilt, to bring in everlasting righteousness, to confirm the prophetic vision, and to anoint the Most Holy Place. Now listen and understand! Seven sets of seven plus sixty-two sets of seven will pass from the time the command is given to rebuild Jerusalem until a ruler—the Anointed One—comes. Jerusalem will be rebuilt with streets and strong defenses, despite the perilous times.
>
> "After this period of sixty-two sets of seven, the Anointed One will be killed, appearing to have accomplished nothing, and a ruler will arise whose armies will destroy the city and the Temple. The end will come with a flood, and war and its miseries are decreed from that time to the very end. The ruler will make a treaty with the people for a period of one set of seven, but after half this time, he will put an end to the sacrifices and offerings. And as a climax to all his terrible deeds, he will set up a sacrilegious object that causes desecration, until the fate decreed for this defiler is finally poured out on him."

This passage is loaded with prophetic insight. Note that the angel Gabriel said to Daniel: "Daniel, I have come here to give you insight and understanding" (Daniel 9:22). Gabriel came to inform Daniel of what lay ahead in the immediate and distant future for his people, the Jews. Recall that Gabriel is portrayed elsewhere in Scripture as bringing revelation to God's people regarding God's purpose and program. He not only appeared to Daniel (Daniel 8:16; 9:21), but 500 years later he brought the message to Zechariah about the birth of John the Baptist, and announced the birth of Jesus to the Virgin Mary (Luke 1:11-17,26-38).

Gabriel informed Daniel that "a period of seventy sets of seven" (also popularly known as "seventy weeks") had been decreed for the Jewish people. As Gabriel explained what would take place during these "seventy sets of seven," he provided Daniel a prophetic timetable for the nation of Israel. More specifically, Israel's timetable was divided into 70 groups of seven years, totaling 490 years (that's 7 multiplied by 70). At the end of these 490 years, 6 things will have occurred:

1. Israel's apostasy will end at the second coming of Jesus Christ, when she repents of her rejection of Jesus Christ as divine Messiah.
2. Israel's sin will be removed upon placing her trust in Jesus Christ (see Ezekiel 37:23; Romans 11:20-27).
3. As Israel repents of her rejection of Jesus Christ at the second coming, the atonement He wrought at the cross will bring salvation to the Jews.
4. In the millennial kingdom, Christ will bring about perfect righteousness in His covenant people (see Isaiah 60:21; Jeremiah 23:5-6).
5. All the covenant promises to Israel in the Old Testament will be "sealed"—that is, fully realized in the millennial kingdom. (In this context, an "unsealed" prophecy is an unfulfilled prophecy.)
6. The most holy place in the millennial kingdom will be consecrated (see Ezekiel 41–46).

Gabriel drew a distinction between the first 69 "sets of seven" and the last "set of seven." In other words, he kept the first 483 years

(69 multiplied by 7) distinct from the last 7 years (which is one "set of seven").

Here is Gabriel's point: There was to be a 483-year period from the issuing of a decree to rebuild Jerusalem up till the time the Messiah came (that is, the first coming of Jesus Christ, not the second). The day on which Jesus rode into Jerusalem on a donkey to proclaim Himself Israel's Messiah was exactly 483 years to the day after the command to restore and rebuild Jerusalem had been given.

Following these 483 years—at the coming of the Messiah—God's prophetic clock was to stop. Daniel described a gap between these 483 years and the final 7 years of Israel's prophetic timetable.

Certain events were to take place during this gap, according to Daniel 9:26: (1) The Messiah would be killed (or "cut off"); (2) the city of Jerusalem and its temple would be destroyed (which occurred in AD 70); and (3) the Jews would encounter difficulty and hardship from that time on.

Gabriel then informed Daniel of the much-further prophetic future. He described what would constitute the beginning of the last seven years (or the last "set of seven"): "The ruler will make a treaty with the people for a period of one set of seven" (Daniel 9:27).

What this means is that the final set of seven years will begin for Israel in the end-times future when the antichrist confirms a treaty or a covenant for seven years (Daniel 9:27). When this peace pact is signed, this will signal the beginning of the tribulation period, which will last seven years. To be clear, then, this will mark the beginning of a seven-year countdown to the second coming of Christ at the end of the tribulation.

It is significant that the treaty signed by the antichrist is called a "strong covenant" (Daniel 9:27 ESV). This can also be translated "firm covenant" (HCSB) and "strong and firm covenant" (AMP). This has led some prophecy scholars to conclude that the antichrist will bring about an *imposed* peace in the Middle East. It will be a *compelled* covenant, or a *forced* covenant. Mark Hitchcock observes that "as the head of a powerful, multinational confederation, he [the antichrist] will have the power and skill to initiate, formulate, and impose a peace covenant on Israel and possibly her neighbors."[1] John Walvoord put it this way:

> When a Gentile ruler [the antichrist] over the ten nations imposes a peace treaty on Israel, it will be from superior strength and will not be a negotiated peace treaty, but it apparently will include the necessary elements for such a contract. It will include the fixing of Israel's borders, the establishment of trade relations with her neighbors—something she does not enjoy at the present time, and, most of all, it will provide protection from outside attacks, which will allow Israel to relax her military preparedness.[2]

It is interesting to observe that the seven-year time frame for the tribulation is reflected in other ancient Jewish literature. Renald Showers, in his helpful book *Maranatha: Our Lord Come!*, writes:

> The Babylonian Talmud states, "Our Rabbis taught: In the seven-year cycle at the end of which the son of David will come…at the conclusion of the septennate the son of David will come."
>
> Raphael Patai, writing on the Messianic texts, said, "The idea became entrenched that the coming of the Messiah will be preceded by greatly increased suffering…This will last seven years. And then, unexpectedly, the Messiah will come."[3]

As the angel Gabriel instructed Daniel about this seven-year period, he warned that "after half this time [that is, after three-and-a-half years of the seven-year period], he [the antichrist] will put an end to the sacrifices and offerings" (Daniel 9:27, inserts added for clarification). The Jews will rebuild their temple during the first part of the seven-year tribulation (Matthew 24:15-16; see also Daniel 9:27; 12:11), and the Jewish sacrificial system will be reinstated. But in the middle of the tribulation period, the antichrist will put a stop to Jewish sacrifices. From this point onward, no one on earth will be permitted to worship anyone but the antichrist, who will set himself up as deity and demand worship from all (see 2 Thessalonians 2:4). In this way, the antichrist will take on the character of Satan, who energizes him (see 2 Thessalonians 2:9; see also Ezekiel 28:11-19; Isaiah 14:12-17).

Gabriel then warned of the antichrist's sacrilege: "As a climax to all his terrible deeds, he will set up a sacrilegious object that causes desecration" (Daniel 9:27). Later, in Daniel 11:31, we read a similar prophecy about the antichrist: "His army will take over the Temple fortress, pollute the sanctuary, put a stop to the daily sacrifices, and set up the sacrilegious object that causes desecration."

The phrase "sacrilegious object that causes desecration" conveys a sense of outrage or horror at the witnessing of a barbaric act of idolatry within God's holy temple (Daniel 9:27; 11:31; 12:11). Such an abomination took place once before in Israel's history. Antiochus Epiphanes desecrated the Jewish temple by erecting an altar to Zeus in it, and then sacrificed a pig—an unclean animal—upon the altar.

We find further clarity on the future "sacrilegious object that causes desecration" in the New Testament. This desecration will take place at the midpoint of the tribulation when the antichrist—the "man of lawlessness" (2 Thessalonians 2:3)—sets up an image of himself inside the Jewish temple (see Daniel 9:27; Matthew 24:15). This amounts to the antichrist enthroning himself in the place of deity, displaying himself as God (compare with Isaiah 14:13-14 and

Ezekiel 28:2-9). This blasphemous act will utterly desecrate the temple, making it abominable, and therefore desolate. The antichrist—the world dictator—will then demand that the world worship and pay idolatrous homage to him. Anyone who refuses will be persecuted and martyred.

The Tribulation Period Is the "Day of the Lord"

The future seven-year tribulation period is one and the same as the future "day of the Lord." This means that the antichrist's signing of the covenant with Israel not only marks the beginning of the tribulation period, it also marks the beginning of the day of the Lord.

The term "day of the Lord" is used in several senses in Scripture. The Old Testament prophets sometimes used the term of an event to be fulfilled in the near future. At other times, they used the term of an event in the distant eschatological future (that is, the future tribulation period). The immediate context of the biblical text generally indicates which sense is intended.

In both cases, the day of the Lord refers to God actively intervening supernaturally in order to bring judgment against sin in the world. The day of the Lord is a time in which God will actively control and dominate history in a direct way, instead of working through secondary means.

Among the New Testament writers, "day of the Lord" is generally used of the judgment that will climax in the end-times seven-year tribulation period (see 2 Thessalonians 2:2; Revelation 16–18), as well as the judgment that will usher in the new earth in the end times (2 Peter 3:10-13; Revelation 20:7–21:1; see also Isaiah 65:17-19; 66:22; Revelation 21:1). It is this theme of end-times judgment against sin that runs like a thread through many of the references to the day of the Lord.

Isaiah 34:1-8 describes a day of the Lord in which God will judge all nations of the earth ("the Lord is enraged against the nations. His fury is against all their armies. He will completely destroy them, dooming them to slaughter"—verse 2). None of the past days of the Lord ever involved divine judgment upon all the nations. This indicates that the day of the Lord of Isaiah 34 must be yet future—that is, the tribulation period.

Similarly, Joel 3:1-16 and Zechariah 14:1-3,12-15 speak of a future day of the Lord that will involve God's judgment upon the armies of all the nations when they gather to wage war against Israel at the end of the tribulation. Revelation 19:11-21 reveals that Christ will wage war against these nations when He comes from heaven to earth as King of kings and Lord of Lords.

The apostle Paul, in 1 Thessalonians 5:1-11, also reveals that this eschatological day of the Lord is yet future. Paul warned that this day would bring sudden, inescapable destruction upon the unsaved of the world. The context of 1 Thessalonians 5 clearly points to the end-times tribulation period.

This will be a completely unique time of judgment, unlike any other period in human history. Randall Price writes,

> The exceptional nature of the Tribulation is earmarked by such phrases as "that day is great, there is none like it" (Jer. 30:7), or "such as never occurred since there was a nation until that time" (Dan. 12:1). These expressions emphasize the uniqueness of this specific judgment, while the accompanying contextual descriptions of the effects such judgments have on both God and Israel, affirm that this is a time unparalleled in Israel's previous history.[4]

Moreover, Scripture reveals that Israel must suffer through the *entire* seven-year period. "The experience of end-time judgment in the Tribulation is depicted by the travail of childbirth...Just as the woman must endure the entire period of labor before giving birth, so Israel must endure the entire seven-year period of Tribulation."[5]

Thankfully, Christians will escape this day via the rapture (see John 14:1-3; 1 Corinthians 15:51-53; 16:22; 1 Thessalonians 1:10; 4:13-18; 5:9,23; 2 Thessalonians 2:1,3; Revelation 3:10.). This is one reason Scripture calls the rapture "our blessed hope" (Titus 2:13-14 ESV).

The Nature of the Tribulation Period (Day of the Lord)

The word *tribulation* literally means "to press" (as grapes), "to press together," "to press hard upon," and refers to times of oppression, affliction, and distress. The Greek word (*thlipsis*) is translated variously as "tribulation," "affliction," "anguish," "persecution," "trouble," and "burden." The word has been used in relation to (1) those "hard pressed" by the calamities of war (Matthew 24:21); (2) a woman giving birth to a child (John 16:21); (3) the afflictions of Christ (Colossians 1:24); (4) those "pressed" by poverty and lack (Philippians 4:14); (5) great anxiety and burden of heart (2 Corinthians 2:4); and (6) a period in the end times that will have unparalleled tribulation (Revelation 7:14).

All Christians may expect a certain amount of general tribulation in their lives. Jesus Himself said to the disciples, "In the world you will have tribulation" (John 16:33 ESV). Paul and Barnabas also warned that "through many tribulations we must enter the kingdom of God" (Acts 14:22 ESV). But such general tribulation is to be distinguished from the tribulation period of the end times, based on the following facts:

1. Scripture refers to a definite period of time at the end of the age (Matthew 24:29-35).

2. It will be of such severity that no period in history past or future will equal it (Matthew 24:21).
3. It will be shortened for the elect's sake (Matthew 24:22), as no flesh could survive it.
4. It is called the time of Jacob's trouble, for it is a judgment on Messiah-rejecting Israel (Jeremiah 30:7; Daniel 12:1-4). Israel will be singled out for suffering in that day.
5. The Gentile nations will also be judged for their sin and rejection of Christ during this tribulation (Isaiah 26:21; Revelation 6:15-17).
6. This tribulation period is seven years in length (Daniel 9:24,27).
7. It will be so bad that people will want to hide and even die (Revelation 6:16).

The tribulation period—the "day of the Lord"—is characterized by wrath (Zephaniah 1:15,18), judgment (Revelation 14:7), indignation (Isaiah 26:20-21), trial (Revelation 3:10), trouble (Jeremiah 30:7), destruction (Joel 1:15), darkness (Amos 5:18), desolation (Daniel 9:27), overturning (Isaiah 24:1-4), and punishment (Isaiah 24:20-21). Simply put, no passage can be found that alleviates, to any degree whatsoever, the severity of this time that will come upon the earth.

Scripture reveals that this tribulation will come upon the *whole* world. Revelation 3:10 describes this period as "the hour of trial that is coming on the whole world, to try those who dwell on the earth." Isaiah likewise says, "Behold, the LORD will empty the earth and make it desolate, and he will twist its surface and scatter its inhabitants" (Isaiah 24:1). He continues along the same lines in verse 17: "Terror and the pit and the snare are upon you, O inhabitant of the earth!"

Regarding the actual source of the tribulation, Scripture reveals that this is a time of both divine wrath and satanic wrath—especially divine wrath. We are told that the tribulation is "the day of the wrath of the LORD" (Zephaniah 1:18). The earth will experience "the wrath of the Lamb" (Revelation 6:16). "The LORD is coming out from his place to punish the inhabitants of the earth for their iniquity" (Isaiah 26:21). Satan's wrath is evident in Revelation 12:4,13,17.

The purpose of the tribulation is threefold:

1. To Purge the Jewish People

The tribulation will bring purging upon the Jewish people, and prepare them for the restoration and the regathering that will take place in the millennial reign of Christ following the second coming (see Isaiah 6:9-13; 24:1-6; Zechariah 13:7-9; Ezekiel 20:34,37-38; John 12:37-41; Romans 11:26-27).[6] Ultimately it will produce a messianic revival among the Jewish people scattered throughout the world (Deuteronomy 4:27-30; Matthew 24:14; Revelation 7:1-4). This Jewish element of the tribulation period is made clear by Gerald Stanton in his book *Kept from the Hour*:

> The tribulation is primarily Jewish. This fact is borne out by Old Testament Scriptures (Deut. 4:30; Jer. 30:7; Ezek. 20:37; Dan. 12:1; Zech. 13:8-9), by the Olivet Discourse of Christ (Matt. 24:9-26), and by the book of Revelation itself (Rev. 7:4-8; 12:1-2; 17, etc.). It concerns "Daniel's people," the coming of "false Messiah," the preaching of the "gospel of the kingdom," flight on the "sabbath," the temple and the "holy place," the land of Judea, the city of Jerusalem, the twelve "tribes of the children of Israel," the "son of

> Moses," "signs" in the heavens, the "covenant" with the Beast, the "sanctuary," the "sacrifice and the oblation" of the temple ritual—these all speak of Israel and prove that the tribulation is largely a time when God deals with His ancient people prior to their entrance into the promised kingdom. The many Old Testament prophecies yet to be fulfilled for Israel further indicate a future time when God will deal with this nation (Deut. 30:1-6; Jer. 30:8-10, etc.).[7]

2. To Bring Judgment

The tribulation will also serve to bring judgment against the Christ-rejecting nations of the world (Isaiah 13:9; 24:19-20; Ezekiel 37:23; Zechariah 13:2; 14:9; Deuteronomy 30:7; Matthew 25:31-46). There will be far fewer wicked people on earth at the end of the tribulation period than there were at the beginning of it. "This violent reduction of the world's unbelieving population will result from the divine judgments unleashed throughout the Tribulation (Rev. 6–18), climaxing with the battles of Armageddon under King Messiah (Rev. 19), and His purge of both rebel Jews and oppressive Gentiles at the end of the Tribulation (Ezek. 20:33-38; Matt. 25:31-46)."[8]

3. To Conclude the Times of the Gentiles

The tribulation will bring a close to "the times of the Gentiles" (Luke 21:24—see Isaiah 24:21-23; 59:16-20; see also Matthew 24:29-31; Mark 13:24-27; Romans 11:25). The phrase "times of the Gentiles," which Christ used in Luke 21:24, refers to the time of Gentile domination over Jerusalem. This period began with the Babylonian captivity that took place in 605 BC, and it was well entrenched by AD 70 when Titus and his Roman warriors overran Jerusalem and destroyed the Jewish temple. This does not rule out the possibility of temporary Jewish control over Jerusalem, but such control will be temporary until the second coming.

The times of the Gentiles will last into the seven-year future tribulation period (Revelation 11:2), and will not end until the second coming of our Lord Jesus Christ.

God Brings Good out of Evil

Since the time of the Jewish rejection of Christ in the first century AD, Israel has experienced a judicial blindness and hardening as a judgment from God. The apostle Paul wrote, "I do not want you to be unaware of this mystery, brothers: a partial hardening has come upon Israel, until the fullness of the Gentiles has come in [that is, until the full number of Gentiles who will be saved have, in fact, become saved]" (Romans 11:25 ESV).

The backdrop is that the Jews in Israel had sought a relationship with God not by faith but by works (see Galatians 2:16; 3:2,5,10). Of course, attaining righteousness by observing the law requires that the law be kept perfectly (James 2:10), which no person is capable of doing. The Jews stumbled over the "stumbling stone," who is Jesus Christ (see Romans 9:31-33). Jesus did not fit their preconceived ideas about the Messiah (Matthew 12:24), so they rejected Him. The result of this rejection of the Messiah is that a partial judicial blindness and hardness has come upon Israel. The nation thus lost her favored position before God, and the gospel was then preached to the Gentiles with a view toward causing the Jews to become jealous and then become saved (Romans 11:11).

Since then, Gentiles who have placed their faith in Jesus have become members of God's church. Believing Jews, too, have become members of God's church in the current age (see Ephesians 3:3-5,9; Colossians 1:26-27).

Ultimately, the good news is that Israel's hardening and casting off is only temporary. As Israel is threatened at Armageddon, toward the end of the tribulation period, she will finally recognize Jesus as her Messiah and turn to Him for rescue from the invading forces of the antichrist (Zechariah 12:10; see also Romans 10:13-14). At that time, a remnant of Israel will be saved (Romans 11:25).

As noted previously, however, this will not happen *until God purges Israel through the tribulation*, during which time two-thirds of the Jews will die. Prophecy scholar John Walvoord wrote,

> The purge of Israel in their time of trouble is described by Zechariah in these words: "And it shall come to pass, that in all the land, saith Jehovah, two parts therein shall be cut off and die; but the third shall be left therein. And I will bring the third part into the fire, and will refine them as silver is refined, and will try them as gold is tried" (Zechariah 13:8, 9). According to Zechariah's prophecy, two thirds of the children of Israel in the land will perish, but the one third that are left will be refined and be awaiting the deliverance of God at the second coming of Christ.[9]

In their book *Israel Under Fire*, John Ankerberg, Dillon Burroughs, and Jimmy DeYoung put all this into perspective for us:

> The ancient Jewish prophet Zechariah says that during this time of testing, two out of every three Jews will be killed (Zechariah 13:8). At the present Jewish population in our world, that would be something in the area of over 8 million Jews. This will be the worst holocaust to ever take place upon the face of the earth. All of these prophecies will come to their fulfillment as the Jewish people come under fire during the tribulation period.[10]

So—even though many Jews are returning to Israel today, and even though a remnant of the Jews will be saved in the end, Israel must first pass through the tribulation period to purge her and bring her to repentance before Jesus. All that is presently taking place in Israel and the Middle East may be viewed as a prelude to the time of Israel's suffering during the tribulation period. Even though it's exceedingly difficult to think about, a majority of the Jews who have returned to Israel (Ezekiel 37)—assuming they're still alive at the beginning of the tribulation period—will *not* be alive by the end of it. Two-thirds will tragically lose their lives during this horrific time.

And yet the good news is that the believing remnant of Jews will enter into Christ's millennial kingdom and enjoy all the blessings promised in the Abrahamic, Davidic, and new covenants. That will be a grand day!

10

THE CONFLICT OVER REBUILDING THE JEWISH TEMPLE

The temple has always been at the very heart of Jewish worship. David, Israel's shepherd-king, had sought to build the first temple for God. But he was disqualified from doing so because he was a warrior. His son, Solomon, was blessed to perform this task (1 Kings 6–7; 2 Chronicles 3–4).

Solomon built the temple based on plans received directly from God. The temple had both a holy place and a Holy of Holies. The holy place was the main outer room. In it were placed the golden incense altar, the table of showbread, five pairs of lampstands, as well as various utensils used for sacrifices. Double doors led into the Holy of Holies. In this room was placed the ark of the covenant. The ark was placed between two wooden cherubim or angels, each standing ten feet tall. Scripture tells us that God manifested Himself in the Holy of Holies in a cloud of glory (see 1 Kings 8:10-11). Tragically for the Jewish people, Solomon's temple was eventually destroyed by King Nebuchadnezzar and his Babylonian army in 587 BC. Nebuchadnezzar's men looted all the valuable utensils that were found within the temple.

These utensils were sacred objects. The Babylonians believed that the seizing of them represented the victory of Babylon's gods over the God of Israel. Little did the Babylonians know, however, that it was actually the one true God of Judah who handed His own people over to them for chastisement (see Deuteronomy 28:64; Jeremiah 25:8-14).

First Kings 7:48-51 tells us that the sacred objects of the temple included "the golden altar, the golden table for the bread of the Presence, the lampstands of pure gold...the lamps, and the tongs, of gold; the cups, snuffers, basins, dishes for incense, and fire pans, of pure gold; and the sockets of gold, for the doors of the innermost part of the house, the Most Holy Place, and for the doors of the nave of the temple" (ESV).

After being in exile in Babylon for 70 years, the Jews were permitted by King Cyrus of Persia to return to Jerusalem. They were allowed to take with them the various temple utensils that Nebuchadnezzar's men had looted.

The returned exiles started out well in rebuilding the temple in 538 BC, but they soon ran out of steam. They became discouraged. One of the primary tasks of the prophets Haggai and Zechariah was to encourage them to carry on. The temple was finally completed in 515 BC. But it was not anywhere nearly as magnificent as Solomon's original temple. This was discouraging to the returned Jews. "Many of the older priests, Levites, and other leaders who had seen the first Temple wept aloud when they saw the new Temple's foundation" (Ezra 3:12). It had little of its former glory and was a dim reflection of the original. This temple was also without the ark of the covenant, which had never been recovered. It also had only one seven-branched lampstand (Solomon's ten lampstands were never recovered). This lesser temple lasted about 500 years.

Fast-forward to New Testament times. In 19 BC, King Herod the Great began a massive rebuilding effort on the temple. He believed that an incredible-looking temple would both ingratiate his Jewish subjects to him as well as impress the Roman authorities. This temple was completed in AD 64. It was far larger and more resplendent—with much more gold—than even Solomon's temple. It was an enormous, cream-colored edifice that shone exceedingly bright during the day. It measured 490 yards north to south by 325 yards east to west.

A mere six years after this magnificent temple was completed, it was destroyed by Titus's Roman armies. How ironic that those whom Herod sought to impress in Rome were the very ones who ended up destroying the temple.

The Tribulation Temple

Herod's temple isn't the last one to stand on the Temple Mount. Indeed, the ancient prophets revealed that there will be another Jewish temple during the future seven-year tribulation period.

We know there will be an end-times temple because Jesus, in His Olivet Discourse,* warned of a catastrophic event that would take place involving the antichrist and the temple: "The day is coming when you will see what Daniel the prophet spoke about—the sacrilegious object that causes desecration standing in the Holy Place...Then those in Judea must flee to the hills" (Matthew 24:15-16).

I briefly touched on this object of desecration in the previous chapter. The "sacrilegious object that causes desecration" refers specifically to the defiling of the Jewish temple by the antichrist, who will not only personally sit within the temple, but will also set up an image of himself (see Revelation 13:14-15; 14:9,11; 15:2; 16:2; 19:20; 20:4). This will take place at the midpoint of the tribulation.

Imagine if you were a Jew and you witnessed this heinous act.

---

* So named because Jesus "sat on the Mount of Olives" when He delivered this discourse (Matthew 24:3).

Prophetic Scripture reveals that this barbaric act of idolatry will cause Jews to feel outrage and horror. It will utterly profane and desecrate the temple. The Hebrew word used to describe this act literally means "to make foul" or "to stink." Thus it refers to something that makes one feel nauseous, and by implication, something morally abhorrent and detestable.

As noted in the previous chapter, an abomination took place on a lesser scale in 168 BC. At that time, Antiochus Epiphanes—who ruled the Seleucid Empire from 175 BC until his death in 164 BC and was a cruel persecutor of the Jews—erected an altar to Zeus in the temple and sacrificed a pig (an unclean animal) upon it. Antiochus may be considered a prototype of the future antichrist.

The image of the antichrist that will be set up in the temple will somehow be given "life" by the false prophet, who is the first lieutenant of the antichrist. We are told that the image will be able to speak (Revelation 13:15). This verse has led to no small amount of discussion among prophecy enthusiasts. Some believe the beast's image will merely give the impression of breathing and speaking by mechanical means, like computerized talking robots today. Others suggest that perhaps a holographic deception may be employed. Still others see the supernatural involved. Do not forget that Satan has great intelligence and also has a limited ability to manipulate the forces of nature, as happened when he afflicted Job (see Job 1–2). So perhaps with his scientific knowledge and his ability to manipulate the forces of nature, he is able to give the appearance of the image being alive in some deceptive way. Whatever the explanation, many people on earth will be deceived by what they perceive to be supernatural.

One cannot help but notice that the "life" in the image, and its ability to speak, sets it apart from typical idols. Psalm 135:15-17 speaks of idols that have no true life: "The idols of the nations are merely things of silver and gold, shaped by human hands. They have mouths but cannot speak, and eyes but cannot see. They have ears but cannot hear, and mouths but cannot breathe." Habakkuk 2:19 likewise says: "What sorrow awaits you who say to wooden idols, 'Wake up and save us!' To speechless stone images you say, 'Rise up and teach us!' Can an idol tell you what to do? They may be overlaid with gold and silver, but they are lifeless inside."

The image of the antichrist—which will be able to speak, unlike the dead idols in Old Testament times—will seem god-like to people during the tribulation period. The goal of placing this supernatural image of the antichrist within the Jewish temple will be to induce people worldwide to worship the antichrist. The antichrist will seek the same kind of worship given to Christ in New Testament times (see Matthew 2:11; 28:9,17; John 9:38; 20:28).

Exodus 34:14 tells us, "You must worship no other gods, for the LORD, whose very name is Jealous, is a God who is jealous about his relationship with you." Because the antichrist demands worship, he is quite obviously placing himself in the position of deity. The image in the temple is a symbol of his alleged deity. It is this that will utterly defile and desecrate the temple, as prophesied by Jesus (Matthew 24:15).

Here is something else to think about: The fact that the antichrist claims to be god is in keeping with the reality that he is energized by Satan (2 Thessalonians 2:9). After all, Satan had earlier sought the place of God (see Isaiah 14:13-14). The antichrist will take on the character of the one who energizes him.

Recall also that during His three-year ministry, Jesus cleansed the temple (Mark 11:15-19). By contrast, the antichrist will defile the temple when he sits "in the temple of God, claiming that he himself is God" (2 Thessalonians 2:4). Truly the antichrist is the antithesis of Christ.

When the antichrist claims to be god, things will turn south rapidly for the Jews who are living in Jerusalem. Jesus, in His Olivet Discourse, points to how bad things will be, and how the Jews in the city will need to flee for their lives:

> The day is coming when you will see what Daniel the prophet spoke about—the sacrilegious object that causes desecration standing in the Holy Place. (Reader, pay attention!) Then those in Judea must flee to the hills. A person out on the deck of a roof must not go down into the house to pack. A person out in the field must not return even to get a coat. How terrible it will be for pregnant women and for nursing mothers in those days. And pray that your flight will not be in winter or on the Sabbath (Matthew 24:15-21).

In other words, when these horrific circumstances begin to unfold, Jesus urges the Jews living in Jerusalem at that time to forget about their personal belongings and get out of town with utmost haste. Time spent gathering things might mean the difference between life and death. From this point onward, the distress for Jewish people will escalate dramatically (see Jeremiah 30:7).

Jewish Sacrifices Reinstated and Then Terminated

Animal sacrifices will be offered in the Jewish temple during the first half of the tribulation. But then the antichrist will cause them to cease. We read in Daniel 9:27 that he "will make a treaty with the people for a period of one set of seven [seven years], but after half this time [that is, after three-and-a-half years], he will put an end to the sacrifices and offerings" (inserts added for clarification). John Walvoord explains that the entire Levitical system will be restored in Jerusalem for three-and-a-half years. But after the antichrist gains worldwide political power, "he will assume power in the religious realm as well and will cause the world to worship him" (2 Thes. 2:4; Rev. 13:8). To receive such worship, he will terminate all organized religions. Posing as the world's rightful king and god and as Israel's prince of peace, he will then turn against Israel and become her destroyer and defiler."[1]

Current Efforts Toward Rebuilding the Temple

Prophecies regarding the tribulation temple—a *rebuilt* temple—will likely not be fulfilled until the tribulation period begins. However, the stage is now being set for this rebuilding.

Just as tremors (or foreshocks) often occur before major earthquakes, so preliminary manifestations of prophecies related to the rebuilt temple are emerging even now. Someone observed that prophecies cast their shadows before them. I believe this is true. Prophecies that relate specifically to the rebuilding of the temple are presently casting their shadows before them, in our present day.

Gershon Salomon, a descendant of ten generations of Jerusale-mites and the founder and leader of the Temple Mount and Land of Israel Faithful Movement, believes not only that the Messiah is coming soon, but that God has called him to help prepare the way. He founded the Temple Mount Faithful in 1967 with a view to (1) liberating the Temple Mount from Islamic occupation, (2) consecrating the Temple Mount, and (3) rebuilding the Jewish temple. For the past four decades, Salomon has been busy writing and speaking throughout Israel, teaching any who will listen about the importance of establishing the Jewish temple before the Messiah returns—which, he believes, could be very soon.[2]

Rabbi Yisrael Ariel is another who is dedicated to the rebuilding of the temple. He founded the Temple Institute in 1987:

> The Temple Institute is a collective of scholars headed up by Rabbi Israel Ariel. These leaders have studied the Old Testament requirements for preparing the priest, the priestly garments, the musical instruments, and the implements for the sacrifices and worship at the temple. These rabbis have already commissioned artisans to make the items needed to operate the Third Temple.[3]

Ariel's desire is to educate people about the temple, pursue the rebuilding of the temple, and create temple utensils and other items. He says, "All of these items are fit and ready for use in the service of the Holy Temple." This includes the seven-branched candelabra, the golden incense altar, the golden table of the showbread, priestly garments, the pure gold crown worn by the high priest, fire pans and shovels, the mitzraq (vessel used to transport the blood of sacrificial offerings), the copper laver, stone vessels to store the ashes of the red heifer, and the like. These items are being prefabricated by the Temple Institute in Jerusalem so that when the temple is finally rebuilt, everything will be ready for it.[4]

The Temple Institute has been working behind the scenes for some 30 years, preparing for the rebuilding of the temple:

> The Temple Institute is dedicated to doing everything possible to build the third Jewish Temple on the Temple Mount...It is incumbent on every one of us, at all times, to prepare for the rebuilding of the Holy Temple. With the work of the Temple Institute over the last three decades, preparation for the Temple is no longer a dream, it's a reality, in which everyone can play a part.[5]

Three times a day, many Jews pray at the Western Wall in Jerusalem, crying out, "May our temple be rebuilt in this day here in the holy city."[6] Many Jews see a connection between the building of this temple and the return of the Messiah. Meir Kahana, an Orthodox Jew, said, "I know that the day the Third Temple is completed, the Messiah will come."[7]

Moreover, as alluded to above, the Jews want to rebuild the temple *on the actual Temple Mount* in Jerusalem. Rabbi Ben-Dahan affirms: "We are all here to declare that we have returned to Jerusalem, and God-willing we will prepare the hearts [of the people] to return to the Temple Mount as well and to rebuild the Temple. We aren't embarrassed to say it: We want to rebuild the Temple on the Temple Mount."[8]

This is a quite exciting development for prophecy enthusiasts. For Bible prophecy students, the Temple Mount movement evidences a powerful sign of the soon coming of the Messiah. "Though there has been a desire to build another temple in Jerusalem over the last 2,000 years, there has never been so much progress toward making it happen. For many, this is strong evidence that the Lord's return truly is near."[9]

At present, of course, the Temple Mount area is a dangerous, highly volatile place. Joel Rosenberg explains it this way:

> Security experts now believe that the Temple Mount is the most dangerous square mile on the planet. Israeli police and intelligence forces maintain tight security around the site to prevent Jewish or other extremists from trying to blow up the Dome of the Rock and the Al-Aksa Mosque. After all, not only would such an attack be morally wrong, it would be incredibly dangerous. For if the dome and the mosque were somehow destroyed by a terrorist attack, this could unleash a war of horrific proportions as the wrath of a billion Muslims turned against Israel.[10]

Some prophecy students have suggested that perhaps the Jewish temple could be built without disturbing the Dome of the Rock. The two structures could stand side by side. Such an idea is infeasible. Muslims would not stand for a Jewish holy place right next door, nor would Jews stand for an Islamic holy place alongside the temple. Besides, the Dome of the Rock is on the exact spot where the previous Jewish temples stood. So the tribulation-era temple *must* be built there.

There are other recent developments that portend the soon rebuilding of the Jewish temple. For example, the Sanhedrin—after 1,600 years of absence—has been reestablished. In Bible times, the Sanhedrin was the supreme court and legislative body of the Jews, made up of 71 rabbis.

The reinstitution ceremony took place in the Israeli town of Tiberias, on the western shore of the Sea of Galilee. This was the exact location of the council's last meeting in AD 425.

I think David Reagan is right when he says that "with regard to the prophetic significance of these events, I see the revival of the Sanhedrin as one more step toward the rebuilding of a Jewish Temple."[11] Thomas Ice likewise notes, "The reinstitution of the Sanhedrin is seen as a harbinger for the rebuilding of the Temple and the coming of Messiah. Orthodox Jews believe that a body like the Sanhedrin is needed today to oversee the rebuilding of the Temple and to identify Messiah should he appear on the scene."[12]

Everything seems to be lining up for the soon rebuilding of the temple. As Arnold Fruchtenbaum says,

> The Temple Institute in Jerusalem has reconstructed the instruments for Jewish Temple worship; Jewish men determined to be descendants of Aaron, known as the Kohanim, are being trained in ritual practices to serve as

> Temple priests; and now we have the establishment of an authoritative body to speak to the nation of Israel on matters of Jewish religion.[13]

The new Sanhedrin now meets monthly in Jerusalem. Presumably the council will seek to become the supreme governing body for modern Israel.

One reason for the necessity of a new Sanhedrin with regard to the temple is that "only the Sanhedrin can select the man who will serve as the high priest of the temple."[14] Now that the Sanhedrin is in place, the selection of the high priest will be an easier task to accomplish, once it becomes necessary.

Of course, there can't be a rebuilding of the temple unless architectural plans are first drawn up. Toward this end, the new Sanhedrin has issued a call for such plans: "The group will establish a forum of architects and engineers to begin plans for rebuilding the Temple—a move fraught with religious and political volatility."[15] Meanwhile, they are "calling on the Jewish people to contribute toward the acquisition of materials for the purpose of rebuilding the Temple—including the gathering and preparation of prefabricated, disassembled portions to be stored and ready for rapid assembly, 'in the manner of King David.'"[16]

As noted earlier, the one big obstacle standing in the way of rebuilding the temple is the presence of the Muslim Dome of the Rock, which rests on the exact spot where the temple must be built. This structure must go before the temple can be rebuilt.

It seems likely to me that the rebuilding of the Jewish temple will be made possible in the aftermath of God's destruction of the Muslim armies during the Ezekiel invasion. If the Muslims were still in power in the early part of the tribulation period, it would be very difficult for Israel to build its temple. But if all the Muslim armies are decimated by God prior to the beginning of the tribulation (or, at the very latest, right at the beginning of the tribulation), then this major obstacle is thereby removed.

It is entirely possible that the Ezekiel invasion will take place three-and-a-half years prior to the beginning of the tribulation period (see chapter 7). This would mean that the Muslim armies would be destroyed well before the beginning of the tribulation period.

Another feasible scenario is that the antichrist himself—following God's destruction of the Muslim invaders—will grant permission to the Jews to rebuild their temple as a part of the "strong covenant" he will make with Israel (Daniel 9:27). Mark Hitchcock suggests that "a key element in that plan would have to include Israeli sovereignty over the Temple Mount area."[17] Once this covenant is enacted—and backed by the full force of the antichrist—it would take only a year or so to dismantle the Muslim structures and rebuild the Jewish temple.

Dr. Randall Price, in his book *The Coming Last Days Temple*, writes,

> What does this say to you and me? It says that not only have the Jews already begun the ascent to their goal, but they are only one step away from accomplishing it!... The current conflict over the Temple Mount and the resolve of the Jewish activists to prepare for the conclusion of this conflict have provided the momentum for the short distance that remains of "the climb." We live in a day that is on the brink of the rebuilding effort, and with it the beginning of the fulfillment of the prophecies that will move the world rapidly to see as a reality the coming Last Days Temple.[18]

The Significance of It All

From a prophetic standpoint, I find all these developments highly significant. To review:

- A key prerequisite to the rebuilding of the Jewish temple—Israel back in her homeland as a nation—has been a reality since 1948.
- The Jews have been streaming back to the Holy Land from around the world ever since (as prophesied in Ezekiel 36–37).
- Items to be used in temple worship are presently being fabricated.
- The Sanhedrin has been reestablished.
- The Sanhedrin has called for architectural plans to be drawn up for the rebuilding of the temple.
- Many Jews and Jewish rabbis desire and pray not only for the temple to be rebuilt, but for it to be rebuilt on the Temple Mount.

The stage is being set.

11

GOD'S END-TIME JEWISH WITNESSES DURING THE TRIBULATION

There are two groups of Jewish witnesses mentioned in the book of Revelation. Both will be very active during the future tribulation period. I am referring to the 144,000 Jewish witnesses of Revelation 7 and 14, and the two prophetic witnesses of Revelation 11. During the darkest days to ever come upon humanity, God will still have His representatives on the earth, pointing people to the way of salvation. These two groups of Jewish witnesses will not necessarily need to be on high alert, as will be other Jews during the tribulation period, for God will supernaturally protect them during the time of their respective ministries. Let's consider some scriptural details.

God's 144,000 Jewish Witnesses

In Revelation 7:2-8 we read:

> I saw another angel coming up from the east, carrying the seal of the living God. And he shouted to those four angels, who had been given power to harm land and sea, "Wait! Don't harm the land or the sea or the trees until we have placed the seal of God on the foreheads of his servants."

> And I heard how many were marked with the seal of God—144,000 were sealed from all the tribes of Israel:
>
> from Judah 12,000
>
> from Reuben 12,000
>
> from Gad 12,000
>
> from Asher 12,000
>
> from Naphtali 12,000
>
> from Manasseh 12,000
>
> from Simeon 12,000
>
> from Levi 12,000
>
> from Issachar 12,000
>
> from Zebulun 12,000
>
> from Joseph 12,000
>
> from Benjamin 12,000

In ancient times, a seal was a symbol of ownership (2 Corinthians 1:22) as well as a symbol of protection (Ephesians 1:14; 4:30). These Jewish believers will be "owned" by God, and by His sovereign authority He will protect them during their time of service during the tribulation period (Revelation 14:1,3-4; see also 13:16-18).

The seal that God's Jewish servants receive seems to be a counterpart to the "mark of the beast" that will be imprinted on all who follow the antichrist during the tribulation period (see Revelation 13:17; 14:11; 16:2; 19:20). Prophecy experts Thomas Ice and Timothy Demy suggest that "God's seal of His witnesses most likely is invisible and for the purpose of protection from the antichrist. On the other hand, antichrist offers protection from the wrath of God—a promise he cannot deliver—and his mark is visible and external." They note, "For the only time in history, an outward indication will identify those who reject Christ and His gospel of forgiveness of sins."[1]

The 144,000 sealed Jews will be "from all the tribes of Israel" (Revelation 7:4). Some modern Christians have taken this as metaphorically referring to the church. However, the context indicates the verse is referring to 144,000 Jewish men—12,000 from each tribe—who live during the future tribulation period (see Revelation 14:4). The fact that specific tribes are mentioned along with specific numbers for those tribes (12) removes all possibility that this is a figure of speech. Nowhere else in the Bible does a reference to 12 tribes of Israel mean anything but 12 tribes of Israel.

Some object that these must not be the literal tribes of Israel because the Old Testament tribes of Dan and Ephraim are omitted, and—unlike the Old Testament listings—the tribe of Levi is included. In response, the Old Testament has no fewer than 20 variant lists of the tribes, and these lists include anywhere from 10 to 13 tribes, though the number 12 is predominant (see Genesis 49; Deuteronomy 33; Ezekiel 48). Hence, no list of the 12 tribes of Israel must be identical. Twelve seems to be the ideal number when the tribes are listed, and Revelation 7 and 14 maintain this ideal number.

It seems apparent that the reason Dan's tribe was omitted was because that tribe was guilty of idolatry on many occasions. As a result, the tribe was largely obliterated (Leviticus 24:11; Judges 18:1,30; see also 1 Kings 12:28-29). To commit unrepentant idolatry is to cut oneself off from God's blessing.

The same was true of the tribe of Ephraim, which was involved in idolatry and paganized worship (Judges 17; Hosea 4:17), and was hence omitted from the list in Revelation 7. The readjustment of the list to include Joseph and Manasseh to complete the 12 thus makes good sense.

As for why Levi's tribe was included in Revelation 7, we must keep in mind that the priestly functions of the tribe of Levi ceased with the coming of Jesus Christ—the ultimate High Priest. Indeed, the Levitical priesthood was fulfilled in the person of Christ (Hebrews 7–10). Because there was no further need for the services of the tribe of Levi as priests, there was no further reason for keeping this tribe distinct and separate from the others. Hence, they were properly included in the tribal listing in the book of Revelation. Again, then, it seems clear from the context that the 144,000 refers not to the church but to the actual tribes of Israel.

It is interesting to observe that God had originally chosen the Jews to be His witnesses, their appointed task being to share the good news of God with all other people around the world (see Isaiah 42:6; 43:10). The Jews failed at this task—so much so they did not even recognize Jesus as the divine Messiah during His short ministry on earth. During the future tribulation, these 144,000 Jews—who become believers in Jesus as the divine Messiah—will finally fulfill this mandate from God, as they will be His witnesses all around the world.

These witnesses will no doubt preach the gospel of the kingdom during the tribulation period. Indeed, Matthew 24:14 tells us that during the tribulation, "the Good News about the Kingdom will be preached throughout the whole world, so that all nations will hear it." Even though persecution and affliction will be widespread, and even though many will have hearts hardened against God, the Lord, in His mercy, will have witnesses on earth who are committed to spreading His message about Jesus Christ and the coming kingdom.

Just as John the Baptist and Jesus preached often that the kingdom of God is near, so will God's witnesses do the same during the tribulation. Jesus will be presented as the divine Messiah, the King who will rule in the soon-coming millennial kingdom. The gospel of the kingdom is the good news that Christ is coming to set up His kingdom on earth, and that those who receive Him by faith will enjoy the blessings of His millennial rule.

Christians debate about precisely when these 144,000 Jews will begin their ministry. My assessment is that they will emerge on the scene near the beginning of the tribulation. It is likely that they will engage in their work of evangelism early in the tribulation because the believing martyrs of Revelation 6:9-11—those who become believers as a result of the ministry of the 144,000—are executed by the forces of the antichrist during the first half of the tribulation.

It is likely that these Jews will become believers in Jesus in a way similar to that of the apostle Paul, himself a Jew. Acts 9:1-9 reveals that Paul had an encounter with the risen Christ on the road to Damascus. A bit later, according to 1 Corinthians 15:8, the apostle Paul referred to himself—in his conversion to Christ—as having "been born at the wrong time." This can also be translated as "one untimely born" (ESV). Paul may have been alluding to his 144,000 Jewish tribulation brethren, who would be spiritually "born" in a way similar to him—only Paul was spiritually born far before them. These Jewish witnesses, like Paul, will be mighty witnesses of Jesus Christ.

We are told that these 144,000 Jewish witnesses will "have kept themselves as pure as virgins, following the Lamb wherever he goes" (Revelation 14:4). As celibates, these men will focus their full attention on serving Christ (see 1 Corinthians 7:26; also Matthew 19:12).

We are then told that they are "firstfruits for God and the Lamb" (Revelation 14:4 ESV). As "firstfruits," these 144,000 may be the first of many to enter directly into Christ's millennial kingdom in their mortal bodies (not yet resurrected). Or perhaps they are firstfruits in the sense that they are like "firstfruit sacrifices" to God, being blameless and perfect—the cream of the crop, as it were.

Scripture affirms of these witnesses, "They have told no lies; they are without blame" (Revelation 14:5). They are truth-tellers in a tribulation environment filled with the antichrist's deception (Revelation 12:9; 13:14; 19:20; see also Philippians 2:15; Hebrews 9:14; 1 Peter 1:19; Jude 24).

A bit later in the book of Revelation, we are told that an unimaginably large company of hideous demons will be released from the bottomless pit (Revelation 9:2). These demonic spirits will inflict tortuous wounds on people all over the world. However, these evil spirits cannot go beyond what God will allow them (as the book of Job reminds us). We are told that the 144,000 Jewish evangelists will be kept safe from the torment of these spirits. We might surmise that the converts of the 144,000 will also likely be kept safe. It seems in keeping with God's mercy and grace that all who have trusted the Lord for salvation will be sealed in some special way and protected from torment.

Still later, in Revelation 14:1-5, we are provided a preview of what will take place following the second coming of Jesus Christ. John, in a panoramic vision, witnesses Jesus, the Lamb of God, standing on Mount Zion. He is portrayed as being with the 144,000 Jewish witnesses. This "Mount Zion" is apparently the literal Mount Zion in earthly Jerusalem. Mount Zion typically refers to the hill in Jerusalem upon which the Jewish temple was built.

These Jewish witnesses will have had the protective seal of God on them all through the tribulation (Revelation 7:3-4), and hence they could not be killed. This means they will still be alive on earth at the end of the tribulation. Following the second coming, they are invited directly into Christ's earthly millennial kingdom.

I think it is highly likely that these 144,000 Jewish witnesses will be directly connected with the judgment of the nations (Matthew 25:31-46), which will take place following the second coming of

Christ. The nations are comprised of the sheep and the goats, representing the saved and the lost among the Gentiles. According to Matthew 25:32, they will be intermingled and will require separation by a special judgment.

These Gentiles will be judged based upon how they treated Christ's "brothers." Who are these brothers? It is likely that they are the 144,000 Jews mentioned in Revelation 7—Christ's Jewish brothers who bear witness of Him during the tribulation. Stan Toussaint, professor of Bible exposition at Dallas Theological Seminary, writes, "It seems best to say that 'brothers of Mine' is a designation of the godly remnant of Israel that will proclaim the gospel of the kingdom unto every nation of the world."[2]

Merrill F. Unger likewise writes,

> During the tribulation period, God will sovereignly call and save 144,000 Jews...So glorious and wonderful will be the ministry of the 144,000 saved Jews and so faithful will be their powerful testimony, the King on His throne of glory will not be ashamed to call them "My brothers." More than that, He will consider Himself so intimately united to them that what was done or not done to them is the same as being actually done or not done to Himself.[3]

J. Dwight Pentecost observes that the 144,000 Jews

> will be under a death sentence by the beast. They will refuse to carry the beast's mark, and so they will not be able to buy and sell. Consequently, they will have to depend on those to whom they minister for hospitality, food, and support. Only those who receive the message will jeopardize their lives by extending hospitality to the

> messengers. Therefore what is done for them will be an evidence of their faith in Christ, that is, what is done for them will be done for Christ.[4]

So even though the antichrist and the false prophet will wield economical control over the world during the tribulation period (Revelation 13), God will still be at work. God's redeemed will come to the aid of Christ's Jewish brethren as they bear witness to Christ all around the world. These brethren will be invited into Christ's millennial kingdom.

God's Two Prophetic Witnesses

Aside from the 144,000 Jewish witnesses, God will also raise up two mighty prophetic witnesses who will have the same kinds of powers as Moses and Elijah. In Revelation 11:3 God affirms, "I will give power to my two witnesses, and they will be clothed in burlap and will prophesy during those 1,260 days." These two witnesses will testify to the true God, His judgment, and His salvation with astounding power. It is noteworthy that in the Old Testament, two witnesses were required to confirm testimony (Deuteronomy 17:6). David Jeremiah observes:

> Two angels testified to the resurrection of the Savior. Two men in white testified to His ascension. God often dispatches His people in twos as well. Think of Moses and Aaron, Joshua and Caleb, Zerubbabel and Joshua, Peter and John, Paul and Silas, Timothy and Titus. The disciples were sent out two by two, and the seventy were also told to travel in pairs. These two witnesses will follow that pattern as they proclaim one of the most important calls to repentance of all time.[5]

These two witnesses will carry out their task for 1,260 days—which measures out to precisely three-and-one-half years. This period is elsewhere defined as "42 months" (Revelation 11:2) and "a time, times and half a time" (12:14). (A "time" is one year, "times" is two years," and "half a time" is half a year.)

Bible expositors debate whether this is the first or last three-and-one-half years of the tribulation. My assessment is that the two witnesses do their miraculous work during the first three-and-one-half years, for the antichrist's execution of them (see below) seems to fit best with other events that will transpire at the midpoint of the tribulation, such as the antichrist's exaltation of himself to godhood. Moreover, the resurrection of the two witnesses—after being dead for three days—would make a bigger impact on the world at the midpoint of the tribulation than at the end, just prior to the glorious second coming of Christ.

Notice that the two witnesses will be "clothed in burlap" (Revelation 11:3). The "burlap" is essentially clothing made of goat or camel hair—which, in Bible times, symbolically expressed mourning (see Genesis 37:34). The mourning of the two prophets will be over the wretched condition and lack of repentance in the world.

There will undoubtedly be many who would like to see these witnesses put to death during their time of ministry. However, as Revelation 11:5 says, "If anyone tries to harm them, fire flashes from their mouths and consumes their enemies. This is how anyone who tries to harm them must die." It is worth noting that, in the Bible, fire often points to the wrath of God. Scripture tells us that God's "rage blazes forth like fire" (Nahum 1:6). God said, "My anger will burn like an unquenchable fire" (Jeremiah 4:4). Those who stand against God's two prophets will come face to face with God's wrath.

The two witnesses are thus sustained by the supernatural

protection of God during the years of their ministry. This is similar to how Jesus was providentially protected during His ministry. Once Jesus's ministry was over, God allowed for Him to be put to death on the cross. Until that time, Jesus continually affirmed, "My time has not yet come" (John 7:8).

In similar fashion, it is only when the ministry of these two witnesses is complete that they will finally be executed by the forces of the antichrist. Up till the time their task is over, they will be immune from danger. Their ministry will be unstoppable for three-and-one-half years, until "they complete their testimony" (Revelation 11:7).

Scripture reveals that these two prophetic witnesses have miraculous powers similar to those of Moses and Elijah: "They have power to shut the sky so that no rain will fall for as long as they prophesy. And they have the power to turn the rivers and oceans into blood, and to strike the earth with every kind of plague as often as they wish" (Revelation 11:6). In both the Old and New Testaments, God often used miracles to authenticate His messengers (Acts 2:43; Romans 15:18-19; 2 Corinthians 12:12). In the tribulation period, when the world is overrun by supernatural demonic activity, false religion, murder, sexual perversion, and unrestrained wickedness, the supernatural signs performed by these two witnesses will mark them as true prophets of God.

Is it possible that these two witnesses will actually be Moses and Elijah? Many think so. Among their reasons:

1. Daniel 9 reveals that just as the first 69 weeks of Daniel dealt with the Jews, so the 70th week—the tribulation period—will deal with the Jews. Moses and Elijah are unquestionably the two most influential figures in Jewish history. It would thus make good sense that they be on the scene during the tribulation. No two men in

Israel's entire history would receive greater respect and appreciation than Moses and Elijah. Timothy J. Demy and John C. Whitcomb explain that "Moses was God's great deliverer and lawgiver for Israel (Deuteronomy 34:10-12)...And God raised up Elijah to confront Israel in a time of great national apostasy."[6] Many thus view them as ideally suited for ministry during the tribulation period.

2. Both Moses (Deuteronomy 18:15,18) and Elijah (Malachi 4:5) were expected to return in the future.
3. Both Moses and Elijah appeared on the Mount of Transfiguration with Jesus—which shows their central place in the unfolding of God's plan. It would thus be appropriate for them to be on the scene during the future tribulation period.
4. The miracles performed by the two prophetic witnesses are quite similar to those performed by Moses and Elijah in Old Testament times (see Exodus 7–11; 1 Kings 17).
5. The Old Testament reveals that both Moses and Elijah left the earth in unusual ways. Elijah never died, but rather was transported to heaven in a fiery chariot (2 Kings 2:11-12). God supernaturally buried Moses's body in a location unknown to man (Deuteronomy 34:5-6).

In view of such facts, it may be that during the tribulation, God will send two of His mightiest servants: Moses, the great deliverer and spiritual legislator of Israel, and Elijah, a prince among Old Testament prophets. During Old Testament times, these individuals rescued Israel from bondage and idolatry. They may appear again during the tribulation to warn Israel against succumbing to the false religion of the antichrist and the false prophet.

But Moses and Elijah are not the only dynamic duo suggested in fulfillment of Revelation 11. Some suggest the two witnesses will be Enoch and Elijah. Keep in mind that both Enoch and Elijah were righteous men who were directly raptured to heaven. Neither one of them passed through death's door. Both were also prophets—one a Gentile (Enoch) and the other a Jew (Elijah). The church fathers held to this view, which remained popular for the next 300 years of church history. Perhaps God will ordain one of the witnesses to speak to the Jews and the other to speak to the Gentiles.

There are other Bible expositors who are convinced that the two prophetic witnesses of Revelation 11 will not involve biblical personalities of the past. After all, it is reasoned, wouldn't Scripture specify these individuals if indeed they were famous personalities of the past? These expositors conclude the two witnesses will likely be new prophets whom God specially raises up for ministry during the tribulation.

In any event, Revelation 11:7-10 tells us:

> When they complete their testimony, the beast that comes up out of the bottomless pit will declare war against them, and he will conquer them and kill them. And their bodies will lie in the main street of Jerusalem, the city that is figuratively called "Sodom" and "Egypt," the city where their Lord was crucified. And for three and a half days, all peoples, tribes, languages, and nations will stare at their bodies. No one will be allowed to bury them. All the people who belong to this world will gloat over them and give presents to each other to celebrate the death of the two prophets who had tormented them.

The two witnesses will minister for a total of 1,260 days, or three-and-a-half years. It is only when they "complete their testimony" that God will permit them to be killed. God's obedient servants will be immortal until their work is done. Once they are finished, they will be executed by the antichrist.

The Greek word translated "complete" in this verse is, interestingly enough, the same word used by Jesus upon the cross when He said, "It is finished!" (John 19:30). Christ died after He had finished His work of redemption. The two witnesses will die after they complete their work of redemptive ministry. And just as Jesus was executed in Jerusalem, so will the two witnesses be executed in Jerusalem.

Scripture reveals that their bodies will lie lifeless in Jerusalem. Jerusalem is figuratively called "Sodom" and "Egypt" because of the people's apostasy and rejection of God. Sodom was a city brimming with perverted sex, while Egypt was known for its persecution of God's people. Both cities were viewed as rebellious against God. The description of Jerusalem as no better than Sodom and Egypt indicates that this once-holy city will be in the same league as those known for their hatred of the true God and His Word.

Television and the Internet will apparently enable "all peoples, tribes, languages, and nations" to stare at the dead bodies for three-and-a-half days (Revelation 11:9). The news feeds will be instantaneous.

The refusal to bury a corpse was, in biblical times, a way of showing contempt (see Acts 14:19). The Old Testament prohibits this practice (Deuteronomy 21:22-23). By leaving the dead bodies in the street, the people of the world render the greatest possible insult to God's spokesmen. This was considered among the greatest indignities that someone could perpetrate on another person (see Psalm

79:2-3). It is equivalent to the people of the world collectively spitting upon the corpses.

The people of the earth will rejoice and will "give presents to each other to celebrate the death of the two prophets" (Revelation 11:10). These worldlings will essentially have a satanic Christmas celebration when the witnesses are put to death.

But then something amazing will happen. As Revelation 11:11 puts it, "After three and a half days, God breathed life into them, and they stood up!" The Christmas celebration quickly gives way to fear as people witness a mighty act of God. The lifeless corpses suddenly stand up, alive, in full view of television and Internet feeds. Clips of this event will no doubt be replayed over and over again through various media. It will no doubt "go viral" on the Internet.

God will then call His two prophetic witnesses up to heaven, in sight of everyone (verse 12). Their resurrection and ascension will serve as a huge exclamation point to their prophetic ministry. And their enemies will see it all, and will likely hate them all the more as a result. As well, the whole world will surmise that the antichrist's murderous activities have just been overruled by heaven.

Henry M. Morris, in his book *The Revelation Record: A Scientific and Devotional Commentary on the Prophetic Book of the End Times*, says this:

> All [the witnesses'] enemies, all those who had rejected their word and rejoiced when they died, especially the beast who had hunted them to death...will gaze transfixed as they watch them ascend far up into the heavens and into the presence of their Lord. The word for "beheld" (Greek *theoreo*) is a strong word, implying a transfixed stare. The sight will be enough to strike terror into the hearts of the most arrogantly rebellious of their enemies. A moment before, such men were

> rejoicing in supreme confidence that Christ was finally defeated and Satan's man was on the victor's throne. But now Christ had triumphed again. The ascent of the prophets into heaven was a dire prediction that even greater judgments were about to descend from heaven. The three-and-a-half-day festivities were about to be followed by another three-and-a-half years of judgments more severe than ever.[7]

The Results of Their Ministry

God's two sets of witnesses—the 144,000 of Revelation 7 and 14, and the two witnesses of Revelation 11—will have important roles during the tribulation. Even though the world will be under judgment, God, in His grace, will continue to testify to the truth. And many will become converted. In fact, Revelation 7:9-14 says,

> After this I saw a vast crowd, too great to count, from every nation and tribe and people and language, standing in front of the throne and before the Lamb. They were clothed in white robes and held palm branches in their hands. And they were shouting with a great roar, "Salvation comes from our God who sits on the throne and from the Lamb!"
>
> And all the angels were standing around the throne and around the elders and the four living beings. And they fell before the throne with their faces to the ground and worshiped God. They sang, "Amen! Blessing and glory and wisdom and thanksgiving and honor and power and strength belong to our God forever and ever! Amen."
>
> Then one of the twenty-four elders asked me, "Who are these who are clothed in white? Where did they come from?"

> And I said to him, "Sir, you are the one who knows."
>
> Then he said to me, "These are the ones who died in the great tribulation. They have washed their robes in the blood of the Lamb and made them white."

Hence, as John MacArthur says, "While the tribulation period will be a time of judgment, it will also be a time of unprecedented redemption (see v. 14; 6:9-11; 20:4; Isa. 11:10; Matt. 24:14)."[8] Charles Ryrie agrees: "In these difficult days, many will find Christ as Savior."[9] This is "an innumerable crowd rejoicing because they are secure in Christ and all tears and sorrows have ended."[10]

This multitude of believers will be comprised of many different ethnic groups from around the world. God's love knows no boundaries. People from every nation will come to know the Lord in that day.

How glorious!

12

THE ANTICHRIST'S CAMPAIGN TO ANNIHILATE THE JEWS

Adolf Hitler (1889–1945) was the infamous dictator of the German Reich. Under his leadership and his racially motivated ideology, the Nazi regime executed about six million Jews whom he and his followers deemed *untermenschen* ("subhumans"). During the future seven-year tribulation period, the antichrist will *far exceed* Hitler's efforts in targeting the Jewish people for extermination. He will be driven by a Satan-inspired hatred for the Jewish people (see 2 Thessalonians 2:9).

The Antichrist and His Double-Cross of Israel

The antichrist will sign a covenant with Israel that is supposed to remain in effect for the full seven-year tribulation period—the 70th week of Daniel (Daniel 9:27). Among other things, it will stipulate that the Jews can offer sacrifices in their temple. But then the antichrist will double-cross Israel. We are told that "after half this time, he will put an end to the sacrifices and offerings." In other words, after the covenant has been in effect for three-and-a-half years, he will renege on it and cause Israel's temple sacrifices to cease.

At the midpoint of the tribulation, the antichrist—having already attained political power—will seek to assume power in the religious realm as well (Revelation 13). He will set up an image of himself in the temple. This will amount to enthroning himself in the place of deity, displaying himself as God (Matthew 24:15; compare with Isaiah 14:13-14 and Ezekiel 28:2-9). The antichrist will demand that the people of the world worship him (see 2 Thessalonians 2:4; Revelation 13:8). In order for that to happen, he must destroy all competing religious systems—including the Jewish religion, with its Levitical sacrifices and offerings.

This means that after the antichrist professes to be Israel's *protector*, he will become Israel's *persecutor*. After he promises to be Israel's *defender*, he will become Israel's *defiler*. He will do this by setting up an image of himself in the Jewish temple (Daniel 9:26).

Understandably, all this will be utterly detestable to the Jewish people. Jesus warned that as soon as they witness this event, *they must leave Jerusalem immediately*:

> "The day is coming when you will see what Daniel the prophet spoke about—the sacrilegious object that causes desecration standing in the Holy Place." (Reader, pay attention!) "Then those in Judea must flee to the hills. A person out on the deck of a roof must not go down into the house to pack. A person out in the field must not return even to get a coat. How terrible it will be for pregnant women and for nursing mothers in those days. And pray that your flight will not be in winter or on the Sabbath. For there will be greater anguish than at any time since the world began. And it will never be so great again" (Matthew 24:15-21).

The bottom line is that when these horrific circumstances unfold in Jerusalem, the Jews who live there should have no concern for personal belongings, but rather they should make haste with utmost speed.

The "Great" Tribulation

We learn a great deal about the antichrist's targeting of the Jews in the two apocalyptic books in the Bible—Daniel and Revelation. In the book of Daniel, we discover that the angel Gabriel gave Daniel specific revelations about the antichrist and the Jews. Daniel 7:21 describes the future work of the antichrist as one who "made war with the saints and prevailed over them" (ESV). In this verse, the word "saints" apparently refers to the nation of Israel (compare with verse 18). The antichrist will launch great persecution against the Jewish people during the tribulation (see Matthew 24:15-22; 2 Thessalonians 2:4).

Daniel 7:25 then affirms that the antichrist "shall wear out the saints of the Most High...and they shall be given into his hand for a time, times, and half a time" (ESV). The antichrist will persecute, oppress, and even kill the Jewish people. As the one who is "against Christ," the antichrist is certainly against the race that gave birth to Christ.

This persecution will last "a time, times, and half a time," which is three-and-a-half years. A comparison with other prophetic passages indicates that the antichrist's persecution of the saints (Jews) will begin at the midpoint of the tribulation (Revelation 13:7-10; Daniel 7:21), and last for the duration of the tribulation. As Daniel 7:22 says, the persecution will last until "the time arrived for the holy people to take over the kingdom"—that is, until Christ's millennial kingdom begins (see Zechariah 14:1-9; Revelation 19:11–20:6).

Scripture reveals that the last three-and-a-half years of the tribulation period is "the great tribulation." This is because the second half of the tribulation will be especially intense. Jews living during that time will find life and survival extremely difficult.

Some have claimed there is a contradiction between saying that the second half of the tribulation is three-and-a-half years long and

Jesus's end-time affirmation recorded in Matthew 24:21-22: "There will be greater anguish than at any time since the world began. And it will never be so great again. In fact, unless that time of calamity *is shortened*, not a single person will survive. But *it will be shortened* for the sake of God's chosen ones" (emphasis added).

The question is this: Was Jesus saying He would make the Great Tribulation *shorter* than three-and-a-half years, or was He saying that three-and-a-half years is, in itself, the shortened time? To answer this question, we turn to the parallel passage in Mark 13:20: "Unless the Lord shortens that time of calamity, not a single person will survive. But for the sake of his chosen ones he has shortened those days." Greek scholars note that the two verbs in this verse—"shortens" and "has shortened"—express action that was taken by God *in the past*. This means that God, in eternity past, sovereignly decreed a limit on the length of the Great Tribulation.

The decrees are God's eternal purpose. As Henry C. Thiessen says, God "does not make His plans or alter them as human history develops. He made them in eternity, and, because He is immutable, they remain unaltered (Ps. 33:11; James 1:17)."[1] We conclude that Jesus was teaching that God, in the past, had *already* shortened the Great Tribulation, sovereignly decreeing that it would end after three-and-a-half years, as opposed to letting it continue indefinitely. In His omniscience, God knew that if the Great Tribulation were to continue indefinitely, all humanity would ultimately perish. To prevent that from happening, God "sovereignly fixed a specific time for the Great Tribulation to end—when it had run its course for three and one-half years or 42 months or 1,260 days. That fixed time cannot be changed."[2]

Antiochus Epiphanes: A Type of the Antichrist

In Daniel 8 we find a discussion of Antiochus Epiphanes, whom many scholars believe to be a type of the antichrist. A type is an Old Testament institution, event, person, object, or ceremony which has reality and purpose in biblical history, but which also by divine design foreshadows something yet to be revealed.

In Daniel 8:10 we are told that Antiochus threw "some of the stars to the ground" and trampled them. There is no small controversy among Bible expositors as to what this means. However, a consensus has emerged among many that the term "stars" likely refers to the Jewish people. Hence, this metaphorical language apparently describes Antiochus's relentless persecution of the Jewish people. Support for the idea that "stars" refers to the Jewish people is found in Joseph's dream: "Listen, I have had another dream...The sun, moon, and eleven stars bowed low before me!" (Genesis 37:9). In this dream, the sun (Joseph's father), the moon (Joseph's mother), and the eleven stars (Joseph's eleven brothers) would one day bow before him. These astronomical terms refer to the whole clan of Israel.

Likewise, in Revelation 12:1 we encounter a metaphorical description of Israel as a woman who has a "crown of twelve stars." The twelve stars represent the twelve tribes of Israel. We conclude, then, that Antiochus's trampling of the stars refers to his trampling of the Jewish people. And history reveals that Antiochus did in fact brutally persecute the Jewish people from 170–164 BC.

Daniel 8:11 then tells us that Antiochus "challenged the Commander of heaven's army." Antiochus, by his actions, was putting himself in the place of God. This, of course, is not the first time in the book of Daniel that a human leader set himself up as God. Recall how Nebuchadnezzar spoke of himself in divine terms (Daniel 3:1-7). Darius, too, was prayed to as a god for a time (6:6-9).

Antiochus then stopped the daily sacrifices in the Jewish temple, thereby halting Israel's religious practices (Daniel 8:11). He also defiled the temple by slaughtering a pig within the Holy of Holies. Apparently he was seeking to destroy the Jewish faith.

Antiochus then trashed the law of Moses, which was communicated to Moses by God (Daniel 8:12). This act essentially amounted to trashing God. Speaking of Antiochus, 1 Maccabees 1:56-57 informs us: "The books of the law which they found they tore in pieces and burned with fire. Where the book of the covenant was found in the possession of anyone, or if anyone adhered to the law, the decree of the king condemned them to death."

This wicked Jew-hater prospered in some of his plans—but only for a time, according to the divine timetable (see Daniel 8:14). One of God's angels—a "holy one"—announced that Antiochus's defiling of Israel and her temple would last only 2,300 evenings and mornings—from 171 BC to 165 BC.

A bit later in Daniel, Antiochus is called "a fierce king, a master of intrigue" (verse 23). History reveals that he took the throne through deceit and guile. Verse 25 tells us: "He will be a master of deception and will become arrogant; he will destroy many without warning." He was not only deceitful, he was also cunning, full of guile, treacherous, and unscrupulous. Many of the people he destroyed were Jewish.

We are also told in verse 25 that Antiochus "will even take on the Prince of princes in battle." Antiochus, a pagan king, raised himself up as a divine being against Israel's king, the Most High God, the Ruler of heaven and earth.

Not unexpectedly, we are then told that Antiochus "will be broken, though not by human power" (verse 25). Antiochus would be destroyed by God's hand. God sovereignly determines the day a person dies. As Job said to God: "You have decided the length of our lives. You know how many months we will live, and we are not given a minute longer" (Job 14:5; see also Psalm 139:16; Acts 17:26). Scripture also reveals that God sometimes inflicts premature death as a judgment (see Acts 5:1-10; 12:23; 1 Corinthians 11:30; 1 John 5:16).

Now, given this backdrop, it is easy to see how Antiochus was a type of the antichrist. Just as Antiochus set himself up as God and defiled the Jewish temple, so will the antichrist set himself up as God and defile the Jewish temple. Just as Antiochus was a fierce persecutor of the Jews, so will the antichrist persecute the Jews. Just as Antiochus's power was great, so will the antichrist's power be great. Just as Antiochus operated through deceit and guile, so will the antichrist. Just as Antiochus was destroyed by God, so will the antichrist be destroyed by God—that is, by Jesus Christ at the second coming (Revelation 19:11-21).

Michael—the Protector of Israel

Daniel 12:1 tells us, "At that time Michael, the archangel who stands guard over your nation, will arise. Then there will be a time of anguish greater than any since nations first came into existence." The phrase "at that time" refers to the same time frame as the latter part of Daniel 11—the future seven-year tribulation period.

Michael is said to stand guard "over your nation"—that is, the nation of Israel, the Jews. Clearly God has assigned Michael the role of "guardian of Israel" during the future tribulation period (compare with Psalm 91:11-12).

Recall from Daniel 10:13 that Michael was one of the angels who did battle with "the spirit prince of the kingdom of Persia"—a demonic spirit no doubt seeking to influence Persia's leadership to move against Israel. (Ancient Persia is the same as modern Iran.) Even then, Michael was watching out for Israel's interests (see also Revelation 12:7).

Michael's guardianship will be especially needed during the

tribulation—"a time of anguish greater than any since nations first came into existence" (Daniel 12:1). Earlier in this book I noted that the word *tribulation* literally means "to press" (as grapes), "to press together," "to press hard upon," and refers to times of oppression, affliction, and distress. In the New Testament the word is translated "tribulation," "affliction," "anguish," "persecution," "trouble," and "burden." The horror of this era cannot be overstated. Michael will have his hands full during the tribulation period. Though there will be countless Jewish casualties (Zechariah 13:8), a remnant will survive till the very end, and this, no doubt, will be largely due to Michael's protective ministry.

Satan's Role in Persecution

Scripture reveals that Satan plays a constant role in the persecution of God's people—including the Jewish people. In Revelation 2:10, the Lord Jesus warns the church in Smyrna: "Don't be afraid of what you are about to suffer. The devil will throw some of you into prison to test you. You will suffer for ten days." God's faithful servant Antipas was martyred in Pergamum, "the city where Satan has his throne" (verse 13). The devil certainly sought to kill the Jewish Messiah, Jesus Christ (Revelation 12:4).

Those living on earth during the tribulation period are warned, "The devil has come down to you in great anger, knowing that he has little time" (Revelation 12:12). Verse 13 then tells us that Satan "pursued the woman who had given birth to the male child." The male child is Jesus Christ. The mention of the dragon seeking to devour the child likely alludes to the massacre of male children commanded by Herod when he attempted to kill Jesus (Matthew 2:13-18).

The woman represents Israel, building on Old Testament imagery in which Israel was viewed as the wife of God (Isaiah 54:5-6; Jeremiah 3:6-8; 31:32; Ezekiel 16:32; Hosea 2:16). Revelation 12:13

thus graphically depicts Satan's persecution of the Jews during the tribulation period. Satan will do whatever he can to destroy all of the Jewish people in the last half of the tribulation, which is referred to as the "great tribulation" by Jesus in Matthew 24:21 (ESV). He will seek to persecute the Jews, from whose lineage the Messiah had been born. Understandably, John 8:44 warns that Satan "was a murderer from the beginning."

Of great significance is the fact that the antichrist will be energized by Satan (2 Thessalonians 2:9). Just as Satan is a persecutor of the Jews, so the antichrist will be a persecutor of the Jews. In fact, Satan will persecute the Jews *through the antichrist.*

David Jeremiah, in his book *Agents of the Apocalypse*, suggests that "the devil hates Israel because, from a biological perspective, Christ came from this nation. Satan wants to destroy Israel, denying its people a home when the Messiah returns to earth and establishes His promised Kingdom."[3] He notes that Satan has always wanted to destroy Israel:

> Knowing from prophecy that the Promised One would spring from Israel, the adversary did everything he could to keep that nation from being formed. He incited Esau to attempt to kill his brother, Jacob, who would father the twelve tribes of Israel...He incited Pharaoh to murder all the Jewish baby boys in Egypt. Had either Jacob or Moses not survived, the nation of Israel would never have existed...Satan incited the wicked Haman to plot the extermination of all the Jews. But God raised up Esther "for such a time as this" to expose Haman's scheme, and the promised seed was spared (Esther 4:14)...When the prophesied Child was finally born, Satan instilled fear and hatred in King Herod, who had all the babies in Bethlehem murdered. He thought that

> surely the promised seed would be slain in this insidious act of infanticide (Matthew 2:16).[4]

It is interesting to observe that Scripture reveals that Jesus will come again *only* when the Jewish people are endangered at Armageddon, and the Jewish leaders cry out for deliverance from Him, their divine Messiah (see Zechariah 12:10). In his perverted thinking, Satan may be reasoning that if he can destroy the Jews, then he can prevent the second coming of Christ and save himself from defeat.

Revelation 12:14, however, assures us, "She [the woman—that is, Israel] was given two wings like those of a great eagle so she could fly to the place prepared for her in the wilderness. There she would be cared for and protected from the dragon for a time, times, and half a time." Wings often represent protection and deliverance in the Bible (see Psalm 91:4; Isaiah 40:31). For example, in the Exodus account, when God delivered the Jews from Egyptian bondage, God said, "You have seen what I did to the Egyptians. You know how I carried you on eagles' wings and brought you to myself" (Exodus 19:4). Hence, the "two wings" in Revelation 12:14 point to God's supernatural delivering power.

John Walvoord, in *The Bible Knowledge Commentary*, tells us that the "two wings" bring the Jews to a safe place: "This hiding place was not clearly identified. Some suggest that it might be Petra, fortress capital of the Nabateans in Edom, south of the Dead Sea." Walvoord notes that "this city has a narrow access which could easily be blocked but which opens up into a large canyon capable of caring for many thousands of people."[5]

Now, even though God will preserve a remnant of Jews through this persecution, this should not be taken to mean that virtually all Jews will survive, for they will not. In Zechariah 13:8-9, we are prophetically told, "'Two-thirds of the people in the land will be cut off and die,' says the LORD. 'But one-third will be left in the land. I will bring that group through the fire and make them pure. I will refine them like silver and purify them like gold. They will call on my name, and I will answer them. I will say, "These are my people," and they will say, "The LORD is our God."'"

God will take care of the Jewish remnant for a time, and times, and half a time (Revelation 12:14). This refers to the last three-and-a-half years of the tribulation period. As noted earlier, "a time" equals one year, "times" equals two years, and "half a time" equals half a year (Daniel 7:25; 12:7). During this time, God will progressively purge out the unbelievers among the Jews. "Like the metallurgist, the Lord will use the fire of the tribulation to purge out the unfaithful."[6]

We are then told that "the dragon tried to drown the woman with a flood of water that flowed from his mouth" (Revelation 12:15). Some Bible expositors take this to mean that Satan will cause a flood in an attempt to dislodge and destroy the Jews. Others take the flood metaphorically, suggesting that a satanically driven army will rapidly advance against the Jews like a flood. It may also refer more broadly to an outpouring of hatred and anti-Semitism.

The good news is that "the earth helped her by opening its mouth and swallowing the river that gushed out from the mouth of the dragon" (Revelation 12:16). Whichever of the above interpretations is correct, the earth will come to the aid of the Jews, under God's providence. If the flood is literal water, perhaps God will cause the earth to open up and swallow the water. If the flood is a rapidly advancing army (or militant anti-Semitics), perhaps they will be destroyed by an earthquake that causes the ground to open up beneath them (keep in mind there will be numerous earthquakes during the end times—see Matthew 24:7; Revelation 6:12; 8:5; 11:13,19; 16:18). Recall that God promised the Jews in Isaiah 54:17,

"No weapon turned against you will succeed"—not even water, literal or metaphorical.

This understandably will make the devil furious (Revelation 12:17). In view of his utter failure to destroy the Jews, an infuriated Satan will then resort to war against a related group—that is, believers in the Lord Jesus Christ, who are ultimately the spiritual offspring of the woman Israel (see Galatians 3:29).

The Jews at Armageddon

Toward the end of the tribulation period, the greatest series of battles ever to be known to humankind will explode on the scene. It is called Armageddon. One of the antichrist's goals at Armageddon will be to finally and definitively destroy the Jewish people. He will first decide to attack Jerusalem. We read about this in Zechariah 14:1-2:

> Watch, for the day of the Lord is coming when your possessions will be plundered right in front of you! I will gather all the nations to fight against Jerusalem. The city will be taken, the houses looted, and the women raped. Half the population will be taken into captivity, and the rest will be left among the ruins of the city.

I want to draw your attention to how all the nations of the world gather against Jerusalem. Many prophecy scholars believe that because "all the nations" will be gathered against Jerusalem, this necessarily means that the United States will be among them. It is not unexpected that following the rapture of the church (when all Christians are snatched off the earth by Christ), the United States will likely become an ally of the revived Roman Empire—the United States of Europe.

In any event, Jerusalem will fall and be ravaged in the face of this overwhelming attack force. The antichrist's armies will gain initial victory. However, as we will see, the Jewish remnant will later attain ultimate victory through the direct intervention of their Messiah.

As noted previously, many Jews will exit Jerusalem—literally running for their lives—at the midpoint of the tribulation when the antichrist breaks his covenant with Israel and puts an image of himself in the Jewish temple (Matthew 24:16-31). Apparently they will flee to the deserts and mountains (see verse 16), perhaps in the area of Bozrah/Petra, about 80 miles south of Jerusalem.

Once Jerusalem is destroyed, the antichrist will target this remnant of Jews. The Jews will sense impending doom about to descend upon them as the forces of the antichrist gather in the rugged wilderness, poised to attack and annihilate them. They will be helpless, and, from an earthly perspective, will be utterly defenseless.

It is here that something wonderful will happen. Scripture reveals that at this point spiritual blindness will be removed from all the Jews and—under the guidance of the Jewish leaders of the remnant—they will call out to their Messiah, Jesus Christ. This remnant will experience national regeneration. *They will become saved!*

Recall that in Romans 11:25 the apostle Paul—himself a Jew who turned to the Messiah—wrote, "I want you to understand this mystery, dear brothers and sisters, so that you will not feel proud about yourselves. Some of the people of Israel have hard hearts, but this will last only until the full number of Gentiles comes to Christ [that is, until the full number of Gentiles who will be saved have, in fact, become saved]." Romans 9:31-33 tells us that Israel had "tried so hard to get right with God by keeping the law," but did not succeed. Why not? "They were trying to get right with God by keeping the law instead of by trusting in him. They stumbled over the great rock in their path," which is Jesus Christ (Romans 9:31-33).

In other words, Israel had sought a relationship with God via a righteousness earned by keeping the law. Instead of seeking a faith-relationship with God, through Christ, the people instead sought to do everything that the law prescribed so they could earn a relationship with God in that way (see Galatians 2:16; 3:2,10).

It is inescapable that the Jews would fail, for attaining a righteousness by observing the law requires it to be kept perfectly (James 2:10), which no man is capable of doing. To make matters worse, the Jews had refused to admit their inability to perfectly keep the law. Instead, they had rejected Jesus Christ as the Messiah, refusing to turn to Him in faith because He did not fit their preconceived ideas about the Messiah (see, for example, Matthew 12:24). *They "stumbled" over Him.*

All this led to a partial judicial blindness or hardness of heart coming upon Israel. The nation thus lost her favored position before God, and the gospel was then preached to the Gentiles with the intent of causing the Jews to become jealous and then become saved (Romans 11:11). Israel's hardening and casting off is thus only temporary.

Now, fast-forward to the campaign of Armageddon. The armies of the antichrist are gathered in the desert wilderness, poised to attack the Jewish remnant. It is at this desperate point that the blindness of the Jews will be removed and they will finally repent and turn to their divine Messiah, seeking to be rescued by Him. As Thomas Ice puts it:

> Many Christians are surprised to learn that the second coming is a rescue event. Jesus will return to planet earth in order to rescue the believing Jewish remnant that is on the verge of being destroyed during the Campaign of Armageddon. I think this is what Paul speaks of in Romans 10 when he tell us, "'Whoever will call upon the name of the Lord will be saved.' How then shall

> they call upon Him in whom they have not believed? And how shall they believe in Him of whom they have not heard? And how shall they hear without a preacher?" (Rom. 10:13-14). In other words, the Jewish people are going to have to be believers in Jesus as their Messiah in order to be rescued by Him at the second advent. This is exactly what will happen.[7]

This turning to the Lord is a precondition to the Lord coming to the aid of the Jewish remnant. The Lord says, "I will return to my place *until they admit their guilt and turn to me.* For as soon as trouble comes, they will earnestly search for me" (Hosea 5:15, emphasis added). The apostle Peter wrote, "Now repent of your sins and turn to God, so that your sins may be wiped away. *Then* times of refreshment will come from the presence of the Lord, and he will again send you Jesus, your appointed Messiah. For he must remain in heaven until the time for the final restoration of all things, as God promised long ago through his holy prophets" (Acts 3:19-21, emphasis added).

Many passages teach the future conversion of the Jews to Jesus as their Messiah (Psalm 79:1-13; 80:1-19; Isaiah 53:1-9; 59:20-21; 61:8-9; 64:1-12; Jeremiah 30:3-24; 31:31-40; 32:37-40; 50:4-5; Ezekiel 11:19-20; 16:60-63; 34:25-26; 36:24-32; 37:21-28; Hosea 6:1-3; Joel 2:28-32; Zechariah 9:11; 12:10–13:9; Romans 11:25-27). It is a common but oft-neglected theme in Scripture.

The Old Testament reveals that the Jewish leaders will call for the people of the nation to collectively repent: "Come, let us return to the LORD. He has torn us to pieces; now he will heal us. He has injured us; now he will bandage our wounds. In just a short time he will restore us, so that we may live in his presence. Oh, that we might know the LORD! Let us press on to know him. He will respond to us as surely as the arrival of dawn or the coming of rains in early spring" (Hosea 6:1-3).

Just as it was the Jewish leaders who led the Jewish people to reject Jesus as their Messiah in the first century AD (see Matthew 12), so then will the Jewish leaders urge repentance, and instruct all to turn to Jesus as their Messiah. This the remnant will do, and they will be saved. This reminds us of Joel 2:28-29, where we find a description of the spiritual awakening that will come upon the Jewish remnant.

To sum up, then, the restoration of Israel will include the confession of Israel's national sin (Leviticus 26:40-42; Jeremiah 3:11-18; Hosea 5:15), following which Israel will be saved, thereby fulfilling Paul's prophecy in Romans 11:25-27. In dire threat from the forces of the antichrist at Armageddon, Israel will plead for their newly found Messiah to return and deliver them (they will "mourn for him as for an only son"—Zechariah 12:10; Matthew 23:37-39; see also Isaiah 53:1-9), at which point their deliverance will surely come (see Romans 10:13-14). Israel's leaders will have finally realized the reason that the tribulation has fallen on them—perhaps due to the Holy Spirit's enlightenment of their understanding of Scripture, or the testimony of the 144,000 Jewish evangelists, or perhaps the testimony of the two prophetic witnesses.

Later, in the millennial kingdom, Israel will finally experience a full possession of the Promised Land and the reestablishment of the Davidic throne. It will be a time of physical and spiritual blessing, the basis of which is the new covenant (Jeremiah 31:31-34; more on this in chapter 14).

All this means that the prayers of the Jewish remnant will be answered! The Messiah will return personally to rescue His people from danger. The very same Jesus who ascended into heaven will come again at the second coming (Acts 1:9-11), and He will save His people.

The second coming will involve a visible, physical, bodily coming of the glorified Jesus. It's worth noting that the Greek word *apokalupsis* is used to describe the second coming of Christ in the New Testament, and the word carries the basic meaning of "revelation," "visible disclosure," "unveiling," and "removing the cover" from something that is hidden. This word is used in 1 Peter 4:13: "These trials make you partners with Christ in his suffering, so that you will have the wonderful joy of seeing his glory when it is *revealed* to all the world" (emphasis added).

Another notable Greek word used of Christ's second coming is *epiphaneia*, which carries the basic meaning of "to appear," "to shine forth," or "to reveal." In Titus 2:13 Paul speaks of "that wonderful day when the glory of our great God and Savior, Jesus Christ, *will be revealed*" (emphasis added; see also 1 Timothy 6:14).

Every eye on earth will witness the event. Revelation 1:7 says, "Look! He comes with the clouds of heaven. And everyone will see him—even those who pierced him. And all the nations of the world will mourn for him." Matthew 24:30 says, "Then at last, the sign that the Son of Man is coming will appear in the heavens, and there will be deep mourning among all the peoples of the earth. And they will see the Son of Man coming on the clouds of heaven with power and great glory."

There will be magnificent signs in the heavens when Christ returns (Matthew 24:29-30). He will come as the King of kings and Lord of lords, and there will be many crowns on His head—crowns that represent His absolute sovereignty. His eyes will be like blazing fire, and He will come to "release the fierce wrath of God" (Revelation 19:11-16).

Scripture reveals that Jesus will return first to the mountain wilderness of Bozrah/Petra, where the Jewish remnant is endangered (Isaiah 34:1-7; 63:1-6; Habakkuk 3:3; Micah 2:12-13). They will not be endangered for long, for Jesus will confront the antichrist and his forces, and slay them with the word of His mouth. The description of the second coming makes it clear that the enemies of Christ will suffer instant defeat:

> Then I saw heaven opened, and a white horse was standing there. Its rider was named Faithful and True, for he judges fairly and wages a righteous war. His eyes were like flames of fire, and on his head were many crowns. A name was written on him that no one understood except himself. He wore a robe dipped in blood, and his title was the Word of God. The armies of heaven, dressed in the finest of pure white linen, followed him on white horses. From his mouth came a sharp sword to strike down the nations. He will rule them with an iron rod. He will release the fierce wrath of God, the Almighty, like juice flowing from a winepress. On his robe at his thigh was written this title: King of all kings and LORD of all lords (Revelation 19:11-16).

This means that instant deliverance will come to the Jewish remnant, and all who stand against Israel will be defeated. The antichrist will be slain. In 2 Thessalonians 2:8 we are told that Jesus Christ "will slay him with the breath of his mouth and destroy him by the splendor of his coming."

As mighty as the antichrist will be during the tribulation period, and despite his claims to deity, he will be shown impotent and powerless in the face of the true Christ. All the forces of the antichrist will also be destroyed, from Bozrah/Petra all the way back to Jerusalem (Joel 3:12-13; Zechariah 14:12-15; Revelation 14:19-20). What a wondrous day that will be!

Jesus will then victoriously ascend to the Mount of Olives:

> Then the LORD will go out to fight against those nations, as he has fought in times past. On that day his feet will stand on the Mount of Olives, east of Jerusalem. And the Mount of Olives will split apart, making a wide valley running from east to west. Half the mountain will move toward the north and half toward the south (Zechariah 14:3-4).

How wondrous it will all be! Against all earthly odds, the Jewish remnant will be rescued by their divine Messiah, the Lord Jesus Christ. Their blindness will finally be gone—*forever*. And they will have the privilege of entering into Christ's millennial kingdom, where they will enjoy the fulfillment of God's ancient covenant promises to Israel.

13

THE END OF THE TIMES OF THE GENTILES

The phrase "the times of the Gentiles"—which is stated by Christ in Luke 21:24 (ESV)—refers to the time of Gentile domination over Jerusalem. It is an extended period that began with the Babylonian captivity that started in 605 BC.

Daniel himself was taken captive as a youth to Babylon by King Nebuchadnezzar in 605 BC. As providence had it, he spent the rest of his life there. There were two more deportations, with the second taking place in 597 BC and the third in 586 BC, at which time the Babylonians destroyed both Jerusalem and its temple, and took the remaining Jews into captivity.

Nebuchadnezzar's Dream and the Times of the Gentiles

Nebuchadnezzar had a dream that provided supernatural insights on the unfolding of the times of the Gentiles, beginning with the dominion of Babylon. When Nebuchadnezzar had the dream, he did not know what it meant. Neither did Babylon's diviners, magicians, or occultists. But with God's help, Daniel provided the correct interpretation to Nebuchadnezzar.

The dream spanned Gentile history and dominion, starting with the Babylonian kingdom and continuing to the various kingdoms that would follow, up to the days preceding the coming of Israel's Messiah in the distant prophetic future. The dream revealed that the sequence of Gentile kingdoms would come to an end with the appearance of God's eternal kingdom.

In the dream, Nebuchadnezzar saw a great image that was rather frightening. Daniel recounted the dream to Nebuchadnezzar this way:

> In your vision, Your Majesty, you saw standing before you a huge, shining statue of a man. It was a frightening sight. The head of the statue was made of fine gold. Its chest and arms were silver, its belly and thighs were bronze, its legs were iron, and its feet were a combination of iron and baked clay. As you watched, a rock was cut from a mountain, but not by human hands. It struck the feet of iron and clay, smashing them to bits (Daniel 2:31-34).

Daniel revealed that Nebuchadnezzar—the king whom God had put into power in Babylon—was represented by the head of gold (verse 38). Because Babylon under Nebuchadnezzar's leadership had brought Judah into captivity, "the times of the Gentiles" began with Babylon.

The dream then focused on "another kingdom" (Daniel 2:39). Nebuchadnezzar was a finite being. He would not live forever. Hence, there would be another kingdom after his. This next kingdom was represented by a "chest and arms" of silver. The two arms represented the rise of the Medes and Persians, who would conquer Babylon in 539 BC. Though the Medo-Persian empire was strong and would last more than 200 years, it was nevertheless inferior to the kingdom of Babylon, just as silver is inferior to gold.

In the dream, yet another kingdom was to arise after the

Medo-Persian Empire. This is represented by the "belly and thighs" of bronze and refers to the Greek Empire which, under the leadership of Alexander the Great, conquered the Medo-Persian Empire between 334 and 330 BC.

A fourth kingdom was to arise after the Greek Empire, represented by legs of iron. This refers to the Roman Empire, which conquered the Greeks in 63 BC. Just as iron is the strongest among metals, so this empire would be stronger than all the previous ones. So strong was Rome that it was able to conquer many peoples and subdue any rebellion.

In Daniel 2:41, Daniel then recounted a strange part of the dream: "The feet and toes you saw were a combination of iron and baked clay, showing that this kingdom will be divided. Like iron mixed with clay, it will have some of the strength of iron." Scholars have debated this verse and those that follow, some ascribing them to the Roman Empire of old, and others ascribing them to the revived Roman Empire in the end times, over which the antichrist will rule.

There are several reasons that the latter view makes more sense. First, it would seem contextually that the ten toes in Daniel 2:41 represent the same kings as the 10 horns in Daniel 7 (more on Daniel 7 shortly). These revelations belong together. These kings will exercise rule in the revived Roman Empire in the end times.

Second, prophecy scholars have noted that the ten-toe stage of Nebuchadnezzar's image has *not yet been fulfilled in history*, and therefore must relate to the prophetic future. As John Walvoord observed, "According to Daniel's prophecy, the kingdoms represented by the ten toes existed side by side and were destroyed by one sudden catastrophic blow. Nothing like this has yet occurred in history."[1] But this will occur as the revived Roman Empire is shattered at the second coming of Jesus Christ in glory.

Third, it is not uncommon for Old Testament prophecies to gloss over long periods of time. For example, there are prophecies in the Old Testament that lump together predictions concerning the first and second comings of Christ without regard for the extended time between the two comings. This being so, there is no difficulty in seeing the leg portion of Nebuchadnezzar's image referring to the Roman Empire of old, but the toes portion pointing forward to the revived Roman Empire in the end times.

Based on Nebuchednezzar's dream, we can say that this latter-days Roman Empire will not attain true unity or cohesiveness, as indicated by the mixture of iron and clay. Just as iron is strong, so the revived Roman Empire will be strong. But just as iron and clay do not naturally mix with each other, so this revived empire will have some divisions.

A point that we need to keep in mind at this juncture is that all these kingdoms—Babylon, the Medo-Persian Empire, Greece, and Rome were *dominant over Jerusalem*. Clearly, then, the Gentile rule over Jerusalem is quite extended. All of this constitutes the "times of the Gentiles."

In Daniel 2:44 we find a prophecy that speaks of the end of this Gentile dominion: "The God of heaven will set up a kingdom that will never be destroyed or conquered. It will crush all these kingdoms into nothingness, and it will stand forever." This speaks of the overthrow of all earthly kingdoms, including the revived Roman Empire of the end times. In Nebuchadnezzar's dream, this was represented by the "rock...that crushed to pieces that statue of iron, bronze, clay, silver, and gold" (verse 45). The term "rock" is often used in reference to the Messiah, Jesus Christ (see Psalm 118:22; Isaiah 8:14; 28:16; 1 Peter 2:6-8). So Christ will not only overthrow earthly kingdoms, but will—following the second coming—set up His own millennial kingdom that will last 1,000 years on earth

(Revelation 11:15; 19:11-20; 20:4). Following the millennial kingdom, Christ will continue His reign forever and ever in what is called the *eternal state*.

Daniel then affirmed that the interpretation he gave Nebuchadnezzar of the dream is certain. After all, the source of the interpretation was God Himself, the Revealer of divine mysteries (see Daniel 2:19,23,28,30).

Daniel's Dream and the Times of the Gentiles

Daniel 7:1 reveals that Daniel also had a dream that had similarities to Nebuchadnezzar's. Daniel said, "In my vision that night, I, Daniel, saw a great storm churning the surface of a great sea" (verse 2). The word "sea" in Scripture often represents nations and peoples (see Isaiah 17:12-13; 57:20). Hence, Daniel's vision focuses on God's providential actions among the Gentile nations. Details are provided in the verses that follow.

Daniel 7:3-8 makes reference to four beasts—representing four kingdoms—that play an important role in the unfolding of biblical prophecy. You will notice three things: (1) These nations were previously identified in Nebuchadnezzar's dream (Daniel 2:31-35); (2) the nations are increasingly violent; (3) all these nations exercised dominion over Jerusalem. They are all central to "the times of the Gentiles."

The first beast, Daniel said, "was like a lion with eagles' wings," but "its wings were pulled off" (Daniel 7:4). This imagery represents Babylon's lion-like qualities of power and strength. It is interesting to note that winged lions guarded the gates of Babylon's royal palaces. It is also interesting that some biblical passages represent Nebuchadnezzar as a lion (see Jeremiah 4:7; 49:19; 50:17,44). The wings on the lion indicate rapid mobility, while the pulling off of the wings indicates a removal of that mobility—perhaps a reference to Nebuchadnezzar's insanity, or to Babylon's deterioration following his death.

Daniel then referred to "a second beast, and it looked like a bear"—an animal of great strength (verse 5). This represents Medo-Persia. The fact that the bear was "rearing up on one side" indicates that the Persians maintained the higher status in the Medo-Persian alliance. The bear had three ribs in its mouth between its teeth; and it was told, "Get up! Devour the flesh of many people." The "three ribs" are vanquished nations—apparently Babylon (conquered 539 BC), Lydia (conquered 546 BC), and Egypt (conquered 525 BC). Medo-Persia was well-known for its strength and fierceness in battle (see Isaiah 13:17-18).

Daniel then referred to a third beast that was "like a leopard." It had "four bird's wings on its back, and it had four heads. Great authority was given to this beast" (Daniel 7:6). The leopard is an animal known for its swiftness, cunning, and agility. This imagery represents Greece under Alexander the Great (born in 356 BC). The reference to the "four heads" represent the four generals who divided the kingdom following Alexander's death, ruling Macedonia, Asia Minor, Syria, and Egypt.

Finally, in Daniel 7:7, Daniel makes reference to the fourth beast—a mongrel composed of parts of a lion, bear, and leopard that was more terrifying and powerful than the three preceding beasts. This beast was "terrifying, dreadful, and very strong." This wild imagery refers to the Roman Empire. Rome's power was growing all through biblical times, but it fell apart by the fifth century AD.

This empire will be revived in the end times. It will apparently be comprised of ten nations ruled by ten kings ("ten horns"—Daniel 7:7). It is noteworthy that Rome has never consisted of a ten-nation confederacy with ten co-rulers. If it hasn't happened yet, that means this prophecy will know fulfillment later.

Speaking of the prophetic future, Daniel next speaks of an eleventh horn—a small horn (the antichrist)—who starts out apparently in an insignificant way, but grows powerful enough to uproot three of the existing horns (kings). The antichrist will emerge from apparent obscurity. By his profound diplomatic skills, however, he will win the admiration of the political world and compel others to follow his lead. Though he will begin his political career as a "small horn" (verse 8), he will be catapulted into global fame and power by means of brilliant statesmanship. He will quickly ascend to the topmost rung of the political world. And once he gains ascendancy, no one will challenge his political power. His political domain will become global, and all other political leaders will be mere pawns in his hands.

The antichrist, as we saw earlier, will be energized by Satan (2 Thessalonians 2:9). Related to this, in Revelation 12:3 we read of a "large red dragon" who is identified as Satan. The color red may imply bloodshed, which we should expect because Satan has always been a murderer (John 8:44). This dragon (Satan) is described as having "seven heads and ten horns, with seven crowns on his heads." From similar descriptions in Daniel 7:7-8,24 and Revelation 13:1, we infer that this terminology points to Satan's control over world empires during the tribulation period, apparently through the person of the antichrist.

The ten horns represent the ten kings of Daniel 7:7 and Revelation 13:1, over whom the antichrist—empowered by Satan—will gain authority. The ten countries headed by the ten kings will form the nucleus of the antichrist's (and thus Satan's) empire—a revived Roman Empire. The seven heads and seven crowns apparently refer to the principal rulers of this empire.

Many modern Bible scholars see the present European Union as a primary prospect for the ultimate fulfillment of this prophecy.

This confederacy will be characterized by both unity and division. Given the actions of the European Union, it appears that the stage is being set even now for the fulfillment of Daniel 2 and 7. Once the antichrist emerges into power in a revived Rome, it is just a matter of time before he dominates the entire globe.

Scripture tells us the antichrist will be an oratorical genius—a master of the spoken word. Daniel 7:8 says he will have a mouth that boasts arrogantly. He is said to have "the mouth of a lion" (Revelation 13:2), which Bible interpreters believe means he will be a majestic and awe-inspiring speaker. Most world dictators have been persuasive speakers, able to motivate the masses to support their political agenda. Likewise, the antichrist will mesmerize the world through his words.

Revelation 13:5 tells us, "The beast [the antichrist]" will speak "great blasphemies against God." Indeed, he will proclaim "terrible words of blasphemy against God, slandering his name and his dwelling—that is, those who dwell in heaven" (verse 6). The antichrist's blasphemous words are in keeping with his blasphemous nature (see 2 Thessalonians 2:3-11). The root meaning of the Greek word translated "blasphemy" carries the idea of injuring the reputation of another. It can range from a lack of reverence to utter contempt for God. It can also involve making claims of divinity for oneself, as the antichrist will do.

As the head of the revived Roman Empire, the antichrist will sign a covenant with Israel, seemingly as a friend of the nation (Daniel 9:27). But then he will double-cross the Jews at the midpoint of the tribulation and force everyone to worship him as God (see Revelation 13).

The times of the Gentiles will not cease until the end of the Great Tribulation and the second coming of Jesus Christ. And according to Daniel's vision, the antichrist's revived Roman Empire will be destroyed not by another nation, but rather as a result of divine judgment (Revelation 19:20). The empire, along with its wicked leader, the antichrist, will be terminated at Christ's second coming.

This glorious and majestic event will put an end to the times of the Gentiles. It will be a "God thing"—or, more specifically, a "Jesus thing." He will bring about this fulfillment.[2]

Now, perhaps I should add a brief clarification. In our own day, the Israelis control much of Jerusalem, but they do not control the Arab quarter or the Temple Mount area. Hence, it is correct to say that the times of the Gentiles have not yet ended. Jesus Himself will one day assume full control of Jerusalem.

Daniel 7:13-14 provides the backdrop. This passage speaks of "a son of man" and "the Ancient One" (or "Ancient of Days"). The Son of Man, coming with clouds of glory, will approach the Ancient One. The Ancient One is the Father, the first person of the Trinity, and the Son of Man is a messianic title of Jesus Christ, the second person of the Trinity. The "clouds of heaven" that accompany His appearance are apparently a reference to divine glory (see Exodus 16:10; 40:34-35; 1 Kings 8:10-11; Isaiah 6:4).

So the second person of the Trinity (Jesus the Messiah) will appear before the first person of the Trinity (the heavenly Father). Scripture consistently portrays Jesus as being in submission to the heavenly Father: "I have come down from heaven to do the will of God who sent me, not to do my own will" (John 6:38; see also John 4:34; 5:19; 14:31).

We are told of the Son of Man, "He was given authority, honor, and sovereignty over all the nations of the world, so that people of every race and nation and language would obey him. His rule is eternal—it will never end. His kingdom will never be destroyed" (Daniel 7:14).

The four earthly kingdoms headed up by various powerful human leaders had sought dominion on earth. They have been or will be destroyed, and Jesus the Messiah will be given global dominion. All the authority, glory, and power that had been sought by earthly rulers will at last be conferred upon Christ so that He is sovereign "over all the nations of the world." This represents the fulfillment of a promise the Father had earlier made to the Son: "I have placed my chosen king on the throne in Jerusalem, on my holy mountain...I will give you the nations as your inheritance, the whole earth as your possession" (Psalm 2:6-9). All this will find final fulfillment at the second coming of Jesus Christ (see Matthew 24:30; 25:31; Revelation 11:15).

Christ's kingdom will be everlasting. It will never be conquered by another. This reign will be established in the future millennial kingdom. Then it will continue forever throughout the eternal state (1 Corinthians 15:24-28).

And "the times of the Gentiles" will become a thing of the distant past.

14

PEACE AT LAST: GOD'S COVENANTS FULFILLED

There is a day coming when Israel will no longer have to constantly be on high alert. A day is coming in which the term *anti-Semitism* will be relegated to ancient history. A day is coming in which the Jewish people will have complete peace and serenity. In that day, they will have turned to the Lord for salvation, entered into His millennial kingdom, and received the blessed covenant promises God made to them long ago. It is a day to look forward to.

These covenant promises are not obsolete. Their significance has not lessened or faded with the passing of time. They are unconditional covenants that God has promised to fulfill—*God is a promise keeper.* Numbers 23:19 asserts, "God is not a man, so he does not lie. He is not human, so he does not change his mind. Has he ever spoken and failed to act? Has he ever promised and not carried it through?" Prior to his death, an aged Joshua declared, "Every promise of the LORD your God has come true. Not a single one has failed!" (Joshua 23:14). Solomon later proclaimed: "Not one word has failed of all the wonderful promises he gave through his servant Moses" (1 Kings 8:56). *God truly is faithful!*

The fact that God has not yet fulfilled all His covenant promises to Israel does not mean He will fail to do so. Theologian Paul Enns explains how these covenants will find their ultimate fulfillment in the future millennial kingdom, that 1,000-year kingdom on earth over which Christ will personally rule:

> The unconditional covenants demand a literal, physical return of Christ to establish the kingdom. The Abrahamic covenant promised Israel a land, a posterity and ruler, and a spiritual blessing (Gen. 12:1-3); the Palestinian covenant promised Israel a restoration to the land and occupation of the land (Deut. 30:1-10); the Davidic covenant promised a ruler for the throne of David (2 Sam. 7:16); the New Covenant promised Israel forgiveness—the means whereby the nation could be blessed (Jer. 31:31-34). At the Second Advent these covenants will be fulfilled as Israel is regathered from the nations (Matt. 24:31), converted (Zech. 12:10-14), and restored to the land under the rulership of her Messiah.[1]

All of this will take place following the second coming of Christ. When Christ comes again, He will personally set up His 1,000-year kingdom on earth. This kingdom is a common theme in Scripture (see Revelation 20:2-7; Psalm 2:6-9; Isaiah 65:18-23; Jeremiah 31:12-14,31-37; Ezekiel 34:25-29; 37:1-13; 40–48; Daniel 2:35; 7:13-14; Joel 2:21-27; Amos 9:13-14; Micah 4:1-7; Zephaniah 3:9-20).

Only Believers Will Enter Christ's Kingdom

Scripture declares that only saved people will enter into the millennial kingdom, while the wicked will be cut off. In the book of Daniel, for example, we are told that "the saints of the Most High shall receive the kingdom and possess the kingdom" (Daniel 7:18). The word "saints" in Daniel is from an Aramaic word that is derived from a Hebrew root, *Oilp*. This word has the connotation of a divine claim and ownership of the person. It points to that which is distinct from the common or profane. This means that profane people will not enter into the millennial kingdom. Only those who are God's people—those "owned" by God—will enter in, whether redeemed Gentiles or redeemed Jews.

So prior to the millennial kingdom, the Gentiles will face Christ at the judgment of the nations (Matthew 25:31-46). Only those found to be believers will be invited into Christ's millennial kingdom in their mortal bodies (25:34,46). Likewise, only the redeemed remnant among the larger body of Jews will be invited to enter into the millennial kingdom in their mortal bodies (Ezekiel 20:34-38).

Once the kingdom is established, people will enjoy longer lives. Yet despite increased longevity, Scripture reveals that both mortal Jews and Gentiles will continue to age and die (Isaiah 65:20). We are also told that married couples among both groups will continue to have children throughout the millennium. All who die during this time will be resurrected at the end of the millennium (Revelation 20:4).

Of course, the fact that only believers ("saints") enter into the kingdom does not stand against the possibility that some of the children of the saints will not be believers. There will be some in the kingdom who grow to adulthood *rejecting* the Savior-King in their hearts (though outwardly still obeying Him). These unbelievers will likewise get married, and some of their children will not be believers. This process will continue throughout the 1,000 years. Those unbelievers who are still alive by the end of the millennial kingdom will participate in a final revolt against God—a revolt led by Satan, who will be released from the abyss at this time (Revelation 20:3). Meanwhile, so long as these unbelievers continue to render external obedience to the King Jesus, they will be permitted to live in the kingdom.

The Jews Will Take Full Possession of Their Land

The land covenant recorded in Deuteronomy 29:1–30:20 is eternal and unconditional. It was promised that even though Israel would be dispersed all over the world, the Jews would be regathered and restored to the land (see Isaiah 43:5-7; Jeremiah 16:14-18). This will take place at the outset of Christ's millennial kingdom.

Back even further, God made specific land promises to Abraham. We read in Genesis 15:18-21, "The Lord made a covenant with Abram that day and said, 'I have given this land to your descendants, all the way from the border of Egypt to the great Euphrates River—the land now occupied by the Kenites, Kenizzites, Kadmonites, Hittites, Perizzites, Rephaites, Amorites, Canaanites, Girgashites, and Jebusites.'"

God's land promises to Abraham were then passed down through Isaac's line. In Genesis 26:3-4 we read the Lord's very words to Isaac:

> Live here as a foreigner in this land, and I will be with you and bless you. I hereby confirm that I will give all these lands to you and your descendants, just as I solemnly promised Abraham, your father. I will cause your descendants to become as numerous as the stars of the sky, and I will give them all these lands. And through your descendants all the nations of the earth will be blessed.

God's land promises to Abraham then passed to Jacob, Isaac's son. The Lord said to Jacob,

> I am the Lord, the God of your grandfather Abraham, and the God of your father, Isaac. The ground you are

> lying on belongs to you. I am giving it to you and your descendants. Your descendants will be as numerous as the dust of the earth! They will spread out in all directions—to the west and the east, to the north and the south. And all the families of the earth will be blessed through you and your descendants (Genesis 28:13-14).

These land promises are later reaffirmed throughout the rest of the Old Testament. For example, in Psalm 105:8-11 we read, "He always stands by his covenant—the commitment he made to a thousand generations. This is the covenant he made with Abraham and the oath he swore to Isaac. He confirmed it to Jacob as a decree, and to the people of Israel as a never-ending covenant: 'I will give you the land of Canaan as your special possession.'"

Following the second coming, believing Jews from around the world will be gathered and they will finally come into full possession of the land that God promised them long ago. John Ankerberg, Dillon Burroughs, and Jimmy DeYoung, in their book *Israel Under Fire*, comment,

> There are 38 different passages in the Bible that give the biblical borders of Israel. A compilation of these 38 passages of the land God has promised to give them would indicate the Jewish people will ultimately be given one half of modern-day Egypt, all of Israel, Lebanon, Syria, Jordan, and Kuwait, three-fourths of Iraq, and three-fourths of Saudi Arabia. This is a prophecy that will be fulfilled in what is called the kingdom period, when Jesus sets up the millennial kingdom.[2]

A New Temple Will Be Built

Ezekiel 40–48 prophesies that a millennial temple will be built

(Joel 3:18; Isaiah 2:3; 60:13), and animal sacrifices will be reinstituted (Isaiah 56:7; 60:7; Jeremiah 33:17-18; Zechariah 14:19-21). This has caused no small debate among biblical scholars—especially over whether these prophecies should be understood literally or figuratively.

Some expositors understand these chapters in Ezekiel as symbolically referring to the church. But they do not agree amongst themselves what the chapters intend to say about the church.

A policy that many Bible scholars use for interpreting prophecy is this: When the plain sense makes good sense, seek no other sense lest you end up in nonsense. To me, the chapters make perfect sense when read in a literal sense. After all, we read about precise dimensions, specifications, and instructions for building the temple—just as specific as those for the tabernacle and the temple of Solomon in Old Testament times. That being so, I believe there will, in fact, be a millennial temple and millennial animal sacrifices.

I think it is fair to say that the millennial temple will be the final temple for Israel. The dimensions provided for this temple make it significantly larger than any other temple built in Israel's history—Solomon's temple, the postexilic temple, and the tribulation temple.

Contextually, it appears that this temple will represent God's personal presence among His people during the millennium (see Ezekiel 37:26-27). Apparently the restoration of Israel as a nation will also entail a restoration of God's presence (and glory) reentering the temple and being with His people in a visible sense. This temple is where Jesus Christ will be worshipped during the entire millennium. It will be built at the beginning of the messianic kingdom (Ezekiel 37:26-28) by Christ (Zechariah 6:12-13), redeemed Jews (Ezekiel 43:10-11), and even representatives from the Gentile nations (Zechariah 6:15; Haggai 2:7).

Ezekiel 37:26-28 provides us with a description of the temple as God's dwelling place among the people:

> I will give them their land and increase their numbers, and I will put my Temple among them forever. I will make my home among them. I will be their God, and they will be my people. And when my Temple is among them forever, the nations will know that I am the LORD, who makes Israel holy.

It is noteworthy that even redeemed Gentiles will worship in this millennial temple (see Isaiah 60:6; Zephaniah 3:10; Zechariah 2:11). The worship of Jesus Christ in this future temple is a key aspect of divine revelation on this subject (see Jeremiah 33:15-22; Ezekiel 40–48; Zechariah 14:16-21).

The question that naturally arises in the minds of many Bible students is this: Why will animal sacrifices be reinstated? After all, Christ's once-for-all sacrifice has taken away sin, and has caused the Mosaic law of sacrifices to be abolished (see Hebrews 7–10).

Several answers have been offered. Some suggest that the millennial sacrifices will be a kind of Jewish memorial of the awful price that Christ—the Lamb of God (who will be living in their midst)—had to pay for the salvation of these believing-but-not-yet-glorified Jews. (They are still in their mortal bodies, having entered into the millennial kingdom following the tribulation period, which they survived.) The temple system will thus allegedly function much like the Lord's Supper does today, as a memorial ritual (1 Corinthians 11:25-26; see also Isaiah 56:7; 66:20-23; Jeremiah 33:17-18; Ezekiel 43:18-27; 45:13–46:24; Malachi 3:3-4).

One theologian describes it this way:

> According to this view the sacrifices offered during the earthly reign of Christ will be visible reminders of His work on the cross. Thus, these sacrifices will not have any efficacy except to memorialize Christ's death. The primary support for this argument is the parallel of the Lord's Supper. It is argued that just as the communion table looks back on the Cross without besmirching its glory, so millennial sacrifices will do the same.[3]

While this explanation has some merit, the problem is that Ezekiel informs us that the sacrifices are to "make atonement for the people...making them right with the LORD" (Ezekiel 45:15-17). Hence, the "memorial" viewpoint seems to fall short of explaining these sacrifices.

Perhaps the best explanation for the reinstituted sacrifices is that they are intended to remove ceremonial uncleanness and prevent defilement from polluting the purity of the temple environment. According to this view, such will be necessary because Yahweh will again be dwelling on the earth in the midst of sinful (and therefore unclean) mortal people. Remember, those believers who survive the tribulation period will enter the millennial kingdom in their mortal bodies—still in full retention of their sin natures, even though redeemed by Christ as believers. They will already have been saved by Christ. Yet the sacrifices will serve to remove ceremonial uncleanness *in the temple*. The rationale of this view is described by one theologian this way:

> Because of God's promise to dwell on earth during the millennium (as stated in the New Covenant), it is necessary that He protect His presence through sacrifice...It should further be added that this sacrificial system will be a temporary one in that the millennium

> (with its partial population of unglorified humanity) will last only one thousand years. During the eternal state all inhabitants of the New Jerusalem will be glorified and will therefore not be a source of contagious impurities to defile the holiness of Yahweh.[4]

Understood in this way, the millennial animal sacrifices should not be viewed as a return to the Mosaic law. The law has forever been done away with through Jesus Christ (Romans 6:14-15; 7:1-6; 1 Corinthians 9:20-21; 2 Corinthians 3:7-11; Galatians 4:1-7; 5:18; Hebrews 8:13; 10:1-14). Salvation continues to be by faith in Christ alone. The sacrifices will relate only to the removing of ritual impurities in the temple as fallen-though-redeemed human beings remain on earth.

Christ Will Rule from the Davidic Throne

God long ago promised David that one of his descendants would rule forever on the throne of David (2 Samuel 7:12-13; 22:51). God's covenant with David was unconditional, meaning that it did not depend on David in any way for its fulfillment. God made a promise, and *He will keep that promise.*

The wording of the covenant is important. The three key words are "kingdom," "house," and "throne." Such words point to the political future of Israel. The word "house" here carries the idea of a royal dynasty.

God's promise to David will find its fulfillment in Christ's future millennial kingdom. Christ, who was born from the line of David (Matthew 1:1), will rule from the throne of David in Jerusalem during the millennial kingdom (Ezekiel 36:1-12; Micah 4:1-5; Zephaniah 3:14-20; Zechariah 14:1-21). This reign will extend beyond the

Jews to include all the Gentile nations as well. This is a consistent theme in Scripture (Psalm 72:8; Isaiah 9:6-7; Daniel 7:13-14).

It is highly relevant that when the angel Gabriel appeared to the young virgin Mary to inform her that the Messiah was to be born through her womb, he spoke to her in terms of the Davidic covenant:

> Do not be afraid, Mary, for you have found favor with God. And behold, you will conceive in your womb and bear a son, and you shall call his name Jesus. He will be great and will be called the Son of the Most High. And the Lord God will give to him the throne of his father David, and he will reign over the house of Jacob forever, and of his kingdom there will be no end (Luke 1:30-33 ESV).

Notice the three key words Gabriel uses to describe Christ's future reign—"throne," "house," and "kingdom." These very words are found in the covenant God made with David in which God promised that one from his line would rule forever (2 Samuel 7:16).

Mary, a devout young Jew, must have immediately understood the significance of the angel's words. Gabriel's revelation constituted a clear announcement that Mary's son would come into this world to fulfill the promise given to David that one of his descendants would sit on David's throne and rule over David's kingdom.

Characteristics of Christ's Government

Christ's government during the millennial kingdom will be perfect in every way. First and foremost, His rule will extend to the entire planet—to "all the nations of the world," and to the "people of every race and nation and language" (Daniel 7:14).

This government will be centered in Jerusalem. Indeed, "the LORD's teaching will go out from Zion; his word will go out from Jerusalem" (Isaiah 2:3). "In that day Jerusalem will be known as 'The Throne of the LORD.' All nations will come there to honor the LORD" (Jeremiah 3:17). "The LORD's voice will roar from Zion and thunder from Jerusalem" (Joel 3:16). The LORD affirms, "I, the LORD, will rule from Jerusalem as their king forever" (Micah 4:7).

Christ's government will also be effective. As Isaiah 9:6-7 puts it, "The government will rest on his shoulders. And he will be called: Wonderful Counselor, Mighty God, Everlasting Father, Prince of Peace. His government and its peace will never end. He will rule with fairness and justice from the throne of his ancestor David."

As the Prince of Peace, Christ's government will bring lasting global peace: "The LORD will mediate between peoples and will settle disputes between strong nations far away. They will hammer their swords into plowshares and their spears into pruning hooks. Nation will no longer fight against nation, nor train for war anymore. Everyone will live in peace and prosperity, enjoying their own grapevines and fig trees, for there will be nothing to fear. The LORD of Heaven's Armies has made this promise!" (Micah 4:3-4).

In short, Christ's government will produce an ideal environment for living on earth. He will succeed where all human governments have failed!

Physical Blessings Will Abound

Christ's millennial kingdom will feature abundant physical blessings on the earth:

> Even the wilderness and desert will be glad in those days. The wasteland will rejoice and blossom with spring crocuses. Yes, there will be an abundance of flowers and

> singing and joy! The deserts will become as green as the mountains of Lebanon, as lovely as Mount Carmel or the plain of Sharon. There the LORD will display his glory, the splendor of our God (Isaiah 35:1-2).

There will never be a lack of rain for the ground, and animals will never go hungry. "The LORD will bless you with rain at planting time. There will be wonderful harvests and plenty of pastureland for your livestock. The oxen and donkeys that till the ground will eat good grain, its chaff blown away by the wind" (Isaiah 30:23-24).

Contrary to the way things are today, the animal kingdom will live in perfect harmony. Apparently their predatory and carnivorous natures will be removed. "In that day the wolf and the lamb will live together; the leopard will lie down with the baby goat. The calf and the yearling will be safe with the lion, and a little child will lead them all. The cow will graze near the bear. The cub and the calf will lie down together. The lion will eat hay like a cow" (Isaiah 11:6-7).

One great benefit for human beings is that people will live longer lives. "No longer will babies die when only a few days old. No longer will adults die before they have lived a full life" (Isaiah 65:20). Longevity will be restored.

Moreover, physical infirmities and illnesses will be removed. "In that day the deaf will hear words read from a book, and the blind will see through the gloom and darkness" (Isaiah 29:18). "The people of Israel will no longer say, 'We are sick and helpless'" (Isaiah 33:24).

Prosperity will fill the earth, and people will be joyful and glad.

> They will come home and sing songs of joy on the heights of Jerusalem. They will be radiant because of the LORD's good gifts—the abundant crops of grain, new wine, and olive oil, and the healthy flocks and herds. Their life

> will be like a watered garden, and all their sorrows will be gone. The young women will dance for joy, and the men—old and young—will join in the celebration. I will turn their mourning into joy. I will comfort them and exchange their sorrow for rejoicing. The priests will enjoy abundance, and my people will feast on my good gifts. I, the Lord, have spoken! (Jeremiah 31:12-14).

These and many other physical blessings will be abundantly present during the future millennial kingdom.

Spiritual Blessings Will Abound

The blessings on earth will not just be physical—they will be spiritual as well. How could it be otherwise when one considers that Jesus Himself will dwell among His people? "As the waters fill the sea, so the earth will be filled with people who know the Lord" (Isaiah 11:9). When one combines this fact with the reality that Satan will be bound during the millennial kingdom (Revelation 20:1-3), we can scarcely imagine the depth of spiritual blessings that will prevail on earth during this time.

The abundance of spiritual blessings during the millennial kingdom are rooted in the new covenant (Jeremiah 31:31-34). As an outworking of this wondrous covenant, abundant spiritual blessings will virtually shower the earth. Perhaps the best example of this is that the Holy Spirit will be present and will indwell all believers: "I will put my Spirit in you so that you will follow my decrees and be careful to obey my regulations" (Ezekiel 36:27). "I will put my Spirit in you, and you will live again and return home to your own land. Then you will know that I, the Lord, have spoken, and I have done what I said. Yes, the Lord has spoken!" (Ezekiel 37:14).

God promises, "I will pour out my Spirit on your descendants, and my blessing on your children" (Isaiah 44:3). The Holy Spirit will be "poured out on us from heaven" (Isaiah 32:15). Indeed, God affirms, "I will pour out my Spirit upon all people. Your sons and daughters will prophesy. Your old men will dream dreams, and your young men will see visions. In those days I will pour out my Spirit even on servants—men and women alike" (Joel 2:28-29).

How awesome it will be!

Righteousness Will Abound

No longer will every country on earth be permeated with criminal activities. No longer will Israel be criminally targeted for destruction. Righteousness will prevail everywhere. "All your people will be righteous. They will possess their land forever, for I will plant them there with my own hands in order to bring myself glory" (Isaiah 60:21). "I am ready to set things right" (46:13). "My salvation is on the way. My strong arm will bring justice to the nations" (51:5)

Obedience to the Lord Will Abound

Can you imagine what living in this kingdom will be like? Everyone on earth will obey the Lord! It is hard to fathom, but it will happen. "The whole earth will acknowledge the LORD and return to him. All the families of the nations will bow down before him" (Psalm 22:27). "I will put my instructions deep within them, and I will write them on their hearts. I will be their God, and they will be my people" (Jeremiah 31:33). Not only will obedience to the Lord abound, but holiness will also abound around the entire planet (Isaiah 35:8-10; Joel 3:17).

Faithfulness Will Abound

Though hard to believe, faithfulness will also abound everywhere. "The LORD says: I am returning to Mount Zion, and I will live in

Jerusalem. Then Jerusalem will be called the Faithful City; the mountain of the LORD of Heaven's Armies will be called the Holy Mountain" (Zechariah 8:3). In that day, "unfailing love and truth" will meet together. And "righteousness and peace" will kiss (Psalm 85:10-11).

Worship of the Lord Will Abound

Prophetic scriptures reveal that there will be a unified worship of the Messiah by the world's residents. "'My name is honored by people of other nations from morning till night. All around the world they offer sweet incense and pure offerings in honor of my name. For my name is great among the nations,' says the LORD of Heaven's Armies" (Malachi 1:11). "I will purify the speech of all people, so that everyone can worship the LORD together" (Zephaniah 3:9; see also Zechariah 8:23).

God's Presence Will Abound

Perhaps best of all, God's presence will abound on the earth. "I will make my home among them. I will be their God, and they will be my people. And when my Temple is among them forever, the nations will know that I am the LORD, who makes Israel holy" (Ezekiel 37:27-28).

In Zechariah 2:10-13 we read,

> The LORD says, "Shout and rejoice, O beautiful Jerusalem, for I am coming to live among you. Many nations will join themselves to the LORD on that day, and they, too, will be my people. I will live among you, and you will know that the LORD of Heaven's Armies sent me to you. The land of Judah will be the LORD's special possession in the holy land, and he will once again choose Jerusalem to be his own city. Be silent before the LORD,

> all humanity, for he is springing into action from his holy dwelling."

How awesome it will all be!

The Role of Previously Raptured Believers

We've considered the mortal Jews and Gentiles who enter into—and live during—the millennial kingdom. But what about all the believers who were raptured before the tribulation began? Will they have a role to play in the millennial kingdom?

I believe yes! While Scripture promises that Christ Himself will reign from the Davidic throne, it also states that believers will reign with Him. In 2 Timothy 2:12, the apostle Paul said, "If we endure hardship, we will reign with him." Those who endure through trials will one day rule with Christ in His future kingdom.

The idea of reigning with Christ is compatible with what we learn elsewhere in the book of Revelation. In Revelation 5:10, for example, we are told that believers have been made "a Kingdom of priests for our God. And they will reign on the earth." Likewise, Revelation 20:6 affirms, "Blessed and holy are those who share in the first resurrection. For them the second death holds no power, but they will be priests of God and of Christ and will reign with him a thousand years."

Even after the millennial kingdom is over, believers will continue to enjoy the privilege of reigning with Christ. Revelation 22:5 says this of the eternal state: "There will be no night there—no need for lamps or sun—for the Lord God will shine on them. And they will reign forever and ever." What an awesome privilege and blessing!

How will our individual ranks be determined as we reign with Christ? I believe our role will be commensurate with the commitment and faithfulness we exhibit during our earthly life. How wonderful it will be to hear these words from Christ: "Well done, my good and faithful servant. You have been faithful in handling this small amount, so now I will give you many more responsibilities" (Matthew 25:21).

Peace, Peace, and More Peace

In Christ's millennial kingdom, being on high alert will be a thing of the past for Israel. There will only be peace, peace, and more peace.

Christ guarantees it. And we can believe it!

15

REDEEMED JEWS AND GENTILES IN THE NEW JERUSALEM

The New Jerusalem will be the capital city of the eternal state. Prophecy scholar Randall Price says that "the New Jerusalem is described in Scripture as 'the Jerusalem above' (Galatians 4:26), 'the city of the living God, the heavenly Jerusalem,' (Hebrews 12:22) and 'the holy city' that 'comes down out of heaven from God' (Revelation 21:2, 10). In the Old Testament it is seen primarily as the abode of God, whereas in the New Testament it is also the heavenly home of the saints."[1]

The occupants of this glorious city will be angels of all different ranks, church-age believers, and believers of all other ages—and, of course, God Himself. Redeemed Jews and Gentiles from all ages will live together in the New Jerusalem, which will rest upon a new earth in a new universe. Put another way, the New Jerusalem will rest upon a resurrected earth in a resurrected universe.

The Old Heavens and Earth Will Pass Away

The present heavens and earth will one day pass away. The backdrop is that in the Garden of Eden, Adam and Eve sinned against God, and a curse was placed upon the earth by God (Genesis 3:17-18). Romans 8:20 tells us that "all creation was subjected to

God's curse." Commenting on this verse, Bible expositor John MacArthur says that "decay, disease, pain, death, natural disaster, pollution, and all other forms of evil will never cease until the One who sent the curse removes it and creates a new heaven and a new earth (2 Pet. 3:13; Rev. 21:1)."[2]

It makes good sense that before the eternal state begins (with life in the New Jerusalem on a new earth), God must remove all vestiges of sin and darkness from the previous creation. This world that is permeated by sin will be replaced by a world permeated by holiness. This world that is filled with darkness will be replaced by a world filled with light. The world in which people constantly attack and persecute others (such as radical Muslims attacking the Jews) will be replaced by a world in which there is perfect unity and love among all the redeemed, no matter their earthly ethnicity.

That the old creation must be destroyed relates to the harsh reality that Satan has long carried out his evil schemes on earth (see Ephesians 2:2). Thus it must be purged of all the polluted stains resulting from his extended presence. Satan will have no place in the new order—the new heavens and the new earth. All evidence of his influence will be removed—utterly eradicated—when God destroys the earth and the heavens.

It is fascinating to observe how many Bible verses deal with the destruction of the old earth and universe. Psalm 102:25-26, for example, affirms the following words to God about the passing of the old earth and heavens: "Long ago you laid the foundation of the earth and made the heavens with your hands. They will perish, but you remain forever; they will wear out like old clothing. You will change them like a garment and discard them." Isaiah 51:6 likewise says, "Look up to the skies above, and gaze down on the earth below. For the skies will disappear like smoke, and the earth will wear out like a piece of clothing." Jesus was well aware of this common Old

Testament teaching, for He contrasted the temporal universe with the eternal nature of His Word: "Heaven and earth will disappear, but my words will never disappear" (Matthew 24:35).

Perhaps the fullest revelation about the passing of the present earth and universe is found in 2 Peter 3:7-13, where we read these sobering words:

> The present heavens and earth have been stored up for fire...The heavens will pass away with a terrible noise, and the very elements themselves will disappear in fire, and the earth and everything on it will be found to deserve judgment...On that day, he will set the heavens on fire, and the elements will melt away in the flames. But we are looking forward to the new heavens and new earth he has promised, a world filled with God's righteousness.

The good news is that while the present universe stained by sin will be judged and destroyed, God will create new heavens and a new earth for us to dwell in forever. *They will be glorious!*

The First, Second, and Third Heavens

Scripture refers to three heavens. The first and second heavens are earth's atmosphere and the stellar universe (Genesis 3:17; 5:29; Romans 8:20-22). The third heaven is God's domain—His perfect dwelling place (see Isaiah 63:15). The only heavens that have been negatively affected by humankind's fall are the first and second heavens. The third heaven—God's glorious home—remains untouched by human sin. It needs no renewal. This heaven subsists in moral and physical perfection, and it will undergo no change.

After the earth and the universe are cleansed, and God creates the new heavens and a new earth, all vestiges of the original curse and Satan's presence will be utterly and forever removed (Revelation 20:10). There will be a massive change—we will instantly transition from an environment of pain, suffering, darkness, and death to an environment of God-focused blessedness.

A consensus that has emerged among theologians is that once God creates the new heavens and a new earth, these new heavens and earth will become a part of what we now call "heaven" (the third heaven). This means there will one day be a much wider meaning—*a much larger territorial boundary*—for the third heaven. In other words, heaven will one day include the entire redeemed universe.

Heaven and earth will no longer be separate realms, as they are now. They will be forever merged. Believers will thus continue to be in heaven even while they are on the new earth. The new earth will be utterly sinless, and hence bathed and suffused in the light and splendor of God, unobscured by evil of any kind or evildoers of any description.

The Heavenly Country

Hebrews 11 is the Faith Hall of Fame in the Bible. In this pivotal chapter we read of the eternal perspective held by many of the great faith warriors in biblical times:

> All these people died still believing what God had promised them. They did not receive what was promised, but they saw it all from a distance and welcomed it. They agreed that they were foreigners and nomads here on earth. Obviously people who say such things are looking forward to a country they can call their own. If they had longed for the country they came from, they could have gone back. But they were looking for a better place, a

> heavenly homeland. That is why God is not ashamed to be called their God, for he has prepared a city for them (Hebrews 11:13-16).

This passage tells us that the great warriors of the faith were not satisfied with earthly things. They looked forward to a better country. And what a glorious country it will be! Eighteenth-century Bible expositor John Gill contemplates how the heavenly country

> is full of light and glory; having the delightful breezes of divine love, and the comfortable gales of the blessed Spirit; here is no heat of persecution, nor coldness, nor chills of affection; here is plenty of most delicious fruits, no hunger nor thirst; and here are riches, which are solid, satisfying, durable, safe and sure: many are the liberties and privileges here enjoyed; here is a freedom from a body subject to diseases and death, from a body of sin and death, from Satan's temptations, from all doubts, fears, and unbelief, and from all sorrows and afflictions.[3]

Architect of the New Jerusalem: Jesus Christ

The New Jerusalem is the heavenly city where you and I will reside for all eternity (Revelation 21:10). Jesus Christ is the builder of this city. We know this to be true because in John 14:2-3, when Jesus addressed His fear-filled disciples, He spoke these words of comfort to them: "There is more than enough room in my Father's home. If this were not so, would I have told you that I am going to prepare a place for you? When everything is ready, I will come and get you, so that you will always be with me where I am." Jesus is preparing our "place"—and that place, according to the book of Revelation, is the New Jerusalem, the eternal city of God and His children.

That's an incredible promise to think about! After all, Scripture tells us that it was Jesus who created our entire stellar universe. Colossians 1:16 says of Him, "By him all things were created, in heaven and on earth, visible and invisible, whether thrones or dominions or rulers or authorities—all things were created through him and for him" (ESV). John 1:3 likewise says of Jesus: "All things were made through him, and without him was not any thing made that was made" (ESV; see also Hebrews 1:2). Jesus made it all—the planets, the stars, and the galaxies that are staggering distances from each other.

Now, if you're impressed when you look up at the stars at night, then you know that Jesus is quite the Creator! Christ is now creating a splendorous place for us to dwell in for all eternity. The apostle Paul in 1 Corinthians 2:9 tells us that "no eye has seen, no ear has heard, and no mind has imagined what God has prepared for those who love him." And Paul was speaking from experience, for he himself had been caught up to heaven and witnessed its glories firsthand (2 Corinthians 12:1-4).

A Genuine Heavenly City

Perhaps the most inspiring description of the New Jerusalem—the heavenly city—is in Revelation 21:1-5:

> I saw a new heaven and a new earth, for the old heaven and the old earth had disappeared. And the sea was also gone. And I saw the holy city, the new Jerusalem, coming down from God out of heaven like a bride beautifully dressed for her husband. I heard a loud shout from the throne, saying, "Look, God's home is now among his people! He will live with them, and they will be his people. God himself will be with them. He will wipe every tear from their eyes, and there will be no more death or sorrow or crying or pain. All these things are

> gone forever." And the one sitting on the throne said, "Look, I am making everything new!"

This passage tells us that the New Jerusalem will come down out of heaven (where Jesus has constructed it) and will rest upon the newly renovated earth. As this divine city comes down, we are assured that "God's home is now among his people." Both human beings and God will dwell together within the confines of this glorious city.

The book of Revelation portrays the New Jerusalem as a literal city, a real place where real resurrected people and a holy God will dwell together. A city has dwelling places, means of transportation, order (government), bustling activity, various kinds of gatherings, and much more. There is no warrant for taking the descriptions of the New Jerusalem in Scripture as merely symbolic. Every description the Bible gives of the New Jerusalem indicates a real place of residence.

This is in perfect keeping with the fact that you and I will have physical resurrection bodies (1 Corinthians 15:50-55). People with *physical bodies* must live in a *physical place*. And that physical place will be the New Jerusalem (John 14:1-3; Revelation 21:1-4).

The New Jerusalem a Megacity

In the Abrahamic covenant, God promised the Jewish people a Promised Land with large boundaries. They will come into full possession of this land in the millennial kingdom. As awesome as that land will be for the Jewish people, it is small in comparison to the promised New Jerusalem.

Indeed, Revelation 21:16 tells us that the New Jerusalem is gigantic: "Its length and width and height were each 1,400 miles." There is no good reason not to take this figure literally. After all, the eternal city must be large enough to accommodate the redeemed of all ages. Further, a large city is one that would be worthy of God.

Today's skyscrapers are dwarfed when compared to the New Jerusalem. For example, the Empire State Building in New York City is 1454 feet high. The Burj Khalifa in Dubai is much higher—2,722 feet. But the New Jerusalem is 1,400 *miles* high. Because it is so high, it is likely that the city will have numerous levels or stories. In fact, if a single story is calculated to be 12 feet high, then the New Jerusalem could easily have 600,000 stories.

That's big! And with our earthly mortal bodies, that would pose quite a challenge for trying to get around. The good news is that you and I will have resurrection bodies—upgraded bodies—that will have amazing capabilities. These bodies will never get tired or grow weary. And besides, the city will be constructed of such awesomely beautiful materials that we'll marvel during every moment of travel.

The eternal city could either be cube-shaped or pyramid-shaped. Some prefer to consider it shaped as a pyramid, for this would explain how the river of the water of life can flow downward from the throne of God as pictured in Revelation 22:1-2. Others view it as being cube-shaped, possibly modeled after the Holy of Holies within the Jewish temple (which is a perfect cube—see 1 Kings 6:20; 8:10-13; 2 Chronicles 3:8; 5:14–6:2).

A City Void of Imperfections

Today's earthly cities are filled with imperfections of every kind. The environments are not perfect. The governing authorities are not perfect. The water and food are not perfect. No one has perfect health. And those within one city do not have perfect relationships with those in neighboring cities. All these problems and more are well illustrated in today's city of Jerusalem.

Things will be far different in the New Jerusalem. There will be no sin (and no sin nature in human beings), no curse, no influence from Satan or demons, no broken relationships, no hunger or thirst, no distance from God, no night or darkness, no fear, no pain or suffering, no tears, and no death. The very absence of all these things seems impossible to imagine, but this is the glorious reality that awaits each of us as believers.

The Gates Are Always Open

Today's Jerusalem is always on high alert. She is surrounded by Arab and Muslim nations who would like to wipe her off the map. The threat is constant and never-ending. *Such will never be the case in the New Jerusalem.*

Prophetic scripture reveals these details to us: "The city wall was broad and high, with twelve gates guarded by twelve angels. And the names of the twelve tribes of Israel were written on the gates" (Revelation 21:12). Moreover, "the wall of the city had twelve foundation stones, and on them were written the names of the twelve apostles of the Lamb" (verse 14).

Why will the names of the 12 tribes of Israel be inscribed on the gates? We might speculate it is because "salvation comes through the Jews" (John 4:22), and the Messiah Himself came from a Jewish lineage (Matthew 1:1).

We might also wonder why the names of the apostles are inscribed on the foundations of the city. Perhaps it is because the church itself was built upon the foundation of these men of God, and they are therefore worthy of special honor (see Ephesians 2:20).

Having all these names inscribed actually makes good sense. After all, both redeemed Jews and redeemed Gentiles are a part of God's eternal family (Ephesians 2:11-13). It is therefore fitting that the names of the 12 tribes of Israel and the 12 apostles be singled out in the eternal city.

John informs us that the eternal city's gates "will never be closed at the end of day because there is no night there" (Revelation 21:25). This is in obvious contrast to earthly cities, such as today's Jerusalem. Indeed, the nighttime is especially dangerous for earthly cities, for under the cover of darkness, invaders could easily approach by stealth and overcome the city while the people are sleeping. Understandably, the reason for shutting the gates at night was to help provide protection. In the New Jerusalem, however, there will be no night, so the gates will always be open. There will be no external threat from without, for Satan, demons, and unbelievers will be eternally quarantined in the lake of fire. And besides, God Himself will dwell within the eternal city. *Who would dare attack it?*

A Health-Giving Environment

John tells us more about the New Jerusalem: "Then the angel showed me a river with the water of life, clear as crystal, flowing from the throne of God and of the Lamb. It flowed down the center of the main street. On each side of the river grew a tree of life, bearing twelve crops of fruit, with a fresh crop each month. The leaves were used for medicine to heal the nations" (Revelation 22:1-2).

Some Bible expositors take the description of the river with the water of life literally while others take it symbolically. I think it might be both literal and symbolic. Perhaps this is a real and material river that symbolizes the rich abundance of the spiritual life of the redeemed in the eternal city. Just as a real river provides a perpetual ongoing outflow of thirst-quenching water on a sunny day, perhaps the river of the water of life symbolizes the perpetual provision of spiritual satisfaction and blessing to the redeemed, who are now basking in the warm glow of eternal life.

As for the tree of life, it made its last appearance in the first book of the Bible—in Genesis 3, where Adam and Eve are portrayed as having sinned against God. Paradise was lost, and the first couple were barred from access to the tree. Now, in the last book of the Bible, paradise is restored, and we will have access to the tree of life.

The leaves of the tree are said to provide for the healing of the nations. This surely does not mean that in the eternal state the nations will be in need of healing, as if recovering from some kind of conflict (see Revelation 21:4). The Greek word translated "heal" is *therapeia*, from which the English word *therapeutic* is derived. The word carries the basic meaning of "health-giving." In the present context, the word conveys the idea that the leaves on the tree of life are health-giving to the redeemed peoples of the world. What a contrast this is to the current unhealthy state of the entire Middle East.

Good-bye Darkness

Today there seems to be a darkness hovering over the entire Middle East. Jerusalem is on constant high alert. But in the future, in the New Jerusalem, darkness will be forever gone. There will be a plentitude of both physical light and spiritual light.

Revelation 21:23 tells us "the city has no need of sun or moon, for the glory of God illuminates the city, and the Lamb is its light." This brings fulfillment to the prophecy in Isaiah 60:19, where we read this: "No longer will you need the sun to shine by day, nor the moon to give its light by night, for the LORD your God will be your everlasting light, and your God will be your glory."

We are reminded from the Gospel of John that Jesus proclaimed, "I am the light of the world. If you follow me, you won't have to walk in darkness, because you will have the light that leads to life" (8:12). We will never walk in either physical or spiritual darkness in the New Jerusalem.

A City of Holiness

The New Jerusalem is described as "the holy city" in Revelation 21:2. Unlike today's Middle East, there will be no sin or unrighteousness in the New Jerusalem. At last, we will live in a state of moral perfection. Of course, this does not mean you and I must personally attain moral perfection in order to enter heaven. Indeed, all who trust in Jesus Christ for salvation have been imputed with the very righteousness of Christ (see Romans 4:11,22-24). We have been made holy by Christ (Hebrews 10:14).

No More Death

Isaiah 25:8 tells us that God "will swallow up death forever! The Sovereign LORD will wipe away all tears." This verse contains a Hebrew play on words. The ancient Jews often spoke of death as metaphorically swallowing up the living, almost like a big mouth opening in the ground to devour people into the grave. But in Isaiah 25:8, God promises that one day He will reverse things so that death itself will be swallowed up. When that happens, death will be gone forever.

The apostle Paul, himself an Old Testament scholar who was well aware of Isaiah 25:8, made the same point in relation to our future resurrection bodies. He wrote, "When the perishable puts on the imperishable, and the mortal puts on immortality, then shall come to pass the saying that is written: 'Death is swallowed up in victory'" (1 Corinthians 15:54 ESV).

Today in the Middle East it seems like the earth opens up its mouth daily to swallow up the living. But in the eternal state, death itself will be swallowed up, never to return. How awesome that will be!

Contrasting Jerusalem with the New Jerusalem

There are some definite differences between today's earthly

Jerusalem and the New Jerusalem. Below is just a sampling of notable contrasts:

- In today's Jerusalem there is a constant need for various structures to be rebuilt or repaired. No such repair will ever be necessary in the New Jerusalem.
- Today's Jerusalem is populated mostly by unbelieving Jews, though some believers in the Lord Jesus are also present (both Jew and Gentile). The New Jerusalem will be populated only by believers.
- In all earthly cities—including today's Jerusalem—there are some people who go hungry and thirsty. There will never be a sense of hunger or thirst in the New Jerusalem.
- All earthly cities—including today's Jerusalem—have crime. There will be perfect righteousness in the New Jerusalem.
- All earthly cities—including today's Jerusalem—have outbreaks of rebellion, whether often or occasional. There will be no rebellions in the New Jerusalem. Everyone will live in submission to the divine King, Jesus Christ.
- All earthly cities—including today's Jerusalem—have broken relationships among people. All relationships in the New Jerusalem will be perfect and loving.
- All earthly cities—including today's Jerusalem—have people with various diseases. Everyone will know perfect health in the New Jerusalem.
- All earthly cities—including today's Jerusalem—have graveyards. But that won't be the case in the

New Jerusalem. Death will be entirely foreign to our experience in heaven.

- In today's earthly cities—including today's Jerusalem—there can be attacks from without (such is common in the Middle East today). The New Jerusalem will know perfect peace, just as the new earth will know perfect peace.

There are many other contrasts I could draw here. But the point is obvious: Our existence in the New Jerusalem will be completely unlike our experience on earth. The eternal city—the New Jerusalem—is going to be absolutely wonderful, far more so than any human mind could possibly fathom or even begin to imagine (1 Corinthians 2:9).

The redeemed Jews and Gentiles in the New Jerusalem will be incredibly blessed!

POSTSCRIPT

THE CONFLUENCE OF END-TIME PROPHECIES

In this book, we have surveyed the entirety of Israel's existence from the beginning all the way to her glorious future, and we have focused attention on all the trials and tribulations in between. As we look at the world today, it certainly seems as though things are spinning out of control. From a strictly human perspective, Israel's problems seem insurmountable. It seems like it's just a matter of time before Israel goes up in flames. But God still has His sovereign eye on Israel. As one prophecy expert has said:

> If one looks at the contemporary situation relating to Israel, without the aid of the Bible, it appears hopeless for God's covenant nation. However, true reality takes into account the will and plan of God, which means that Israel will not be destroyed as a nation no matter how desperate their situation becomes...No matter how dark it may look for Israel God will keep His promises to the only nation on planet earth that He has made an everlasting covenant with. No matter what happens to the modern nation of Israel in our day, we know that she will not be destroyed or pushed into the sea. The Lord God of Israel is in charge of history and He will keep His

> promise of salvation to His elect nation as they come to realize during the tribulation that Jesus of Nazareth was indeed the stone which the builders rejected. The Jewish people will come to realize that it is only through their Messiah, Jesus, that their sins will be removed and they will be restored to a right relationship with God.[1]

The Stage Is Being Set

It appears that we may very well be living in the day in which God's promises to Israel will come to final and full fruition. The late John Walvoord was confident that

> in the present world scene there are many indications pointing to the conclusion that the end of the age may soon be upon us. These prophecies relating to Israel's coming day of suffering and ultimate restoration may be destined for fulfillment in the present generation...never before in the history of the world has there been a confluence of major evidences of preparation for the end.[2]

This "confluence of major evidences"—all related to the fulfillment of end-time prophecies, or the stage being set for their fulfillment—is impressive indeed. Today we are witnessing...

- a massive falling away from the truth
- a widespread embracing of doctrinal error
- a profound moral decline
- a growing tolerance for all things evil
- a widespread outbreak of a variety of sexual sins and perversions, with no repentance in sight

- the steady diminishing of religious freedom
- the ever-increasing global persecution of God's people
- Israel being a relentless sore spot in the world
- ever-escalating conflict in the Middle East
- efforts being made toward the rebuilding of the Jewish temple
- the stage being set for a massive invasion of Israel by Russia and Muslim nations
- the steady rise and influence of globalism
- political and economic steps toward the establishment of a revived Roman Empire—a United States of Europe
- the emergence of a cashless world in preparation for the antichrist's control of the world economy during the tribulation

And much more.

It is sobering—*even a bit frightening*—to recognize that all these things are taking place in our present day. I agree with Walvoord that the end of the age may soon be upon us.

No Need for Fear

As I consider all that we've covered in this book, it seems to me it is best to end right where we began. In the introduction, I pointed out that God Himself is in ultimate control of human history. He asserts, "Everything I plan will come to pass, for I do whatever I wish" (Isaiah 46:10). And He assures us, "It will all happen as I have planned. It will be as I have decided" (14:24). Theologian Robert Lightner is correct when he says that "when viewed from the perspective of Scripture, history is more than the recording of the events of the past. Rather, what has happened in the past, what is happening now, and what will happen in the future is all evidence of the unfolding of the purposeful plan devised by the personal God of the Bible." In view of all this, Lightner said that "all the circumstances of life—past, present, and future—fit into the sovereign plan like pieces of a puzzle."[3]

Because this is true, we need not fear what is coming upon the world. Jesus, speaking in the context of the prophetic future, instructs His followers: "Don't let your hearts be troubled. Trust in God, and trust also in me" (John 14:1). *Don't worry. Trust God.* That is God's simple recipe for a right outlook in the end times.

Wisdom for Living in These Last Days

Beyond this, Scripture provides three tidbits of wisdom for end-time believers that we'd all be wise to implement:

1. Choose to Live Righteously

God does not give us prophecy to teach us mere intellectual facts about eschatology. Many Bible verses that deal with prophecy are followed by an exhortation to personal purity. For example, Romans 13:11-12 instructs, "Time is running out...The night is almost gone; the day of salvation will soon be here. So remove your dark deeds like dirty clothes, and put on the shining armor of right living." Second Peter 3:10-11 tells us, "The day of the Lord will come as unexpectedly as a thief." In view of this reality, we ought to live "holy and godly lives." First John 3:2-3 tells us that in view of Christ's second coming, "all who have this eager expectation will keep themselves pure, just as he is pure."

2. Maintain an Eternal Perspective

No matter what takes place on this earth, we each have a

splendorous destiny ahead. We are but pilgrims on our way to another land—to the final frontier of heaven, where God Himself dwells (see Hebrews 11:16). So, as Colossians 3:1-2 puts it, "Set your sights on the realities of heaven... Think about the things of heaven, not the things of earth." And seek to follow Jesus's advice in Matthew 6:20-21: "Store your treasures in heaven, where moths and rust cannot destroy, and thieves do not break in and steal. Wherever your treasure is, there the desires of your heart will also be."

3. Pray for the Peace of Jerusalem

Psalm 122:6-7 tells us, "Pray for peace in Jerusalem. May all who love this city prosper. O Jerusalem, may there be peace within your walls and prosperity in your palaces." The name of Jerusalem means "city of peace"—and one day in the prophetic future, it actually *will* be a city of peace.

APPENDIX A:

ISRAEL AND THE CHURCH

At scattered points throughout this book, I've briefly touched on today's debate over whether promises made to Israel in the Old Testament covenants will be fulfilled literally by Israel or allegorically by the church. And I have argued that the covenants will be fulfilled by Israel. Here's why:

Old Testament messianic prophecies that refer to the first coming of Christ have been fulfilled literally. This gives us strong confidence to expect that the prophecies not yet fulfilled will also be fulfilled literally. Hence, the covenant land promises to Israel will be fulfilled literally.

Prophecies about Israel in the Old Testament were also fulfilled literally, including those related to Israel's dispersion (Deuteronomy 28:64; Leviticus 26:33), ongoing persecution (Deuteronomy 28:65), desolation of their land (Deuteronomy 29:22-23), and preservation as a people (Isaiah 66:22; Jeremiah 30:11; 31:35-37). Again, this gives us strong confidence to expect that the prophecies not yet fulfilled will also be fulfilled literally.

The church and Israel are still seen to be distinct throughout the New Testament. For example, we are instructed in 1 Corinthians 10:32, "Don't give offense to Jews or Gentiles or the church of God." Israel and the church are also viewed as distinct throughout the book of Acts, with the word "Israel" being used 20 times and the word "church" 19 times. New Testament scholar S. Lewis Johnson noted that "the usage of the terms Israel and the church in the early chapters of the book of Acts is in complete harmony, for Israel exists there alongside the newly formed church, and the two entities are kept separate in terminology."[1] In view of this continued distinction, it is unreasonable to say the church takes Israel's place, or that the promises made to Israel in the Old Testament will be fulfilled in the church.

The apostle Paul, in New Testament times, affirmed that God still has a plan for Israel (Romans 9–11). From his perspective, God's ancient covenants would yet be fulfilled by Israel, not the church.

Those who say the church replaces Israel typically appeal to Galatians 6:16, where they claim the church is called "the Israel of God" (ESV). But Paul is not calling the entire church "the Israel of God." Rather, he is referring to *saved Jews*—that is, Jews who have trusted in Jesus for salvation. The term "Israel" refers to physical Jews everywhere else in the New Testament (some 65 times). There is no indication in Galatians 6:16 that the term is to be taken any differently than how it is commonly used elsewhere.

Those who say the church replaces Israel also appeal to Galatians 3:29, where they claim the church is called "Abraham's offspring" (ESV). However, this verse does not obliterate any distinction between the church and Israel. It simply states that believers who are a part of the church are *spiritual descendants* of Abraham (they have faith just like he did), and are therefore beneficiaries of some of God's promises to him. More specifically, some of God's promises to Abraham were for the physical descendants of Abraham—the Jews (for example, Genesis 12:1-3,7). Other promises to Abraham were for the spiritual seed of Abraham who are not Jews (see Galatians

3:6-9). Failure to distinguish these groups and the promises given to each results only in confusion.

Those who say the church replaces Israel sometimes appeal to Philippians 3:3, where they say the church is called "the circumcision" (ESV). However, Paul was pointedly referring to the circumcision *of the heart* that occurs the moment a person trusts in Jesus Christ for salvation. It is a huge leap in logic to say that this verse proves that the church becomes the new Israel.

Those who say the church replaces Israel often harp on Joshua 21:43-45, where they claim that God has already given the Israelites their land, and thus there are no future land promises yet to be fulfilled for Israel. Those who consult biblical history will find that God indeed fulfilled His part in giving the Israelites the promised land—*but Israel failed to take full possession of what was promised to the nation by God.* They failed to dispossess all the Canaanites. The land promises still hold for the future. The idea that there are no further land promises to be fulfilled is proven to be false in view of the fact that many prophecies written far after the time of Joshua speak of Israel possessing the land in the future (see Isaiah 60:21; Jeremiah 24:6; 30:18; 32:37-40; 33:6-9; Ezekiel 28:25-26; 34:11-12; 36:24-26; 39:28; Hosea 3:4-5; Micah 2:12; 4:6-7; Amos 9:14-15; Zephaniah 3:20; Zechariah 8:7-8). The truth is, every Old Testament prophet except Jonah spoke of a permanent return to the land of Israel by the Jews. Though Israel *partially* possessed the land at the time of Joshua, it was later dispossessed. Contrary to this, the Abrahamic covenant promised Israel that she would possess the land *forever* (Genesis 17:8). That awaits future fulfillment.

All things considered, then, I believe that in the Bible, *Israel is Israel and the church is the church.*

APPENDIX B:

PROPHETIC VERSES RELATING TO ISRAEL

Abrahamic Covenant (Promise to Israel)

Covenant with Abraham, Isaac, and Jacob will continue forever—Psalm 105:5-11

Many blessings of—Genesis 12:1-3; 15:18-21

Reaffirmed with Isaac—Genesis 17:21

Reaffirmed with Jacob—Genesis 35:10-12

See also Joshua 1:2-6; 21:43-45; 1 Chronicles 16:15-18; Isaiah 49:6; Jeremiah 25:9-12; Ezekiel 37:21-25; Daniel 9:2; Amos 9:14-15; Acts 1:6-7; 3:19-21; 15:14-17; Romans 11:1-32; Hebrews 11:8-10,12-16; Revelation 7:4

Anti-Semitism

Jews ordered out of Rome—Acts 18:1-2

Jews persecuted—Nehemiah 1:1-3

Jews persecuted in end times—Revelation 12:5-6

Plot to destroy Jews—Esther 3:1-6

Blindness, Israel's

Stumbled over "stumbling stone," Jesus Christ—Romans 9:31-33

Refused to turn to Christ in faith—Matthew 12:14,24

Judicial hardening has come upon Israel—Romans 11:25

Gospel consequently preached to Gentiles, causing Jewish jealousy—Romans 11:11

Remnant of Israel becomes saved in present age, members of church—Romans 11:25

End times repentance, turning to Lord—Zechariah 12:10; Matthew 23:37-39; Isaiah 53:1-9

Church and Israel, Distinction of

Church began Day of Pentecost, not in Old Testament—Acts 1:5; 1 Corinthians 12:13

Yet future from time of Jesus—Matthew 16:18; Ephesians 3:1-10

Israel composed of Jews; church composed of Jews and Gentiles—Ephesians 2:15

Israel is earthly political entity; universal church is invisible spiritual body of Christ—Exodus 19:5-6; Ephesians 1:3

National Israel will be restored before Christ returns—Romans 11:1-2,29

One becomes Jew by birth; one becomes member of church by spiritual birth—John 3:3

Unconditional land/throne promises will be literally fulfilled in Israel (not the church)—Genesis 13:1-7; 2 Samuel 7:12ff

Covenant, Antichrist Signs with Israel

Antichrist signs seven-year covenant—Daniel 9:24-27

Gives Israel sense of security/rest, a precondition for Ezekiel invasion—Ezekiel 38:1-6,18

Daniel and the 70 Weeks

First 69 groups of 7 years span decree to rebuild Jerusalem till Messiah comes—Daniel 9:25

Gap then occurs: Messiah killed, Jerusalem/temple destroyed, Jews experience hardship—Daniel 9:26

Final 70th "week" (Tribulation) begins when Antichrist signs covenant—Daniel 9:27

Davidic Covenant

Promised that Davidic descendant would rule forever—2 Samuel 7:12-13; 22:51; 1 Chronicles 17:10-14

Will be fulfilled in Jesus, born from line of David—Matthew 1:1; Luke 1:32-33

Jesus will rule on throne in Jerusalem during millennial kingdom—Isaiah 9:6-7; Jeremiah 23:5-6; 33:17-26; Ezekiel 36:1-12; Amos 9:11-12; Micah 4:1-5; Zephaniah 3:14-20; Zechariah 14:1-21

Ezekiel Invasion Against Israel

All-out invasion into Israel by northern coalition—Ezekiel 38:1-6

Enemies seek wealth of Israel—Ezekiel 38:11-12

God destroys invaders—Ezekiel 38:17–39:8

God watches over Israel—Psalm 121:4

No weapon against Israel will prosper—Isaiah 54:17

Takes place "in the latter years" and "in the last days"—Ezekiel 38:8,16

God, Protector of Israel

God battles Israel's enemies—Exodus 15:3; Psalm 24:8

God is military "LORD of Hosts"—2 Samuel 6:2,18

He who keeps Israel will neither slumber nor sleep—Psalm 121:4

No weapon formed against Israel will prosper—Isaiah 54:17

Israel, Conversion of in End Times

Israel now in state of judicial blindness—Romans 9:32

Gospel now preached to Gentiles, causing Jewish jealousy—Romans 11:11

Israel will repent, turn to Messiah in end times—Isaiah 53:1-9; Zechariah 12:10; Matthew 23:37-39

Israel's Gatherings

First worldwide gathering in unbelief (1948 and following)—Isaiah 11:11-12; Ezekiel 20:33-38; 22:17-22; 36:22-24; 38–39; Zephaniah 2:1-2

Second worldwide gathering in belief (related to millennial kingdom)—Deuteronomy 4:29-31; 30:1-10; Isaiah 27:12-13; 43:5-7; Jeremiah 16:14-15; 31:7-10; Ezekiel 11:14-18; Amos 9:14-15; Zechariah 10:8-12; Matthew 24:31

Israel in Tribulation

Tribulation is "time of Jacob's trouble"—Jeremiah 30:7

Israel to experience purging judgments—Zechariah 13:8-9

Israel partially delivered from Satan in tribulation—Revelation 12:14-17

Remnant of Israel delivered, others martyred in tribulation—Revelation 7:4-17; 13:5-6

Israel, National Rebirth of

Gathered from many nations—Ezekiel 36:24

Converts at Armageddon—Zechariah 12:2–13:1

Will "mourn" for Messiah—Zechariah 12:10; see also Isaiah 53:1-9; Matthew 23:37-39

Israel's national sin will be confessed—Leviticus 26:40-42; Deuteronomy 4:29-31; 30:6-8; Jeremiah 3:11-18; Hosea 5:15

Spiritual awakening—Joel 2:28-29

Towns will be inhabited, ruins rebuilt—Ezekiel 36:10

Vision of dry bones—Ezekiel 37

Will again be prosperous—Ezekiel 36:30

Jacob's Trouble, Time of

Tribulation is "time of Jacob's trouble"—Jeremiah 30:7

Details of distress—Revelation 6–18

Jerusalem, in Millennial Kingdom

City of God's presence—Ezekiel 48:35

City of holiness—Isaiah 33:5; Jeremiah 31:40

City of political rule—Psalm 2:6; 110:2; Isaiah 2:2-4; 24:23; Micah 4:7

City of prominence—Isaiah 2:2-4; Zechariah 14:9-10

City of prosperity—Isaiah 2:2; 60:11; 66:12

City of protection and peace—Isaiah 40:2; 66:20; Jeremiah 31:6

City of worship—Isaiah 60:3; Jeremiah 3:17; Zechariah 8:23

Jewish Temple, Rebuilding

Antichrist will exalt himself as God in tribulation temple—2 Thessalonians 2:4

Temple must be rebuilt for abomination of desolation to occur—Daniel 12:11; Matthew 24:15-16

Land Promises to Israel

Abraham's descendants, numerous as stars—Genesis 12:1-3; 13:14-17

God promised land to Abraham and descendants—Genesis 11:31

Parameters of land promises—Genesis 15:18-21

Promises passed to Isaac's line—Genesis 26:3-4

Promises passed to Jacob's line—Genesis 28:13-14

Promises reaffirmed later—Psalm 105:8-11

Land permanently restored to Israel—Deuteronomy 30:5;

Isaiah 11:11-12; Jeremiah 23:3-8; Ezekiel 37:21-25; see also Isaiah 60:18,21; Jeremiah 23:6; 24:5-6; 30:18; 31:31-34; 32:37-40; 33:6-9; Ezekiel 28:25-26; 34:11-12; 36:24-26; 37; 39:28; Hosea 3:4-5; Joel 2:18-29; Amos 9:14-15; Micah 2:12; 4:6-7; Zephaniah 3:19-20; Zechariah 8:7-8; 13:8-9

Millennial Kingdom

Christ restores Israel—Isaiah 25:7-8; 30:26; 51:11-16; 52:1-12; 65:17-19; Ezekiel 36:24-38; 37:1-28; Hosea 2:16-17,19-23; Zechariah 8:1-17; 9:11-17; Romans 11:25-27; Ephesians 3:11-13

Glory of Israel—Isaiah 60:1-22

God will not rest until Israel is restored—Isaiah 62:1-12; Jeremiah 30:16-24; Zechariah 10:9-12

God purposes to redeem Israel—Isaiah 44:1-23

God will bring salvation to Israel—Isaiah 52:1-6

Israel cleansed, glory restored—Isaiah 4:2-6; see also Zephaniah 3:14-20

Israel elevated—Isaiah 61:4-11

Israel restored as wife of Lord, inherit glory—Isaiah 54:1-17

Israel restored, influential—Isaiah 45:14-25

Israel to rejoice in blessings of restoration—Isaiah 35:1-10; Zephaniah 3:14-20

Israel, restored to land—Jeremiah 30:1-11

Jerusalem will have temple in millennial kingdom—Ezekiel 40–48

Regathering of Israel promised—Jeremiah 23:7-8

Righteous King, reign over Israel—Jeremiah 23:5-6

APPENDIX C:

IF YOU ARE NOT A CHRISTIAN

A personal relationship with Jesus is the most important decision you could ever make in your life. It is unlike any other relationship. If you go into eternity without this relationship, you will spend eternity apart from Him.

If you will allow me, I would like to tell you how you can come into a personal relationship with Jesus.

First you need to recognize that...

God Desires a Personal Relationship with You

God created you (Genesis 1:27). And He did not just create you to exist all alone and apart from Him. He created you with a view to coming into a personal relationship with Him.

God has fellowshipped with His people throughout Bible times (for example, Genesis 18:1-21). Just as God fellowshipped with them, so He desires to fellowship with you (1 John 1:5-7). God loves you (John 3:16). Never forget that fact.

The problem is...

Humanity Has a Sin Problem that Blocks a Relationship with God

When Adam and Eve chose to sin against God in the Garden of

Eden, they catapulted the entire human race—to which they gave birth—into sin. Since that time, every human being has been born into the world with a propensity to sin.

The apostle Paul affirmed that "when Adam sinned, sin entered the world. Adam's sin brought death, so death spread to everyone" (Romans 5:12). We are told that "because one person disobeyed God, many became sinners" (verse 19). Ultimately this means that "death came into the world through a man" (Adam), and "everyone dies because we all belong to Adam" (1 Corinthians 15:21-22).

Jesus often spoke of sin in metaphors that illustrate the havoc sin can wreak in one's life. He described sin as blindness (Matthew 23:16-26), sickness (Matthew 9:12), being enslaved in bondage (John 8:34), and living in darkness (John 8:12; 12:35-46). Moreover, Jesus taught that this is a universal condition and that all people are guilty before God (Luke 7:37-48).

Jesus also taught that both inner thoughts and external acts render a person guilty (Matthew 5:28). He taught that from within the human heart come evil thoughts, sexual immorality, theft, murder, adultery, greed, malice, deceit, envy, slander, arrogance, and folly (Mark 7:21-23). Moreover, He affirmed that God is fully aware of every person's sins, both external acts and inner thoughts; nothing escapes His notice (Matthew 22:18; Luke 6:8; John 4:17-19).

Of course, some people are more morally upright than others. However, we all fall short of God's infinite standards (Romans 3:23). In a contest to see who can throw a rock to the moon, I am sure a muscular athlete would be able to throw it much further than I could. But all human beings ultimately fall short of the task. Similarly, all of us fall short of measuring up to God's perfect holy standards.

Though the sin problem is a serious one, God has graciously provided a solution:

Jesus Died for Our Sins and Made Salvation Possible

God's absolute holiness demands that sin be punished. The good news of the gospel, however, is that Jesus has taken this punishment on Himself. God loves us so much that He sent Jesus to bear the penalty for our sins!

Jesus affirmed that it was for the very purpose of dying that He came into the world (John 12:27). Moreover, He perceived His death as being a sacrificial offering for the sins of humanity (Matthew 26:26-28). Jesus took His sacrificial mission with utmost seriousness, for He knew that without Him, humanity would certainly perish (John 3:16) and spend eternity apart from God in a place of great suffering (Matthew 10:28; 25:41; Luke 16:22-28).

Jesus therefore described His mission in these ways: "The Son of Man came not to be served but to serve others and to give his life as a ransom for many" (Matthew 20:28). "The Son of Man came to seek and save those who are lost" (Luke 19:10). "God sent his Son into the world not to judge the world, but to save the world through him" (John 3:17).

Please be aware that the benefits of Christ's death on the cross are not automatically applied to your life. *To receive the gift of salvation, you must...*

Believe in Jesus Christ the Savior

By His sacrificial death on the cross, Jesus took the sins of the entire world on Himself and made salvation available for everyone (1 John 2:2). But this salvation is not automatic. Only those who personally choose to believe in Christ are saved. This is the consistent testimony of the biblical Jesus. Listen to His words:

- "This is how God loved the world: He gave his one and only Son, so that everyone who believes in him will not perish but have eternal life" (John 3:16).

- "It is my Father's will that all who see his Son and believe in him should have eternal life. I will raise them up at the last day" (John 6:40).
- "I am the resurrection and the life. Anyone who believes in me will live, even after dying" (John 11:25).

Choosing *not* to believe in Jesus, by contrast, leads to eternal condemnation: "There is no judgment against anyone who believes in him. But anyone who does not believe in him has already been judged for not believing in God's one and only Son" (John 3:18).

Free at Last: Forgiven of All Sins

When you believe in Christ the Savior, a wonderful thing happens. God forgives you of all your sins. *All of them!* He puts them completely out of His sight. Ponder for a few minutes the following verses, which speak of the forgiveness of those who have believed in Christ:

- "He is so rich in kindness and grace that he purchased our freedom with the blood of his Son and forgave our sins" (Ephesians 1:7).
- God said, "I will never again remember their sins and lawless deeds" (Hebrews 10:17).
- "Oh, what joy for those whose disobedience is forgiven, whose sin is put out of sight! Yes, what joy for those whose record the Lord has cleared of guilt, whose lives are lived in complete honesty!" (Psalm 32:1-2).
- "His unfailing love toward those who fear him is as great as the height of the heavens above the earth. He has removed our sins as far from us as the east is from the west" (Psalm 103:11-12).

Such forgiveness is wonderful indeed, for none of us can possibly work our way into heaven or be good enough to warrant God's good favor. Because of what Jesus has done for us, we can freely receive the gift of salvation. It is a gift provided solely through the grace of God (Ephesians 2:8-9), and it becomes ours by placing our faith in Jesus.

Don't Put It Off

It is a dangerous thing to put off turning to Christ for salvation, for you do not know the day of your death. What if it happens this evening? "Everyone dies—so the living should take this to heart" (Ecclesiastes 7:2).

If God is speaking to your heart now, then now is your door of opportunity to believe. "Seek the Lord while you can find him. Call on him now while he is near" (Isaiah 55:6).

Follow Me in Prayer

Would you like to place your faith in Jesus for the forgiveness of sins, thereby guaranteeing your eternal place in heaven along His side? If so, pray the following prayer with me.

Keep in mind that it is not the prayer itself that saves you; it is the faith in your heart that saves you. So let the following prayer be a simple expression of the faith that is in your heart:

Dear Jesus:
I want to have a relationship with You.
I know I cannot save myself, because I know I am a sinner.
Thank You for dying on the cross on my behalf.
I believe You died for me and rose from the dead.
I accept Your free gift of salvation.
Thank You, Jesus.
Amen.

Welcome to God's Forever Family

On the authority of the Word of God, I can now assure you that you are a part of God's forever family. If you prayed the above prayer with a heart of faith, you will spend all eternity by the side of Jesus in heaven. Welcome to God's family!

What to Do Next

1. Purchase a Bible and read from it daily. Read at least one chapter a day, followed by a time of prayer. If you've not read the Bible before, I recommend that you obtain an easy-to-understand translation—such as the New Living Translation (NLT). I also recommend starting with the Gospel of Luke.
2. Join a Bible-believing church immediately. Get involved in it. Join a Bible study group at the church so you will have regular fellowship with other Christians. This will bring great blessing to your spiritual life.
3. Send me an email at ronrhodes@earthlink.net. I would love to hear from you if you have made a decision for Christ.

BIBLIOGRAPHY

Ankerberg, John, and Dillon Burroughs. *Middle East Meltdown*. Eugene, OR: Harvest House, 2007.

Barnhouse, Donald Grey. *Revelation: An Expository Commentary*. Grand Rapids: Zondervan, 1971.

Bernis, Jonathan. *A Rabbi Looks at the Last Days*. Minneapolis: Chosen, 2013.

Block, Daniel. *The Book of Ezekiel: Chapters 25–48*. Grand Rapids: Eerdmans, 1998.

Dyer, Charles. *The Rise of Babylon: Sign of the End Times*. Chicago: Moody, 2003.

Feinberg, Charles. *The Prophecy of Ezekiel*. Eugene, OR: Wipf & Stock, 2003.

Fruchtenbaum, Arnold. *The Footsteps of the Messiah*. San Antonio, TX: Ariel, 2004.

Geisler, Norman. *Systematic Theology: Church/Last Things*, Vol. 4. St. Paul, MN: Bethany House, 2005.

Gold, Dore. *The Fight for Jerusalem: Radical Islam, the West, and the Future of the Holy City*. Washington, DC: Regnery, 2007.

Hays, J. Daniel, J. Scott Duvall, and C. Marvin Pate. *Dictionary of Biblical Prophecy and End Times*. Grand Rapids: Zondervan, 2007.

Hindson, Ed. *Revelation: Unlocking the Future*. Chattanooga, TN: AMG, 2002.

Hitchcock, Mark. *Bible Prophecy*. Wheaton, IL: Tyndale House, 1999.

Hitchcock, Mark. *The Coming Islamic Invasion of Israel*. Sisters, OR: Multnomah, 2002.

Hitchcock, Mark. *Iran: The Coming Crisis*. Sisters, OR: Multnomah, 2006.

Hitchcock, Mark. *Is America in Bible Prophecy?* Sisters, OR: Multnomah, 2002.

Hitchcock, Mark. *The Late Great United States*. Colorado Springs: Multnomah, 2009.

Hitchcock, Mark. *The Second Coming of Babylon*. Sisters, OR: Multnomah, 2003.

Hoyt, Herman. *The End Times*. Chicago: Moody, 1969.

Ice, Thomas, and Randall Price. *Ready to Rebuild: The Imminent Plan to Rebuild the Last Days Temple*. Eugene, OR: Harvest House, 1992.

Ice, Thomas, and Timothy Demy. *Prophecy Watch*. Eugene, OR: Harvest House, 1998.

Ice, Thomas, and Timothy Demy. *When the Trumpet Sounds*. Eugene, OR: Harvest House, 1995.

Jeffress, Robert. *Countdown to the Apocalypse*. New York: Faith Words, 2015.

Jeremiah, David. *Agents of the Apocalypse*. Carol Stream, IL: Tyndale House, 2014.

Jeremiah, David. *Escape the Coming Night: An Electrifying Tour of the World as It Races Toward Its Final Days*. Dallas: Word, 1990.

LaHaye, Tim. *The Beginning of the End*. Wheaton, IL: Tyndale, 1991.

LaHaye, Tim. *The Coming Peace in the Middle East*. Grand Rapids: Zondervan, 1984.

LaHaye, Tim, and Thomas Ice. *Charting the End Times*. Eugene, OR: Harvest House, 2001.

LaHaye, Tim, and Jerry Jenkins. *Are We Living in the End Times?* Wheaton, IL: Tyndale, 1999.

The MacArthur Study Bible, ed. John MacArthur. Nashville: Thomas Nelson, 2003.

Newell, William. *Revelation Chapter-by-Chapter*. Grand Rapids: Kregel, 1994.

Pentecost, J. Dwight. *Prophecy for Today*. Grand Rapids: Discovery House, 1989.

Pentecost, J. Dwight. *Things to Come*. Grand Rapids: Zondervan, 1964.

Pentecost, J. Dwight. *The Words and Works of Jesus Christ*. Grand Rapids: Zondervan, 1978.

Pink, Arthur W. *The Antichrist: A Study of Satan's Christ*. Blacksburg, VA: Wilder, 2008.

The Popular Bible Prophecy Commentary, eds. Tim LaHaye and Ed Hindson. Eugene, OR: Harvest House, 2006.

The Popular Encyclopedia of Bible Prophecy, eds. Tim LaHaye and Ed Hindson. Eugene, OR: Harvest House, 2004.

Price, Randall. *Fast Facts on the Middle East Conflict*. Eugene, OR: Harvest House, 2003.

Price, Randall. *Jerusalem in Prophecy*. Eugene, OR: Harvest House, 1998.

Price, Randall. *Unholy War*. Eugene, OR: Harvest House, 2001.

Price, Walter K. *The Coming Antichrist*. Neptune, NJ: Loizeaux Brothers, 1985.

Prophecy Study Bible, ed. Tim LaHaye. Chattanooga, TN: AMG, 2001.

Rhodes, Ron. *40 Days Through Daniel: Revealing God's Plan for the Future*. Eugene, OR: Harvest House, 2013.

Rhodes, Ron. *40 Days Through Revelation: Uncovering the Mystery of the End Times*. Eugene, OR: Harvest House, 2013.

Rhodes, Ron. *The Middle East Conflict: What You Need to Know*. Eugene, OR: Harvest House, 2009.

Rhodes, Ron. *Northern Storm Rising: Russia, Iran, and the Emerging End-Times Military Coalition Against Israel*. Eugene, OR: Harvest House, 2008.

Rhodes, Ron. *The Popular Dictionary of Bible Prophecy*. Eugene, OR: Harvest House, 2010.

Rhodes, Ron. *The Topical Guide of Bible Prophecy*. Eugene, OR: Harvest House, 2010.

Richardson, Joel. *The Islamic Antichrist*. Los Angeles: WND, 2009.

Richardson, Joel. *When a Jew Rules the World*. Washington, DC: WND Books, 2015.

Rosenberg, Joel. *Epicenter: Why Current Rumblings in the Middle East Will Change Your Future*. Carol Stream, IL: Tyndale, 2006.

Rosenberg, Joel. *Israel at War*. Carol Stream, IL: Tyndale House, 2012.

Ruthven, Jon Mark. *The Prophecy that Is Shaping History: New Research on Ezekiel's Vision of the End*. Fairfax, VA: Xulon, 2003.

Rydelnik, Michael. *The Messianic Hope: Is the Hebrew Bible Really Messianic?* Nashville: B&H Publishing Group, 2010.

Ryrie, Charles. *Basic Theology*. Wheaton, IL: Victor, 1986.

Ryrie, Charles. *Dispensationalism Today*. Chicago: Moody, 1965.

The Ryrie Study Bible, ed. Charles Ryrie. Chicago: Moody Press, 2011.

Showers, Renald. *Maranatha: Our Lord Come!* Bellmawr, NJ: The Friends of Israel Gospel Ministry, 1995.

Toussaint, Stanley. *Behold the King: A Study of Matthew*. Grand Rapids: Kregel, 2005.

Unger, Merrill F. *Beyond the Crystal Ball*. Chicago: Moody, 1978.

Walvoord, John F. *End Times*. Nashville: Word, 1998.

Walvoord, John F. *Israel in Prophecy*. Grand Rapids: Zondervan, 1970.

Walvoord, John F. *The Millennial Kingdom*. Grand Rapids: Zondervan, 1975.

Walvoord, John F. *The Prophecy Knowledge Handbook*. Wheaton, IL: Victor, 1990.

Walvoord, John F. *The Return of the Lord*. Grand Rapids: Zondervan, 1979.

Walvoord, John F., and John E. Walvoord. *Armageddon, Oil, and the Middle East Crisis*. Grand Rapids: Zondervan, 1975.

Walvoord, John F., and Mark Hitchcock. *Armageddon, Oil, and Terror*. Carol Stream, IL: Tyndale House, 2007.

Wood, Leon J. *The Bible and Future Events: An Introductory Summary of Last-Day Events*. Grand Rapids: Zondervan, 1973.

Yamauchi, Edwin. *Foes from the Northern Frontier: Invading Hordes from the Russian Steppes*. Eugene, OR: Wipf & Stock, 1982.

NOTES

Introduction: Israel on High Alert

1. Isabel Kershner, "How Long Netanyahu Can Back Settlements and Two-State Solution," *The New York Times*, December 25, 2016.
2. Ali Waked, "Hamas, Islamic Jihad Terror Groups Praise UN Anti-Israel Resolution," *Breitbart*, December26,2016,http://www.breitbart.com/jerusalem/2016/12/26/hamas-islamic-jihad-terror-factions-praise-un-anti-israel-resolution/.
3. Mark Hitchcock, *Isis, Iran, Israel* (Eugene, OR: Harvest House, 2016), iBooks edition.
4. Robert P. Lightner, *Evangelical Theology* (Grand Rapids: Baker Books, 1986), 57.
5. David Reagan, "The Jews in Prophecy," Lamb & Lion Ministries, http://christianprophecy.org/articles/the-jews-in-prophecy/.
6. David Reagan, "The World's Hatred of Israel: Prophecy Fulfilled," Lamb & Lion Ministries, http://christinprophecy.org/articles/the-worlds-hatred-of-israel/.

Chapter 1: Correctly Interpreting Biblical Prophecies About Israel

1. J. Dwight Pentecost, *Things to Come* (Grand Rapids: Zondervan, 1964), iBooks edition.
2. Pentecost, *Things to Come.*
3. David Reagan, "The Jews in Prophecy," Lamb & Lion Ministries, http://christianprophecy.org/articles/the-jews-in-prophecy.
4. Reagan, "The Jews in Prophecy."
5. Charles C. Ryrie, *The Basis of the Premillennial Faith* (Dubuque, IA: ECS Ministries, 2005), iBooks edition.
6. Mark Hitchcock, *Isis, Iran, Israel* (Eugene, OR: Harvest House, 2016), iBooks edition.
7. David Cooper; cited in Arnold Fruchtenbaum, *The Footsteps of the Messiah* (San Antonio, TX: Ariel Ministries, 1983), iBooks edition.
8. Fruchtenbaum, *The Footsteps of the Messiah.*
9. Pentecost, *Things to Come.*

Chapter 2: The Amazing Rebirth of Israel

1. Tim LaHaye and Ed Hindson, *Target Israel* (Eugene, OR: Harvest House, 2015), 64-65.
2. Joel Rosenberg, *Epicenter: Why the Current Rumblings in the Middle East Will Change Your Future* (Carol Stream, IL: Tyndale House, 2006), 27.
3. Randall Price, *Fast Facts on the Middle East Conflict* (Eugene, OR: Harvest House, 2003), 45-46.
4. See Gleason Archer, "Confronting the Challenge of Islam in the 21st Century," *Contend for the Faith* (Chicago: EMNR, 1992), 97.
5. Stephen Neill, 64; cited in Josh McDowell and Don Stewart, *Handbook of Today's Religions* (San Bernardino, CA: Here's Life, 1989), 387.
6. Alhaj Ajijola, *The Essence of Faith in Islam* (Lahore, Pakistan: Islamic Publications, 1978), 79.

7. Gerhard Nehls, *Christians Answer Muslims*, in *The World of Islam* CD-ROM, © 2000 Global Mapping International, compiled from the Answering Islam site at http://answering-islam.org/, insert added.

8. Maurice Bucaille, *The Bible, the Quran, and Science: The Holy Scriptures Examined in the Light of Modern Knowledge* (Pakistan: Darulfikr, 1977), 9.

9. Larry A. Poston with Carl F. Ellis, Jr., *The Changing Face of Islam in America* (Camp Hill, PA: Horizon, 2000), 183.

10. Nelson Glueck, *Rivers in the Desert* (Philadelphia: Jewish Publications Society of America, 1969), 31.

11. William F. Albright; cited in Josh McDowell, *Evidence that Demands a Verdict* (San Bernardino, CA: Campus Crusade for Christ, 1972), 68.

12. Gleason Archer, *A Survey of Old Testament Introduction* (Chicago: Moody, 1964), 19.

13. Paul Little, *Know Why You Believe* (Downers Grove, IL: InterVarsity, 1975), 41.

14. Dan Story, *Defending Your Faith: How to Answer the Tough Questions* (Nashville: Thomas Nelson, 1992), 35.

15. Thomas Ice, "Modern Israel's Right to the Land," Pre-Trib Research Center, http://www.pre-trib.org/articles/view/modern-israels-right-to-land.

16. Tim LaHaye, *The Beginning of the End* (Wheaton, IL: Tyndale, 1991), 44-45.

17. Price, 47.

18. Walid Phares, *Future Jihad* (New York: Palgrave MacMillan, 2005), 93-94.

Chapter 3: Muslim Hostilities Against Jews

1. Aaron Klein, *The Late Great State of Israel* (New York: WND, 2009), 139.

2. Klein, 141.

3. Klein, 150.

4. Paul Wolfowitz, cited in Linda D. Kozaryn, "Wolfowitz: Al Qaeda Is an Infectious Disease with No One-Shot Cure," *American Forces Press Service*, June 26, 2002, http://www.navy.mil/submit/display.asp?story_id=2265.

5. Rachel Ehrenfeld, *Funding Evil: How Terrorism Is Financed—and How to Stop It* (Chicago: Bonus, 2005), 35.

6. George Braswell, *What You Need to Know About Islam and Muslims* (Nashville: Broadman & Holman, 2000), 34.

7. David Goldmann, *Islam and the Bible: Why Two Faiths Collide* (Chicago: Moody, 2004), 118.

8. Ergun Mehmet Caner and Emir Fethi Caner, *Unveiling Islam: An Insider's Look at Muslim Life and Beliefs* (Grand Rapids: Kregel, 2002), 125.

9. Ehrenfeld, 37.

10. Yossef Bodansky, *Bin Laden: The Man Who Declared War on America* (New York: Prima Lifestyles, 2001), 364.

11. Ehrenfeld, 125-26.

12. Klein, 150.

13. Ophir Falk and Henry Morgenstern, *Suicide Terror: Understanding and Confronting the Threat* (New York: Wiley, 2009), 53.

14. Ehrenfeld, 133.

15. Abu Bakr al-Baghdadi; cited in Mark Hitchcock, *Isis, Iran, Israel* (Eugene, OR: Harvest House, 2016), iBooks edition.

16. Klein, x.

Chapter 4: Understanding Islamic Beliefs, Part 1

1. Risaleh-i-Barkhawi, quoted in Gerhard Nehls, *Christians Ask Muslims* (Bellville: SIM International Life Challenge, 1987), 21.

2. The Institute for the Study of Islam and Christianity, *Survey of Islam*, Section Six: "Islam— The Practice," in The World of Islam CD-ROM, © 2000 Global Mapping International.

3. See *Beliefs of Other Kinds: A Guide to Interfaith Witness in the United States* (Atlanta: Baptist Home Mission Board, 1984), 121.

4. Bruce A. McDowell and Anees Zaka, *Muslims and Christians at the Table* (Phillipsburg, NJ: Presbyterian & Reformed, 1999), 60.

Chapter 5: Understanding Islamic Beliefs, Part 2

1. Abd El Schafi, *Behind the Veil: Unmasking Islam* (Mumbai, India: Pioneer Book Company, 1996), 41, 31.

2. Thomas Ice, "Islam Is Not a Peaceful Religion," Pretrib Research Center, http://www.pre-trib.org/articles/view/islam-is-not-peaceful-religion.

3. Joel Rosenberg, *Israel at War* (Carol Stream, IL: Tyndale House, 2012), iBooks edition.

4. Dore Gold, *The Fight for Jerusalem* (Washington, DC: Regnery, 2007), 22.

5. Rosenberg, *Israel at War*.

6. Gold, 231-32.

7. Ali Ansari, *Confronting Iran* (New York: Basic Books, 2006), 3.

8. *U.S. News & World Report*, cited in Mark Hitchcock, *Iran: The Coming Crisis* (Sisters, OR: Multnomah, 2006), 57.

9. Mahmoud Ahmadinejad, cited in Gold, 232.

10. Gold, 232.

11. Joshua Yasmeh, "Ahmadinejad: The Next Hitler?" *Tribe*, February 2, 2007, see at http://jewishjournal.com/culture/lifestyle/kids_and_teens/14383/.

12. Kenneth Timmerman, *Countdown to Crisis* (New York: Three Rivers Press, 2006), 325.

13. Timmerman, 325.

14. "Iran's Ahmadinejad: Israel, U.S. Soon Will Die," NewsMax.com, January 24, 2007, online article no longer available.

15. See Joel C. Rosenberg, "State of the Union: The President Must Lay Out a Clear and Convincing Plan to Stop Iran. Period," *Flash Traffic*, January 23, 2007, online article no longer available.

16. Elaine Sciolino, "A Journalist's Dark Perspective on the Nuclear Deal with Iran," *The Washington Post*, October 21, 2016, https://www.washingtonpost.com/opinions/a-journalists-dark-perspective-on-the-nuclear-deal-with-iran/2016/10/21/c6c549e8-8745-11e6-ac72-a299.793.81495_story.html?utm_term=.bd8cd51a0d6f.

17. George Jahn, "Secret Document Reveals Key Iran Nuclear Constraints Will Ease in 10 Years," *The Times of Israel*, July 18, 2016, http://www.timesofisrael.com/secret-document-reveals-key-iran-nuclear-constraints-will-ease-in-10-years/.

18. Ansari, 2.
19. Jerome Corsi, *Atomic Iran* (Nashville: WND Books, 2005), 180.
20. Corsi, 180.
21. Sciolino, "A Journalist's Dark Perspective on the Nuclear Deal with Iran."
22. Mark Hitchcock, *Isis, Iran, Israel* (Eugene, OR: Harvest House, 2016), iBooks edition.
23. Andre Mitchell, "Humanitarian Warns of the 'Elimination' of Christianity in the Middle East," *Christianity Today*, July 12, 2016, https://www.christiantoday.com/article/humanitarian.warns.of.the.elimination.of.christianity.in.the.middle.east/90262.htm.
24. Maria Abi-Habib, "For Many Christians in Middle East, Intimidation or Worse," *Wall Street Journal*, July 26, 2016, https://www.wsj.com/articles/for-many-christians-in-middle-east-intimidation-or-worse-146.957.3266.
25. Abu Bakr al-Baghdadi; cited in Hitchcock, *Isis, Iran, Israel*.
26. Robert Jeffress, *Countdown to the Apocalypse* (New York: FaithWords, 2015), iBooks edition.
27. Benjamin Netanyahu; cited in Jeffress, *Countdown to the Apocalypse*.
28. See Hitchcock, *Isis, Iran, Israel*.
29. Hitchcock, *Isis, Iran, Israel*.

Chapter 6: The Diminishing Support for Israel

1. "Exclusive Polling on Latest American Attitudes Regarding U.S. Policy Towards Israelis and Palestinians," conducted by McLaughlin & Associates for Joel C. Rosenberg, Joel Rosenberg *Flash Traffic* blog.
2. "The World Facing Trump: Public Sees ISIS, Cyberattacks, North Korea as Top Threats," *Pew Research Center*, January 12, 2017, http://www.people-press.org/2017/01/12/the-world-facing-trump-public-sees-isis-cyberattacks-north-korea-as-top-threats/.
3. Joel Rosenberg, "If Obama's Team Is Hostile to Israel Before the Elections…" *Flash Traffic* blog, October 29, 2014, https://flashtrafficblog.wordpress.com/2014/10/30/if-the-obama-team-is-this-hostile-to-israel-before-the-election-how-bad-will-things-get-after-tuesday-will-the-president-turn-against-israel-appease-iran-analysis/.
4. "Rubio, Cardin Introduce Senate Resolution Condemning Anti-Israel Efforts at United Nations" press release, January 4, 2017, http://www.rubio.senate.gov/public/.
5. David Reagan, "The World's Hatred of Israel: Prophecy Fulfilled," Lamb & Lion Ministries, http://christianprophecy.org/articles/the-worlds-hatred-of-israel/.
6. Tim LaHaye and Ed Hindson, *Target Israel* (Eugene, OR: Harvest House, 2015), iBooks edition.
7. Joel Richardson, cited in "End Times Harbinger: Nations Gang Up on Israel," *WorldNetDaily*, January 14, 2017, http://www.wnd.com/2017/01/end-times-harbinger-nations-gang-up-on-israel/#!.
8. "Paris Meeting to Push for Mideast Peace with Eye on Trump," *Yahoo News*, January 13, 2007, https://sg.news.yahoo.com/paris-meeting-push-mideast-peace-eye-trump-140311246.html.
9. "Paris Summit Urges Two-State Solution to Israeli-Palestinian Conflict," *NPR*, January 15, 2017, http://www.npr.org/sections/thetwo-way/2017/01/15/509939635/dozens-of-diplomats-gather-in-paris-for-israel-palestinian-peace-talks.
10. "End Times Harbinger: Nations Gang Up on Israel."
11. Jan Markell, cited in "End Times Harbinger."
12. Markell, in "End Times Harbinger."
13. LaHaye and Hindson, *Target Israel*.

14. *U.S. News & World Report*; cited in Reagan, "The World's Hatred of Israel."

15. "Adam Lebor, "Exodus: Why Europe's Jews Are Fleeing Once Again," *Newsweek*, July 29, 2014, http://www.newsweek.com/2014/08/08/exodus-why-europes-jews-are-fleeing-once-again-261854.html.

16. Reagan, "The World's Hatred of Israel."

17. Arnold Fruchtenbaum, *The Footsteps of the Messiah* (San Antonio, TX: Ariel Publishers, 2004), 111-12.

18. LaHaye and Hindson, *Target Israel*.

Chapter 7: Northern Storm Rising

1. Mark Hitchcock, *Isis, Iran, Israel* (Eugene, OR: Harvest House, 2016), iBooks edition.

2. Joel Rosenberg, *Epicenter: Why the Current Rumblings in the Middle East Will Change Your Future* (Carol Stream, IL: Tyndale, 2008), 731.

3. Rosenberg, *Epicenter*, 68-69.

4. Arnold Fruchtenbaum, *The Footsteps of the Messiah*, Logos Bible Software.

5. Thomas Ice, "Ezekiel 38 and 39," Part 1, Pre-Trib Research Center, http://www.pre-trib.org/articles/view/ezekiel-38-39-part-1.

6. Ice, "Ezekiel 38 and 39," Part 1.

7. Ilan Berman, *Tehran Rising* (New York: Rowman and Littlefield, 2005), 57-58.

8. Berman, 57-58.

9. Kenneth R. Timmerman, "The Turkey-Russia-Iran Axis," *Front Page*, August 22, 2016, http://www.frontpagemag.com/fpm/263922/turkey-russia-iran-axis-kenneth-r-timmerman.

10. Hazel Torres, "Iran Ready for 'Annihilation' of Israel: 'More than 100,000 Missiles Ready to Strike at the Heart of Jewish Nation,'" *Christianity Today*, July 7, 2016, https://www.christian-today.com/article/iran.ready.for.annihilation.of.israel.more.than.100000.missiles.ready.to.strike.at.the.heart.of.jewish.nation/90017.htm.

11. Torres, "Iran Ready for 'Annihilation' of Israel." See also Majid Rafizadeh, "Iran: 'More than 100,000 Missiles Are Ready to Strike Israel,'" *Front Page*, July 12, 2016, http://www.frontpagemag.com/fpm/263442/iran-more-100000-missiles-are-ready-strike-israel-dr-majid-rafizadeh.

12. Rafizadeh, "Iran: 'More than 100,000 Missiles Are Ready to Strike Israel.'"

13. Elad Benari, "Iranian commander: Ground is ready to destroy 'Zionist regime,'" *Arutz Sheva*, July 7, 2016, http://www.israelnationalnews.com/News/News.aspx/214609.

14. "Iranian Official: We Will Not Recognize Israel," *Middle East Monitor*, June 30, 2016, https://www.middleeastmonitor.com/20160630-iranian-official-we-will-not-recognize-israel/.

15. "As Russia and Turkey Cozy Up, U.S. Influence at Stake in Middle East," *The Kansas City Star*, August 18, 2016, http://www.kansascity.com/opinion/editorials/article96504882.html.

16. "As Russia and Turkey Cozy Up, U.S. Influence at Stake in Middle East."

17. Sergei Karpukhin, "US Apoplectic as Turkey Pivots Eastward," *RT Op-Edge*, August 19, 2016, https://www.rt.com/op-edge/356489-turkey-russia-cooperation-us/, inserts added for clarification.

18. Timmerman, "The Turkey-Russia-Iran Axis."

19. Joel Rosenberg, "Turkey Continues Moving to the Dark Side: Erdogan Cuts Major Military Deal with Russia," Joel C. Rosenberg's *Flash Traffic* blog, July 27, 2017, https://flashtrafficblog.wordpress.com.

Chapter 8: God's Defeat of the Northern Coalition

1. J.I. Packer, *Knowing God* (Downers Grove, IL: InterVarsity, 1983), 126.
2. John F. Walvoord and Roy B. Zuck, eds., *The Bible Knowledge Commentary* (Wheaton, IL: Victor, 1985). Logos Bible Software.
3. Joel Rosenberg, *Epicenter* (Carol Stream: Tyndale, 2006), 163-64.
4. Tim LaHaye and Ed Hindson, *Target Israel* (Eugene, OR: Harvest House, 2015), iBooks edition.
5. Arnold Fruchtenbaum, *The Footsteps of the Messiah* (San Antonio, TX: Ariel Ministries, 2003), Logos Bible Software.
6. John F. Walvoord, *The Return of the Lord* (Grand Rapids: Zondervan, 1979), 139-40.

Chapter 9: The 70 Weeks of Daniel

1. Mark Hitchcock, *Is the Antichrist Alive Today?* (Sisters, OR: Multnomah, 2003), iBook edition.
2. John F. Walvoord, *Major Bible Prophecies: 37 Crucial Prophecies that Affect You Today* (Grand Rapids: Zondervan, 1993), 319.
3. Renald Showers, *Maranatha: Our Lord Come!* (Bellmawr, NJ: Friends of Israel, 1995), 21.
4. Randall Price, "An Overview of the Tribulation," Rapture Ready, http://www.raptureready.com/2015/01/16/an-overview-of-the-tribulation-by-randall-price/.
5. Price, "An Overview of the Tribulation."
6. J. Dwight Pentecost, *Things to Come* (Grand Rapids: Zondervan, 1964), iBooks edition.
7. Gerald Stanton, *Kept from the Hour* (Grand Rapids: Zondervan, 1956), 30-31.
8. Price, "An Overview of the Tribulation."
9. John F. Walvoord, *Israel in Prophecy* (Grand Rapids: Zondervan, 1978), http://walvoord.com/series/319.
10. John Ankerberg, Dillon Burroughs, and Jimmy DeYoung, *Israel Under Fire: The Prophetic Chain of Events That Threatens the Middle East* (Eugene, OR: Harvest House, 2009), Kindle edition.

Chapter 10: The Conflict over Rebuilding the Jewish Temple

1. John F. Walvoord, "Revelation," in *The Bible Knowledge Commentary*, New Testament Edition, eds. John F. Walvoord and Roy B. Zuck (Colorado Springs: David C. Cook, 1983), The Bible App edition.
2. Joel Rosenberg, *Epicenter: Why the Current Rumblings in the Middle East Will Change Your Future* (Carol Stream, IL: Tyndale, 2008), 566.
3. John Ankerberg, Dillon Burroughs, and Jimmy DeYoung, *Israel Under Fire: The Prophetic Chain of Events That Threatens the Middle East* (Eugene, OR: Harvest House, 2009), Kindle edition.
4. Rosenberg, *Epicenter*, 569-74; See also Ed Hindson, *15 Future Events that Will Shake the World* (Eugene, OR: Harvest House, 2014), iBooks edition.
5. Arutz Sheva Staff, "Preparation for Temple No Longer a Dream," *Israel National News*, August 8, 2016, http://www.israelnationalnews.com/News/News.aspx/216112.
6. Ankerberg, Burroughs, and DeYoung, *Israel Under Fire*.
7. Meir Kahana; cited in Ankerberg, Burroughs, and DeYoung, *Israel Under Fire*.
8. Eliran Aharon, "We're Not Embarrassed to Say It: We Want to Rebuild the Temple," *Israel National News*, August 15, 2016, http://www.israelnationalnews.com/News/News.aspx/216358.

9. Ankerberg, Burroughs, and DeYoung, *Israel Under Fire.*
10. Rosenberg, *Epicenter*, 562-63.
11. David Reagan, "The Rebirth of the Sanhedrin: What is its Prophetic Significance?" Lamb & Lion Ministries, http://christianprophecy.org/articles/the-rebirth-of-the-sanhedrin/.
12. Thomas Ice, "Is It Time for the Temple?," http://www.pre-trib.org/articles/view/is-it-time-for-temple.
13. Arnold Fruchtenbaum, *Ariel Ministries Newsletter* (Fall 2004/Winter 2005), 4.
14. Ankerberg, Burroughs, and DeYoung, *Israel Under Fire.*
15. "New 'Sanhedrin' Plans Rebuilding of Temple: Israeli Rabbinical Body Calls for Architectural Blueprint," *WorldNetDaily* (June 8, 2005), http://www.wnd.com/2005/06/30709/.
16. "New 'Sanhedrin' Plans Rebuilding of Temple," *WorldNetDaily.*
17. Mark Hitchcock, *Is the Antichrist Alive Today?* (Sisters, OR: Multnomah, 2003), iBook edition.
18. Randall Price, *The Coming Last Days Temple* (Eugene, OR: Harvest House, 1999), 592.

Chapter 11: God's End-Time Jewish Witnesses During the Tribulation

1. Thomas Ice and Timothy Demy, *The Coming Cashless Society* (Eugene, OR: Harvest House, 1996), 125-26, 80.
2. Stanley Toussaint, *Behold the King: A Study of Matthew* (Grand Rapids: Kregel, 2005), 291.
3. Merrill F. Unger, *Beyond the Crystal Ball* (Chicago: Moody, 1978), 134-35.
4. J. Dwight Pentecost, *The Words and Works of Jesus Christ* (Grand Rapids: Zondervan, 1978), 410. See also J. Dwight Pentecost, *Things to Come* (Grand Rapids: Zondervan, 1978), 418.
5. David Jeremiah, *Agents of the Apocalypse* (Carol Stream, IL: Tyndale House, 2014), iBooks edition.
6. Timothy J. Demy and John C. Whitcomb, "Witnesses, Two," in *The Popular Encyclopedia of Bible Prophecy*, eds. Tim LaHaye and Ed Hindson (Eugene, OR: Harvest House, 2004), 402-3.
7. Henry M. Morris, *The Revelation Record: A Scientific and Devotional Commentary on the Prophetic Book of the End Times* (Carol Stream, IL: Tyndale House, 1983), 204.
8. *The MacArthur Study Bible* (Nashville: Thomas Nelson, 2013), The Bible App edition.
9. *The Ryrie Study Bible* (Chicago: Moody, 2001), The Bible App edition.
10. *The NLT Study Bible* (Wheaton, IL: Tyndale House, 2011), The Bible App edition.

Chapter 12: The Antichrist's Campaign to Annihilate the Jews

1. Henry C. Thiessen, cited in Renald Showers, *Maranatha: Our Lord Come!* (Bellmawr, NJ: Friends of Israel, 1995), 50.
2. Showers, 50.
3. David Jeremiah. *Agents of the Apocalypse* (Carol Stream, IL: Tyndale House, 2014), iBooks edition.
4. Jeremiah. *Agents of the Apocalypse.*
5. *The Bible Knowledge Commentary*, eds. John F. Walvoord and Roy B. Zuck, E-Sword Bible Software.
6. Thomas Ice, "God's Purpose for Israel During the Tribulation," Pre-Trib Research Center, http://www.pre-trib.org/articles/view/gods-purpose-for-israel-during-tribulation.
7. Ice, "God's Purpose for Israel During the Tribulation."

Chapter 13: The End of the Times of the Gentiles

1. John F. Walvoord, *Daniel* (Chicago: Moody, 2012), Kindle edition.
2. Helpful discussions of all this may be found in Ed Hindson, *15 Future Events that Will Shake the World* (Eugene, OR: Harvest House, 2014), chapter 11; John F. Walvoord, *Major Bible Prophecies* (Grand Rapids: Zondervan, 1999), chapters 12-15; and Mark Hitchcock, *The Amazing Claims of Bible Prophecy* (Eugene, OR: Harvest House, 2010), chapter 11.

Chapter 14: Peace at Last

1. Paul Enns, *The Moody Handbook of Theology* (Chicago: Moody Press, 1989), Logos Bible Software.
2. John Ankerberg, Dillon Burroughs, and Jimmy DeYoung, *Israel Under Fire: The Prophetic Chain of Events That Threatens the Middle East* (Eugene, OR: Harvest House, 2009), Kindle edition.
3. Jerry Hullinger, "The Problem of Animal Sacrifices in Ezekiel 40-48," *Bibliotheca Sacra* 152 (July-September 1995), 280.
4. Hullinger, 289.

Chapter 15: Redeemed Jews and Gentiles in the New Jerusalem

1. Randall Price, "The New Jerusalem," World of the Bible, http://worldofthebible.com/wp-content/uploads/2017/03/The-New-Jerusalem.pdf.
2. John MacArthur, *MacArthur New Testament Commentary*, Accordance Bible Software.
3. John Gill, "Hebrews 11:13-15" in The Online Bible (electronic media). Version 2.5.2.

Postscript: The Confluence of End-Time Prophecies

1. Thomas Ice, "Closing in on Israel," Pretrib Research Center, http://www.pre-trib.org/articles/view/closing-in-on-israel.
2. John F. Walvoord, *Israel in Prophecy* (Grand Rapids: Zondervan, 1962), 129.
3. Robert P. Lightner, *Evangelical Theology* (Grand Rapids: Baker Books, 1986), 57.

Appendix A: Israel and the Church

1. S. Lewis Johnson, "Paul and 'The Israel of God': An Exegetical and Eschatological Case Study," in *Essays in Honor of J. Dwight Pentecost*, eds. Stanley Toussaint and Charles Dyer (Chicago: Moody Press, 1986), 189.